JÜRGEN MOLTMANN IN PLAIN ENGLISH

STEPHEN D. MORRISON

BELOVED PUBLISHING · COLUMBUS, OH

Print ISBN: 978-1-63174-172-2

eBook ISBN: 978-1-63174-173-9

Cover design and illustration copyright © 2018 Gordon Whitney Media (www.GordonWhitneyMedia.com)

Beloved Publishing · Columbus, Ohio.

CONTENTS

Introduction   v

Biography   1
An Overview of Moltmann's Works   9
1. Experiences in Theology   13
   SIDEBAR: Ecumenism   29
2. Chapter 2: Theology of Hope   31
   SIDEBAR: Peace with God   45
   SIDEBAR: Economic Inequality   49
3. The Crucified God   53
   SIDEBAR: Political Religion   77
   SIDEBAR: The Death Penalty and Torture   83
4. The Church in the Power of the Spirit   87
   SIDEBAR: The Sacraments   105
5. The Trinity and the Kingdom   109
   SIDEBAR: God, His & Hers   125
   SIDEBAR: Tritheism   133
6. God in Creation   137
   SIDEBAR: Evolution   149
   SIDEBAR: Ecological Responsibility   155
7. The Way of Jesus Christ   161
   SIDEBAR: Nonviolence   171
8. Ethics of Hope   179
   SIDEBAR: Gun Violence   191
9. The Spirit of Life   195
   SIDEBAR: Live Slowly   209
10. The Coming of God   213

A Brief Reading Guide   233
Works Cited   239
About the Author   245
Also by Stephen D. Morrison   247

INTRODUCTION

Jürgen Moltmann is a theological iconoclast. His unrelenting challenge to the status quo is what makes him so worth reading today. Read Moltmann because any theology above reproach is an ideology; because there are few things worse than settling for the status quo. Even if you walk away disagreeing with some of his conclusions, you cannot read Moltmann without his creativity and conviction provoking your thinking.

To read Moltmann is also to be provoked for the cause of God's kingdom. No theological insight is free from its social, political, and personal challenges, and these are often just as arresting as Moltmann's theological challenges. He is not a theologian content with theoretical insights alone but recognizes the significant implications of theological thought. He does not collapse theological thinking into practical action, but neither does he divorce the one from the other. Theology is not for monks in a high-tower, far removed from the concerns of the world. What good is it to have a "perfect" theology if it means nothing for the poor and oppressed?

As an iconoclast in both intellectual and practical matters, Moltmann has naturally been quite controversial in the Church. However, he would have it no other way. Moltmann once lamented over the "nice and pleasant" theologians who turn theology into a "harmless business" (Houtz: "Jürgen Moltmann at 90"). "What we need," he continued, "is dispute!

Why do we need disputes? Because of the truth! It is worth a heated conflict, especially among friends. Tolerance is good, but being tolerated is bad" (ibid.).

Moltmann's theology is no "harmless business," but a sharp prod against the safe and comfortable ways of thinking and acting in the Church today. We need theological iconoclasts, or else we will become internally stagnant and externally irrelevant. In this sense, Moltmann is a modern day prophet for the Church because he shakes us free from the comfortable bondage of the status quo.

AN OUTLINE OF THIS BOOK

Each chapter corresponds to one of Moltmann's ten major books, either from his early "trilogy" or his later "systematic contributions to theology." With two exceptions, we examine these in chronological order.

Chapters: I want to stress that the chapters in this book are *not* summaries of Moltmann's books. That would not only be quite boring to read, but it would defeat the purpose of this book. The last thing it is meant to be is a *replacement* for reading Moltmann yourself. In fact, its primary goal (along with the others in this series) is to help you quickly jump in and discover Moltmann firsthand.

Therefore, each chapter examines only a few of the essential insights from each book. I am not summarizing the text but mining for gold and bringing up a few of the key nuggets I have found helpful. Accordingly, it is best to consider each chapter as initial *explorations,* not summaries. I have taken liberties in exploring what personally interests me about Moltmann—alongside what I find necessary for adequately understanding him —rather than merely repeating him or systematically describing his work.

Sidebar: Following each chapter, you will find what I call "sidebar" sections. These explore the social, political, and personal implications of Moltmann's theology. They also help clarify Moltmann's theology by preemptively answering some of the questions or objections readers may be asking about his work.

Because of the nature of Moltmann's work, this is the most political book I have written. I want to preface the politics I discuss here by asking for your patience and grace. Talking politics can be uncomfortable, especially if you are conversing with someone of another persuasion. I know that not everyone will arrive at the same conclusions I do, but I have attempted to present these conclusions as they explicitly or implicitly correspond with Moltmann's insights. In some cases, I have contextualized Moltmann's political ideas for my American environment, since this is the context I am best able to speak into. However, most of these reflections directly relate to Moltmann's work.

The complexity of any political debate is impossible to capture in such a short space, especially when recognizing that theology, not politics, is the primary concern of this book. In brevity, it is impossible not to seem biased or one-sided. With the political reflections in this book, I am not attempting to make an exhaustive argument for each issue, but I merely hope to draw attention to their connection with Moltmann's theology.

FOR BEGINNERS, BY A BEGINNER

This book was written *for beginners, by a beginner.* I am not a professional theologian; I have never even been to seminary. That is what makes my "Plain English Series" unique: it is the first and only introductory series of its kind. I am not an academic "insider" writing for "outsiders," but an amateur writing for other amateurs. There is nothing wrong with academic work, but the theologians I examine in this series are far too significant to remain locked away in the high-towers of academia; they should be accessible to the Church at large. If an untrained amateur such as myself, with nothing but time and dedication, can read and understand great theologians like Jürgen Moltmann, then so can you. It is in this spirit that I humbly present my attempt at understanding Jürgen Moltmann "in plain English."

Ultimately, God alone is the real subject of theology. Therefore, Moltmann himself is not the primary subject of this book. It is in *conversation* with Moltmann's profound theological insights that we stand together before God as "eternal beginners," awestruck by the love and grace of the Triune God. I pray above all else that this book celebrates the love of God and cultivates unwavering hope in the coming of God's Kingdom "on earth as it is in heaven."

STEPHEN D. MORRISON
TALLINN, 2018

BIOGRAPHY

Jürgen Moltmann was born in Hamburg, Germany, on April 8, 1926. He currently lives in the small university town of Tübingen, where he taught as a professor for many years. Moltmann turned 92 this year (2018), but despite his age, he has remained an incredibly active writer and speaker. In the past three years (2015-18), he has written and published a new book each year, and he often travels across the globe to lecture at conferences or in universities. He is one of the most widely discussed theologians of our time, and rightly so, as he is genuinely a theologian for the modern world.

His success is in a unique ability to speak theologically to modernity without collapsing theology beneath the feet of modernity. As a theologian who suffered through the horrors of World War II, he is undoubtedly among the most significant voices of his generation. No one has wrestled with the questions of our time more seriously, and yet he comes out the other side full of hope, life, and joy. For these reasons, among many others, his legacy will live on as one of the prominent theological figures of the late twentieth and early twenty-first centuries.

Moltmann grew up in a small but unique community just outside of Hamburg. A group of enthusiasts for the simple life formed a settlement there, which was designated only by the curious sign "Im Berge," meaning "in the mountain" (curious, because there were no mountains in the region). It was a garden community made up of teachers who wanted to reconnect with the rudiments of life. Moltmann's parents moved into "Im Berge 4" in 1929. Moltmann recalls spending his childhood tending the garden, roaming the nearby forests, playing games in the car-free streets, and competing in sports.

As a young student, Moltmann loved mathematics and science, though he also read Goethe and learned many of his poems by heart. Faith was not a part of Moltmann's life during these years. Neither his father or mother was religious, and the community as a whole lacked a Church. His father was a gifted historian, with a "fabulous memory" like a "walking encyclopedia" (*A Broad Place*, 12). Moltmann recalls being less than proficient in school. He was often the youngest student in the class, which developed in him "an undue measure of imagination" (ibid., 10).

When he came of age, Moltmann went into the German army as an Air Force auxiliary. The most significant event of this time was his survival of the infamous "Operation Gomorrah." This English military bombing operation brutally destroyed the city of Hamburg (July 24, 1943). At the end of a nine-day "inferno" of bombs, 42,000 civilians were killed (mostly women and children), over 30,000 were injured, and the city was in ruins. On one of the final days of the raid, Moltmann narrowly escaped death. A bomb hit the platform where he stood with his friend, Gerhard Schopper. Miraculously, Moltmann survived but was left to grapple with the fact that his friend did not. One moment they stood together on the platform, then in an instant he was left alone in agony. That night, Moltmann cried out to God:

> During that night I cried out to God for the first time in my life and put my life in his hands. I was as if dead, and ever after received life every day as a new gift. My question was not, 'Why does God allow this to happen?' but, 'My God, where are you?' And there was the other question, the answer to which I am still looking for today: Why am I alive and not dead, too, like the friend at my side? I felt the guilt of survival and searched for the meaning of continued life. I knew that

there had to be some reason why I was still alive. During that night I became a seeker after God.

— A Broad Place, 17

Moltmann survived the bombing but felt "guilty" to be alive and "duty bound to the dead because of my survival" (ibid.). As the war continued, and after a series of further tragedies including the loss of another close friend, Günther Schwiebert, Moltmann ended up as a British prisoner of war from 1945 to 1948.

At first, Moltmann was in despair in the POW camp. He tried to find solace by reciting Goethe, but he now found that the poems he loved so much as a boy "had nothing more to say to me" (ibid., 26). Moltmann gave up his dream of mathematics and physics, because, "What was the point of it all?" (ibid.). It was a time of mental and spiritual torment, a "dark night of the soul."

A turning point came when some of the prisoners were transferred to a camp up north in Scotland. Here Moltmann encountered warmth and kindness from the Scottish overseers and their families, a "hospitality that profoundly shamed us. We heard no reproaches, we were not blamed, we experienced a simple and warm common humanity which made it possible for us to live with the past of our own people, without repressing it and without growing callous. True, we had numbers on our backs and prisoners' patches on our trousers, but we felt accepted as people. This humanity in far-off Scotland made human beings of us once more. We were able to laugh again" (ibid., 28-9).

However, the Scottish camp also opened the eyes of its prisoners to the horrors of the German concentration camps. Some thought it was propaganda and others just could not believe it, but "slowly and inexorably the truth seeped into our consciousness, and we saw ourselves through the eyes of the Nazi victims" (ibid., 29).

Moltmann cites two experiences in the camp that "raised" him from his depression "to a new hope in life" (ibid.). The first was the friendliness of the Scottish oversees, as already mentioned, and the second was Moltmann's encounter with the Bible. An army chaplain distributed Bibles to the prisoners one day, and for a while, Moltmann read it "without much understanding." Eventually, he read Psalm 39 and discovered "an echo from my own soul" (ibid., 30). So then he read Mark's gospel and was apprehended by Jesus' dying cry, "My God, why have you forsaken me?" He writes, "I felt growing within me the conviction: this is someone who understands you completely, who is with you in your cry to God and has felt the same forsakenness you are living in now" (ibid.). God gripped Moltmann's heart, and he began to "understand the assailed, forsaken Christ" who understood him. Because of this realization, Moltmann "summoned up the courage to live again, and I was slowly but surely seized by a great hope" (ibid.).

In 1946, after his experiences in Scotland, Moltmann passed an English exam and was sent to the Norton Camp, an educational camp located near Mansfield (central England). Here Moltmann had a vast library of books to read and discover, and many notable professors and lecturers came to teach the prisoners. For example, Anders Nygren spent two weeks at the camp, and even Dietrich Bonhoeffer's niece, Dorothee Schleicher, came and informed them about his resistance to Hitler. Moltmann recalls the first theological book he read at the camp: Reinhard Niebuhr's *The Nature and Destiny of Man*. It deeply impressed him, though he admits "I hardly understood it" (ibid., 32). Here a whole world of learning was opened up to him. He attended a wide range of lectures in the camp's theology school, including lessons in Greek and Hebrew. In 1947, he decided he would become a pastor. Moltmann summarized his experience in the camp like this: "I have never lived so intensive an intellectual life as I did in Norton Camp. We received what we had not deserved, and lived from a spiritual abundance we had not expected" (ibid., 33).

A profound moment of reconciliation came when a group of Dutch students arrived to speak with them at the camp. They told the prisoners about the horrors they had suffered, as well as the deaths of their Jewish friends. Through it all, however, they said, "Christ was the bridge on which they were coming to meet us, and that without Christ they would not have been able to speak a word to us" (ibid., 34). The German prisoners confessed their guilt and asked for reconciliation. "At the end we all embraced. For me that was an hour of liberation. I could breathe freely again and felt like a human being once more" (ibid.).

On April 19, 1948, Moltmann was officially released from the camp, after more than five years "in barracks, camps, dugouts and bunkers" the dark cloud of war had lifted (ibid.). Looking back at this time Moltmann concludes, "I had experienced something that was to determine my whole life" (ibid.).

Returning to a homeland that he no longer recognized, Moltmann studied theology in Göttingen from 1948-52. Hans-Joachim Iwand was one of the first professors to make an impression on him. Moltmann said he became a kind of "disciple" to Iwand. It was especially Iwand's theology of the cross (which was indebted to Luther) and his doctrine of justification that made such a deep impression. He writes, "It was in his spirit that in 1972 I wrote *The Crucified God*" (ibid., 41). Iwand had also introduced Moltmann to Elisabeth Wendel, who later became his wife.

Moltmann took courses with several notable professors, including Gerhard von Rad (the well-known Old Testament scholar), Ernst Wolf (on Church history), Ernst Käsemann (New Testament), Günter Bornkamm (on the Synoptic Gospels), and even Friedrich Gogarten (on homiletics). In 1949-50, Moltmann approached Elisabeth's doctoral supervisor, Otto Weber, and asked if he could give him a thesis subject. Weber suggested Moyse Amyraut, a seventeenth-century Calvinist known for maintaining a "hypothetical universalism" in the doctrine of predestination (also known as "four-point Calvinism"). From then on, Moltmann attended all of Weber's lectures and considered him an "expert teacher" (ibid., 46). Moltmann recalls a deep appreciation for Weber, saying that he was more than just a supervisor or a teacher to him, "[H]e was a fatherly friend" (ibid., 47). Weber's influence on Moltmann's theology has remained strong, as Moltmann admits, "[W]henever I come to a theological standstill, I read his *Grundlagen der Dogmatik* [Foundations of Dogmatics]" (ibid., 48).

Three of the teachers Moltmann learned from at university (Wolf, Weber, Iwand) were appreciative of Karl Barth's theology. As a result, Moltmann had the impression that "there could be no more theology after Barth, because he had said everything and said it so well—just as in the nineteenth century it was said that there could be no more philosophy after Hegel" (ibid., 47). Thankfully, Moltmann did not remain under Barth's massive shadow for too long but discovered new territory with his *Theology of Hope* (1964).

In July 1950, Moltmann was engaged to be married to Elisabeth, and their wedding took place on March 17, 1952. Moltmann recalls how much he admired her political theology when they first met, "which was radically democratic and pretty far left" (ibid., 45). Elisabeth would later become a well-respected feminist theologian in her own right, and together they were the most famous theological couple in Germany. As far as dialogue partners go, and in a more implicit sense, Elisabeth is undoubtedly the most significant influence in Moltmann's life.

After receiving high marks on his thesis, the Moltmanns searched for a Church. The new couple eventually found themselves in Wasserhorst, from 1953-58. Standing before a congregation of workers and farmers, however, Moltmann felt slightly out of place, "at first like a fool." However, he soon realized that he could preach from the "hard school of life" experiences he shared with these men and women better than he could from his lecture notes. As a result, Moltmann's theology has never been restricted to the academic world but finds its home in the community of the Church. He writes:

> This congregation taught me 'the shared theology of all believers', the theology of the people. Unless academic theology continually turns back to this theology of the people, it becomes abstract and irrelevant. For the fact is that theology is not just something for theological specialists; it is a task laid on the whole people of God, all congregations and every believer.
>
> — A BROAD PLACE, 59

In 1958, Moltmann accepted work as a professor at the Church seminary in Wuppertal, where he stayed until 1964. One of the most important events during this time was his meeting with Ernst Bloch on May 8, 1961. Following Bloch's lecture at the university, they talked together at a nearby pub until midnight. Moltmann recalls how positively Bloch discussed religion with him, leading him to ask, "But you are an atheist aren't you, Herr Bloch?" Bloch responded, "with a twinkle in his eyes, 'I am an atheist for God's sake'" (ibid., 79). Moltmann had read Bloch's *The Principle of Hope* during a vacation in the Swiss mountains (1960), and it captivated him so much that the beautiful scenery "passed me by unnoticed." From this moment on Moltmann "set out to search for a theology of hope" (ibid.). It should be clarified, however, that Moltmann "had no wish to follow Bloch or to fall heir to him" (ibid.). Instead, "What I was looking for was a theological parallel act to his atheistic principle of hope on the basis of the promissory history of the old covenant and the resurrection history of the new" (ibid.). That is important to clarify against Barth's concern that Moltmann had simply "baptized" Bloch's philosophy. Moltmann published *Theology of Hope* in 1964, with an English translation appearing in 1967. In 1963, Moltmann moved from Wuppertal to a position at Bonn University.

Following its publication, *Theology of Hope* was read and discussed widely. Moltmann became a well-known theologian, especially in America. Moltmann spent a year as a visiting professor at Duke University (1967-68). Many newspapers and periodicals such as the *New York Times, Newsweek,* and *Los Angeles Times* published articles on Moltmann's new theology of hope. This initial popularity and the relationships he formed because of it led to many further visits to America throughout his life.

In 1967, Moltmann was invited to the chair of systematic theology in Tübingen. Ernst Käsemann had championed him for the position. He began lectures in 1968, after his guest professorship at Duke. He remained at Tübingen until his retirement in 1994.

Moltmann continued to accept invitations from around the world to lecture, from North America, Latin America, Australia, Japan, and Korea. His theology took on a broader scope as he engaged in a dialogue with theologians from all around the world.

The Crucified God (1972) was perhaps one of Moltmann's most personal books. He describes it as "part of my wrestling with God" (ibid., 189). After that, Moltmann wrote *The Church in the Power of the Spirit* (1975). These first three books mark the end of Moltmann's "early" theology, and from that point on he began focusing on his "systematic contributions to theology" (more on these two periods in the next chapter).

He still lives in Tübingen, travels and speaks semi-regularly around the globe, has roundtable meetings with former colleagues Hans Küng and Eberhard Jüngel, and continues to read and write theology actively.

———

Moltmann published his autobiography in 2006 (English translation, 2009). Sadly, his wife Elisabeth passed away recently, on June 7, 2016. It would be difficult to underestimate the influence she had on him. They authored a few books together, and she was, in her own right, a significant feminist theologian. She lived to be 89.

In an interview, Moltmann once said: "You see before you only half a Moltmann. The other half is Elisabeth. And we shared one hundred percent love, one hundred percent respect, and a lifelong friendship" (Forster: "An Interview with Moltmann").

AN OVERVIEW OF MOLTMANN'S WORKS

Moltmann's ten major books fit within one of two series. The first series includes *Theology of Hope, The Crucified God,* and *The Church in the Power of the Spirit.* These are known as Moltmann's early "trilogy." In these three books, the goal was to re-orient the whole of theology from a particular focal point. Moltmann describes this well:

> The theological method which I used in the three books can be described as: *the whole of theology in one focal point.* In *Theology of Hope* hope, from being an object of theology, became for me the subject of theology. To think theologically out of hope means to see the whole of theology in the light of the future of God. In *The Crucified God* the whole of theology came together for me in the focal point of the cross, and in the perspective of the crucified Christ I learned to understand God and humanity in their common suffering. *The Church in the Power of the Spirit* is in comparison not so strongly concentrated into one perspective, because ecclesiology has to deal with many different themes. [...] Of course, this method gives rise to onesided emphases and exaggerations, but one also sees things which one had not seen before.

> — PREFACE TO BAUCKHAM: MOLTMANN, IX

The second series makes up the longest concentration of Moltmann's career, known as his "systematic contributions to theology." There are seven volumes in total, beginning with the Trinity and concluding with ethics. The focus of this series was to examine particular topics and offer a unique "contribution" without the claim of saying everything that needs to be said. These works are rightly understood when we recognize them as taking part in a *conversation,* rather than as a closed system in itself. Moltmann explains the method for this series:

> I decided then not to go on using this method of concentrating the whole of theology into one focal point, but, conversely, to present *my own part as a contribution to the collective whole of theology.* [...] I have given up the method of focussing on the one focal point at a time and am attempting to contribute my limited understanding to the great conversation of theology about the times of history and the places of the earth.
>
> — IBID., IX-X

It is beneficial if we recognize the distinction between these two series because each has a unique purpose in mind. The two compliment each other well, however, and their difference does not imply they are at odds with each other. While Moltmann indeed grew as a theologian from the beginning of his career to the end, he nevertheless retains many essential insights throughout his work. That is to say, the second series is not a negation of the first but merely has a different method and focus. As we proceed to explore the ten books from both series, the distinctions will become clear.

These are Moltmann's major books, in chronological order:

EARLY TRILOGY

- *Theology of Hope: On the Ground and the Implications of a Christian Eschatology* (chapter 2)
- *The Crucified God: The Cross of Christ as the Foundation and Criticism of Christian Theology* (chapter 3)

- *The Church in the Power of the Spirit: A Contribution to Messianic Ecclesiology* (chapter 4)

SYSTEMATIC CONTRIBUTIONS TO THEOLOGY

- *The Trinity and the Kingdom: The Doctrine of God* (chapter 5)
- *God in Creation: A New Theology of Creation and the Spirit of God* (chapter 6)
- *The Way of Jesus Christ: Christology in Messianic Dimensions* (chapter 7)
- *The Spirit of Life: A Universal Affirmation* (chapter 9)
- *The Coming of God: Christian Eschatology* (chapter 10)
- *Experiences in Theology: Ways and Forms of Christian Theology* (chapter 1)
- *Ethics of Hope* (chapter 8)

1

EXPERIENCES IN THEOLOGY

Summary: Jürgen Moltmann is a theologian of *exodus, dialogue,* and *praxis.* These three categories are helpful for beginning to understand his distinct approach to theology and the Bible.

In Moltmann's own words:

A 'theology of hope' is a theology of questions that can be answered only by the coming of God through the kingdom of his freedom.

— Religion, Revolution, and the Future, 66

The theology of the people of God, wandering in the faith of Abraham and Sarah, is a theology of the way—a *theologia viae*—not yet a theology of the home country, a *theologia patriae*. It is a theology of exile and exodus, and in all its images and concepts it bears the stamp of the far-off land itself out of which these images and concepts are to lead us.

— Experiences in Theology, 50

You never have to ask how [Moltmann's] theology might be applied because his theological work is from beginning to end practical. Indeed, he has taught us that if you have to ask how a theology can be or should be 'applied' to preaching you know such a theology is based on a mistake.

— STANLEY HAUERWAS: THE FUTURE OF THEOLOGY, 26

INTRODUCTION

Theologians often *begin* their major works by explaining their method. Moltmann did the opposite. Moltmann placed his book of methodology at the end of his systematic contributions to theology. We will begin here even though Moltmann does not, because recognizing the unique characteristics of Moltmann's theology from the start will help us better appreciate his ideas. Moltmann's decision to deal with methodology at the end of his contributions works well for his project, but it would make my task here confusing and repetitive. To be clear upfront about the *kind* of theology Moltmann is doing, as well as the *way* he proposes to do it, examining this book first will provide helpful context for the rest of what is to follow.

Moltmann offers a summary of his method and explains why he addresses it at the end of his systematic contributions:

For me, theology was, and still is, an adventure of ideas. It is an open, inviting path. Right down to the present day, it has continued to fascinate my mental and spiritual curiosity. My theological methods therefore grew up as I came to have a perception of the objects of theological thought. *The road emerged only as I walked it.* And my attempts to walk it are of course determined by my personal biography, and by the political context and historical kairos in which I live. I have searched for the right word for the right time. I have not written any theological textbooks. The articles I have contributed to various theological dictionaries and encyclopaedias have seldom been particularly successful. I was not concerned to collect up correct theological notions, because I was much too preoccupied with the perception of new perspectives and unfamiliar aspects. I had no wish to be a disciple of the great theological masters of past generations. Nor have I any desire to found a new theological school. My whole concern has been, and still is, to stimulate other people to discover theology for themselves—to have their own theological ideas, and to set out along their own paths.

— EXPERIENCES IN THEOLOGY, XV

Jürgen Moltmann is probably unlike any theologian you have read before. His sheer originality has led to grave misunderstandings; those who expect him to fit within specific pre-established categories often launch unfair criticisms of his work. If we fail to recognize what makes him so unique, then we risk misreading him.

It is perhaps best to begin by stating that Moltmann's theology is *for outsiders.* Even though his career was quite traditional as a university professor and prolific lecturer, his theology is as popular as it is (and as controversial) because, while in the form of a classic theologian, he is and remains a theologian outside of traditional categories. He is an iconoclast who challenges the status quo at every turn.

The three categories listed here are not exhaustive, but I think they will be helpful for new readers of his work. These are Moltmann's theology 1) of *exodus,* 2) of *dialogue,* and 3) of *praxis* (practice).

THEOLOGY OF EXODUS

For Moltmann, theology is an "adventure of ideas." Theology is thus a journey, an exodus; it is theology "on the way." A theology of exodus is the opposite of *a theology of the homeland.* No attempt is made to say all that there is to say for all times and places. Systematic theology has traditionally attempted to do precisely that: to present doctrines that are universally valid. This notion is present in most great traditions, but it is not the goal of Moltmann's theology.

Since Schleiermacher, however, modern theology often recognizes the permanently *unfinished* character of theology—that is, its unavoidable cultural and historical limitations. The idea of a universally valid theology for every group of people and every period is no longer an image theology can have of itself. Most modern theologians have recognized this, but few have taken it as seriously as Moltmann.

Theology is fundamentally *theologia viatorum,* a theology of pilgrims. Moltmann writes, "My image of theology is not 'A safe stronghold is our God'. It is the exodus of God's people, on the road to the promised land of liberty where God dwells" (*Experiences in Theology,* xx). It is theology *on the way,* a theology which has not yet arrived at perfection. It is not a theology of the safe and comfortable homeland; it presupposes an *unfinished* story in the history of God with the world.

We often prefer to fixate on a single great work, such as Calvin's *Institutes* or Barth's *Dogmatics,* and to let it do our thinking for us. We imagine these masterpieces are like a safe fortress from the changes of time. However, even the most complete systematic theology cannot free us from the "new thing" God is doing in the world (Isa. 43:19). We feel happy to spend our time in these large theological systems, but we risk being left behind. We talk about "Calvinists" and "Barthians" for this reason, and while these terms are sometimes helpful, they can mistakenly imply that either Calvin or Barth have said all there needs to be said. However, this goes against the stated intentions of both theologians, and it contradicts the principle of *theologia viatorum* (theology of pilgrims).

(Barth: "Systematic theology is a contradiction in terms" [*Evangelical Theology,* 180]. Anyone who properly understands Barth will recognize the impossibility of becoming a "Barthian." Moreover, Calvin once sharply noted the difference between "a disciple and an ape": the former goes *beyond* their teacher while the latter merely repeats what they have said; see B.A. Gerrish: *Thinking with the Church,* 122.)

A theology of exodus rejects the idea that we have arrived at the homeland, that we can remain stagnant and unchanged in our thinking and rest in some great theology of the past. Thus, a theology of exodus offers no allegiance to any system of theology as if it were the endgame of all theological discussion. No council, creed, or dogma can have the final word. As Schleiermacher famously said, "The reformation still goes on!" Theology today must recognize that it has not yet arrived at its goal: we see dimly as in a mirror, not yet face to face (1 Cor. 13:12).

The genuinely faithful student of a theological master is not the student who merely repeats what their master has said, but who goes beyond them into new territory. Calvin is not honored best by the "Calvinists" who hold to a reductionistic system created around his ideas, but by those who go beyond him, even if it means leaving some things behind. We must resist the temptation of hiding away in the unfinished tents of past theologians, while the journey of theological history moves on without us. Of course, we must learn from the masters of the past (this entire "Plain English Series" presupposes the importance of that task!), but we cannot camp out at any one place as if we have arrived. Theology reaches its goal only in the *eschaton*, in God's Kingdom, when we see face to face God's glory. Until then, all theology is *preliminary* and *anticipatory,* conditioned and limited by its own time and place. There is no perfect theological system, and so we must be ever on the move. That is the heart of Moltmann's theology of exodus.

Theology is therefore also *existential.* We cannot ignore our own experiences with God in history. I will often reference stories from Moltmann's life to show this connection. An image to keep in mind is the biblical account of Jacob wrestling with God (Gen. 32:22-32). This image describes what theology is as well as the task of the theologian. A theologian's greatest suffering is God, and God is their greatest joy. Moltmann writes:

> Theology is for me a suffering from God and a passion for God's kingdom. For me this is a messianic passion, because it is possessed and moved by the presence of the crucified Christ. For me theology springs from a divine passion—it is the open wound of God in one's own life and in the tormented men, women, and children of this world; from the accusation Job threw at God; from Christ's cry of forsakenness on the cross. We are not theologians because we are particularly religious; we are theologians because in the face of this world we miss God. We are crying out for his righteousness and justice, and are not prepared to come to terms with mass death on earth.
>
> But for me theology also springs from God's love for life—the love for life that we experience in the presence of the life-giving Spirit and that enables us to move beyond our resignation and begin to love life here and now. These are also Christ's two experiences of God, the kingdom of God and the cross, and because of that they are the foundations of Christian theology, as well: God's delight and God's pain.

It is out of the tension between these two that hope is born for the kingdom in which God is wholly in the world and the world is wholly in God. 'Seek first the kingdom of God…'

— A PASSION FOR GOD'S REIGN, 2

An exodus theology is intensely personal because it is our journey together with God in history. This journey is marked by suffering and joy. It is a joy and a pain because it is *God's* joy and pain, together with creation, as we await the final redemption.

An exodus theology is primarily *for* the Church, and it takes place *in* the Church. Theology is a help to the Church and arises from out of the congregation. As Moltmann writes, "Theology is the business of all God's people" (*Experiences in Theology*, 11). Everyone *is* a theologian the moment he or she begins thinking about what he or she believes. The academy is not the center of theological exploration; it is merely an *extension* of the Church's theology. An exodus theology cannot become elitist. Theology is not a sovereign proclamation from the heights of ecclesiastical authority, but it comes "from below," in the congregation. The image of an exodus theology forbids any claims of professional status.

This change in perspective from a leadership-oriented, "top-down" theology to a congregation-oriented, "from below" theology is noteworthy. It means that a "theology of all believers is the foundation for every academic theology," and not the reverse (ibid., 14). Theology begins in the congregation of believers, and there it is sustained; it is not exclusively the task of the academy. Of course, academic work is necessary, but it is at best only an *extension* of theological thinking within the congregation. Academic work is often more precise and systematic, but it is merely an extension of the theological task of all believers. Moltmann shares this vision of the task of academic theology when he writes:

> Academic theology is nothing other than the scholarly penetration and illumination by mind and spirit of what Christians in the congregations think when they believe in God and live in the fellowship of Christ. By scholarly I mean that the theology is methodologically verifiable and comprehensible. Good scholarly theology is therefore basically simple, because it is clear. Only cloudy theology is complicated and difficult.

Whether it be Athanasius or Augustine, Aquinas or Calvin, Schleiermacher or Barth—the fundamental ideas of every good theological system can be presented on a single page. It is true that Barth needed more than 8,000 pages for his *Church Dogmatics*, and even then they were still unfinished, so that kindly disposed critics said, 'surely truth can't be as long as that'. But as we know, theological praise of the eternally bounteous God is never-ending. So the length of a work does not necessarily detract from the simple truth of what it says.

— Experiences in Theology, 13-4

Moltmann's theology fits within this unique kind of academic work. It is not a theology "from above," so to speak, but "from below." It arises in dialogue with the whole body of Christ. Thus, it is an extension of the Church's worship and adoration of the Triune God. Academic theology is dense and lengthy because worship has no end; because we will never finish marveling at God's glory and love. The best theology *is* worship, therefore, and not merely an exercise in abstract thinking. An exodus theology is finally a *doxological theology*, continually discovering new facets of God's goodness and refusing to settle for yesterday's manna.

THEOLOGY OF DIALOGUE

A theology of exodus is an *incomplete* expression of the Church's thinking about God; it remains unfinished until we see God face to face in the new creation. As such, the fragmentary nature of theology means continued *dialogue* with others is necessary and essential. The desire to listen and engage in a broad conversation marks Moltmann's work, and not only within the Church but even outside it. That is why Moltmann was willing to learn from Jewish philosophers such as Ernst Bloch and Abraham Heschel, atheist existentialists such as Albert Camus, and even those whom the Church condemned heretical such as Joachim of Fiore. It is perhaps *the* defining characteristic of Moltmann's theology, but it has also led to controversy. It is useful to recognize that this vision of theology as dialogue is the logical conclusion of an exodus theology. Because we have yet not arrived at the homeland, because there are no experts in the Church, we must humbly listen to a wide range of voices.

Moltmann writes:

> Theology is like a network of rivers, with reciprocal influences and
> mutual challenges. It is certainly not a desert in which every individual is
> alone with himself or herself, and with his or her God. For me,
> theological access to the truth of the triune God is through dialogue. It is
> communitarian and co-operative. *Theologia viatorum*—the theology of
> men and women on the way—is an enduring critical conversation with
> the generations before us and the contemporaries at our side, in
> expectation of those who will come after us. So what I have written is
> not safeguarded from every side. It is sometimes 'foolhardy', as some
> concerned churchmen have thought. In the business of theology it is
> hard not to be controversial.
>
> — EXPERIENCES IN THEOLOGY, XVII

A theology of dialogue presupposes the mutual dependence of
dialogue partners. The primary *modus operandi,* the method of operation,
of a theologian, is in *conversation* and *community* with others. It is for the
sake of stimulating this conversation and engaging in a community that
Moltmann writes. He has no illusions about saying either the first word or
the last word on any subject. His theology takes place inherently and
necessarily in *unhindered dialogue.* Accordingly, Moltmann's theology is
not understood best as the final word in a conversation, but as an *invitation* to an "adventure of ideas."

ON THE BIBLE

This understanding of theology as unhindered dialogue is not hard for
us to accept, but difficulty often comes when we discover that Moltmann
extends this dialogue to include the Bible itself. He does not consider the
Bible to be the final, exhaustive word for all times and places—in the
sense that the Bible alone is enough to guarantee the truth of theology.
The Bible is the authoritative foundation of theology, to be sure, but
Moltmann engages the Bible more as a *stimulant* for theological thinking
than as a *restriction.* Moltmann writes, "A hearer of the texts becomes a
friend of the texts, who discusses with them what they are talking about"

in an ongoing dialogue which never arrives at perfection since we remain pilgrims on the way towards God's future and the Kingdom of Glory.

THEOLOGY OF PRAXIS

We might summarize all that we have said so far about Moltmann's theology by stating that Moltmann is *a theologian of the Kingdom of God*. A Kingdom of God theology is a theology of exodus, of hopeful expectation of the coming Kingdom and its King; it is a theology of dialogue since we have not yet reached the Kingdom; and as such, it is a theology of *praxis*. That is the final characteristic we will consider. In Moltmann's terms, a Kingdom of God theology is a "*missionary* theology," and thus it is a "*public* theology" (*Experiences in Theology*, xx). Therefore, Moltmann writes:

> Kingdom-of-God theology intervenes critically and prophetically in the public affairs of a given society, and draws public attention, not to the church's own interests but to 'God's kingdom, God's commandment and his righteousness', as Thesis 5 of the Barmen Theological Declaration says. That means that kingdom-of-God theology can neither withdraw to its own community of faith in fundamentalist fashion nor adapt itself in modernist style to society's prevailing trends. It is resistingly and productively concerned about the future of life in the whole earthly creation.
>
> — IBID., XX-XXI

Moltmann's theology moves towards this particular end. It is neither apolitical or reclusive. For Moltmann, all theology *is* political and practical, whether we explicitly admit it or not. "A logical and consistent Christian discipleship always has logical political consequences. [...] [A] missionary church cannot be apolitical" (*The Church in the Power of the Spirit*, 15). A Church that is silent in the face of injustice fails to live in the discipleship of Christ consistently. Any Church that attempts to hide under a neutral, apolitical cloak finally lends its support to an oppressive status quo. Kingdom of God theology necessitates political and social action, and this means all theological statements have public consequences.

An insight worth considering in this connection is the political and ethical way Moltmann insists we should read the Scriptures. Moltmann writes, "[T]here is no all-encompassing hermeneutics of the Bible's promissory history of the kingdom of God without ethics and politics—the ethics of life and the politics of the righteousness which puts things to rights and creates rightful justice" (*Experiences in Theology,* 133). To read the Bible as a purely "spiritual" book with nothing to say to the ethical and political dimensions of life is to misread it gravely. The Church is called to stand on the side of the poor and oppressed because it is the messianic fellowship of Jesus Christ. God took up solidarity with the poor and weak in Christ, and the Church is properly the Church when it follows the way of Jesus into solidarity with the oppressed. Moltmann challenges us to read the Bible "with the eyes of the poor" (ibid., 131). That does not mean offering superficial charity but "recognizing 'the messianism of the poor' [...] by listening to them as their own determining subjects of an authentic interpretation of scripture, not as objects of our own endeavours" (ibid., 132).

Moltmann explores this hermeneutic further, writing:

> Reading the Bible with the eyes of the poor is a different thing from reading it with the eyes of the man with a full belly. If it is read in the light of the experiences and hopes of the oppressed, the Bible's revolutionary themes—promise, exodus, resurrection and Spirit—come alive. The way in which the history of Israel and the history of Christ blend with that of the hungry and oppressed is quite different from the way in which they have often been linked with the history of the mighty and rich. However the theology of revolution may be criticized, it has made it patently clear that the political responsibility of Christianity in the present conflicts must definitely take specific form in the people, with the people and for the liberation of the people.
>
> — THE CHURCH IN THE POWER OF THE SPIRIT, 17

The whole of Moltmann's theology ends in *praxis.* It always includes implications for the personal, political, and ethical realms. The Church participates in the public sphere for Christ's sake. Reading the Bible as a purely spiritual book without recognizing its public implications is a disastrous mistake. Moltmann's theology presupposes a political and ethical reading of the Bible, and it is thus a theology of *praxis.*

Throughout this book, we will highlight the many personal, political, and ethical implications of Moltmann's theology, so it will not be necessary to give further examples.

CONCLUSION

Judgments regarding the success of Moltmann's theology should be made within the context of these three characteristics; because to appreciate Moltmann reasonably means appreciating him according to how he sets himself out to be understood. These three characteristics are by no means exhaustive, but I have decided to focus on them here to establish the trajectory of this book. Ideally, these points will also act as an effective defense against critics of his work that fail to take account of his stated method and goals.

The goal of reading Moltmann's theology is not to agree with everything he says. Instead, the goal is to be stimulated by his insights, to be challenged by him, and ultimately to join him on a great journey of discovery in this "adventure of ideas." It would be a mistake to reject him outright merely because we disagree with some of his conclusions. A few disagreements are to be expected and perhaps even encouraged. The goal is not *agreement* but *dialogue* along the way, as we anticipate together the coming of God's Kingdom and worship before the glory of God's grace in Christ. In this sense, Moltmann is a theologian of a particular kind, *sui generis,* and should be appreciated accordingly. His success is not in uniform agreement, but, according to his own stated goals, he succeeds by the conversations he invokes. Critical thinking, not uniformity of thought, is the presupposed goal.

So as we begin to explore the content of Moltmann's theology, it will be crucial to keep these three characteristics in mind. Moltmann's theology is not a "take it or leave it" theology, but an invitation to dialogue. I encourage you to think about all of his proposals within this context.

SIDEBAR: ECUMENISM

It is Moltmann's conviction that "humanly speaking, truth is to be found in unhindered dialogue" (*The Trinity and the Kingdom,* xiii). This conviction makes ecumenical dialogue *essential* for theology; it is vital we have conversations with those outside of our tradition. Moltmann was involved in several ecumenical conferences and conventions throughout his career, and his approach to ecumenical dialogue is noteworthy.

Moltmann defines ecumenism as "the discovery of the other, and reciprocal acceptance of others in their otherness" (*God for a Secular Society,* 203). Ecumenism is possible only when we stand together under the cross of Christ. Ecumenical movements have attempted a wide range of strategies, and Moltmann thinks those that focus on the internal rather than external comparisons are more successful, particularly when we find each other at the foot of the cross. He explains:

> Ecumenism is realized only (but then also world-wide) where we find ourselves beneath the cross of Christ, and mutually discover ourselves beneath his cross as brothers and sisters, as the hungry in shared poverty (Rom. 3:23), as people imprisoned in shared sin. Beneath his cross we all stand there with empty hands. We have nothing to offer God except the burden of guilt and the emptiness of our hearts. Beneath the cross, people are not accounted

Protestants, Catholics and Orthodox. There the godless are justified, enemies reconciled, the imprisoned freed, the poor made rich and the grieving filled with hope. That is why beneath the cross we also discover ourselves as children living from the same freedom in Christ, and as friends in the same fellowship of the Spirit.

'The closer we come to the cross of Christ, the closer we come to one another.' How could we keep alive our divisions and enmities in the face of his bitter suffering and death? How, in the face of 'the open heart' of Christ, could we remain closed to one another, and be afraid for the church? Clasped by the arms of God stretched out in his suffering on the cross, how can we clench our fists, or cling fast with tenacious hands to what we possess in our different denominations?

— IBID., 214-5

Under the cross, we will find each other not in ecclesiastical glory or power, but in weakness and humility. With open and humble hearts we freely embrace each other once again, finding brothers in sisters in all streams and traditions. It is an offense to Christ and His cross when we refuse to fellowship with our brothers and sisters. Narrow-minded fundamentalism, which excludes every perspective but its own, is a lonely road, and it is not the way of Jesus. Open friendship and a shared embrace at the base of the cross—this is His way. May we walk the road of the cross as we begin to see Christ in those we disagree with, as we learn to listen to their perspective and turn those who were once thought to be our enemies into our brothers and sisters.

CHAPTER 2: THEOLOGY OF HOPE

SUMMARY: Christianity is wholly and utterly *hope*. In contrast with escapist hope and utopian hope, it is hope in the transformation of *this* world by the coming of God. Theology is therefore eschatologically oriented towards God's future Kingdom.

IN MOLTMANN'S OWN WORDS:

From first to last, and not merely in the epilogue, Christianity is eschatology, is hope, forward looking and forward moving, and therefore also revolutionizing and transforming the present. The eschatological is not one element *of* Christianity, but it is the medium of Christian faith as such, the key in which everything in it is set, the glow that suffuses everything here in the dawn of an expected new day. For Christian faith lives from the raising of the crucified Christ, and strains after the promises of the universal future of Christ. Eschatology is the passionate suffering and passionate longing kindled by the Messiah. Hence eschatology cannot really be only a part of Christian doctrine. Rather, the eschatological outlook is characteristic of all Christian proclamation, of every Christian existence and of the whole Church. There is therefore only one real problem in Christian theology, which its own object forces upon it and which it in turn forces on mankind and on human thought:

the problem of the future. [...] A proper theology would therefore have to be constructed in the light of its future goal. Eschatology should not be its end, but its beginning.

— THEOLOGY OF HOPE, 16

I had no wish simply to write a theology *about* hope. My purpose was a theology *out of* hope—theology as eschatology, theology of the liberating kingdom of God in the world.

— EXPERIENCES IN THEOLOGY, 93

When we wait and hope for the new creation, we are not seeking another world; we are seeking for this world to be different.

— GOD WILL BE ALL IN ALL, 83

SECONDARY QUOTES:

[Kurt Vonnegut] was the most imaginative contemporary novelist helping us see the absurdity of the normal. Moltmann, I believe, is the Vonnegut of recent theology: he has been willing to force us theologically to imagine our world eschatologically.

— STANLEY HAUERWAS: THE FUTURE OF CREATION, 26

Ascetic Christianity called the world evil and left it. Humanity is waiting for a revolutionary Christianity which will call the world evil and change it.

— WALTER RAUSCHENBUSCH: CHRISTIANITY AND THE SOCIAL CRISIS, 91

INTRODUCTION

Moltmann's *Theology of Hope* re-orients the whole of theology from the focal point of eschatology, the doctrine of hope. Theology has often neglected the theme of hope by placing eschatology in the appendix of faith, deeming hope in the imminent arrival of the Kingdom of God nonessential to the life of the Church. Moltmann's genius, however, is the insight that Christianity is, in essence, forward-looking and moving; *Christianity is hope.* Hope is the fuel of a revolutionary Christianity which calls the world evil and rises to change it. As such, Moltmann's proposal for the eschatological orientation of theology is at once the manifesto for a Church conscious of the political and social implications of the Gospel.

According to Richard Bauckham, the "greatest achievement" of Moltmann's early theology is its ability "to open up hermeneutical structures for relating biblical faith to the modern world" (*The Theology of Jürgen Moltmann,* 26). Moltmann's *Theology of Hope* calls us to *embrace* God's future instead of falling into "reactionary traditionalism" against the changes of history (ibid., 8). Thus Moltmann "wished to show how the modern experience of history as a process of constant and radical change, in hopeful search of a new future, need not be rejected by the church" (ibid.). Eschatological hope leads to a Christianity which no longer resists the progress of history but embraces it with hope in God's coming Kingdom, so that the Church may be *credible* and *relevant* in the modern world. Hope for God's coming draws the Church into the Trinitarian history and mission of God; it pushes the Church into the public sphere.

Theology of Hope is one of Moltmann's best-known works, and it places a defining stamp on the whole of his theology. It is also one of his most difficult books to read, and newcomers to his thought are likely to be put off by its complexity. Its proposal, however, is quite simple: *Christianity is hope.* What this means for specific doctrines is yet to be seen as we explore other facets of Moltmann's theology. Here we will only focus on a few of the critical insights that are necessary to appreciate this eschatological orientation by examining how Moltmann relates eschatology to God's self-revelation and the lordship of Christ. First, however, we have to be clear about what is and is not the content of our hope.

CONTRASTING VISIONS OF HOPE

What is eschatology? Some define it as the doctrine of "last things," but this is not a truly *Christian* understanding of the term. The fearful "last things" are not the subject of Christian eschatology, but the glorious first day of God's new creation. It is not the end that concerns us, but the new beginning. Eschatology is the doctrine of hope. The critical point shaping our eschatology is our definition of hope. What is a genuinely *Christian* hope? We must begin by contrasting this hope against two alternative visions of the future: utopia and escape.

1. UTOPIAN HOPE

A utopian vision of the future is hope in an ideal world extrapolated from the present situation and achieved by humans within history. In other words, utopian hope is that which is possible by human beings; it is thus faith in the progress of history towards an idealized end. It is, for example, Karl Marx's vision of a utopian communist society. It is the idealized projection of what a perfect world could be. It is a *this-worldly* hope which places its trust in the achievements of humanity, not God.

Although Moltmann is indebted to the Marxist philosophy of Ernst Bloch, his denial of utopian hope is the best way to recognize his essential disagreement with Bloch. Bloch's hope is utopian; Moltmann's hope is in the Kingdom. Bloch's hope trusts in the progress of history; Moltmann's hope trusts in God's faithfulness, in God's sovereign grace. That is important to clarify against those who have deemed Moltmann's *Theology of Hope* merely a "baptized" version of Bloch's philosophy (Barth). Moltmann's hope is not a Marxist utopian hope disguised in Christian clothing, but hope thoroughly founded on Christ and His future.

The Kingdom of God is not the result of historical progress. It is "not of this world" (John 18:36). In the *culmination* of history, in the *eschaton* or final *parousia* (arrival) of Christ, God's Kingdom will dwell on this earth. When our hope is in the abilities of powerful leaders or nations to create utopia *within history*, then it is a misplaced hope. God alone is our hope. God will be faithful to the promise. Neither faith in "progress" or the strength of nations will bring about the Kingdom.

That means: no kingdom, nation, or ruler of this earth should take the place of the Kingdom of God. We pledge allegiance to no other Lord but Jesus Christ. No earthly power should be the object of Christian hope. No nation or political agenda can claim Christ's legitimization (there is no such thing as a "Christian nation"). History knows all too well the disastrous effects of misplaced hope: Hitler's Third Reich and Stalin's forced communism, for example. Both leaders slaughtered millions in the name of their false hope. Utopian hope is faith in humanity and the progress of history; Christian hope is hope in the faithfulness of God to the promise, it is hope in the coming Kingdom.

2. ESCAPIST HOPE

Escapist hope gives up on God's coming transformation of this world by resigning its hope to *another world*. In contrast with a worldly utopian hope, escapism is hope in the flight of the soul from all things bodily and worldly. It is hope in "heaven" or a kind of gnostic spirit-world, and this, too, is an illegitimate form of hope.

It is a common error for Christians today, especially in American evangelicalism, to mistake our hope in God's Kingdom for an escapist dream of a pagan afterlife, to place our hope in "heaven." In contrast, true Christian hope is not hope for *another* world but the new creation of *this* world. Hope which gives up on this world is not *Christian* hope. Since the foundation of our hope is Christ and His *bodily* resurrection, our hope is firmly rooted in the *humanity* of Christ. Moltmann writes, "The Christian hope is foundationally and in essence the hope of resurrection" (*The Source of Life*, 81). To deny hope for *this* world is to deny the bodily resurrection of Jesus Christ eschatologically.

We have wrongly placed our hope in "going to heaven" someday when we die, but this is precisely the kind of escapist hope Moltmann cannot accept. "Personally speaking," Moltmann writes, "when I die I have no wish to 'go to heaven'; I expect 'the resurrection of the dead and the life of the world to come,' to put it in the Christian terms of the Nicene Creed" (*The Living God and the Fullness of Life*, 84). He calls the desire to escape earth for a spiritual, heavenly existence a "fantasy" like in "gnostic redemption religion" (ibid.). The notion of going to heaven when we die owes more to paganism than to Christ's resurrection. We will not be redeemed *from* this world but together *with* it. Christian hope must be as bodily and earthly as the risen Christ. The nature of Christ's resurrection points ahead as a foretaste of the coming resurrection and new creation of all things. If we confess that Christ was raised bodily from the grave, and not merely as a spiritual being, then we must also confess hope in the resurrection of the flesh in the world to come. Recognizing this connection protects our hope from gnostic and pagan ideas of a disembodied afterlife.

An escapist way of thinking about the future has paralyzed the Church. That much is clear in the way we talk about salvation. Salvation is regularly restricted to mean the salvation of souls. We talk about "saving souls" in our evangelism efforts, or about death as the release from the "prison" of our bodies. Moltmann, in contrast, widens the scope of salvation. A genuinely *Christian* understanding of redemption includes 1) the whole person (body, soul, mind), 2) the person with others (community), and 3) the whole of creation (the earth and the cosmos). To limit salvation only to the soul is to deny the full scope of Christ's reconciliation. Who are we without the full expression of our being, including body, mind, and soul? If even one aspect of who we are is lost in redemption, is it not indeed redemption but rather a diminution of our existence? Moreover, who are we without the relationships defining our identity, without the loved ones and family members we surround ourselves with? Finally, what is humanity without the earth from which we came, and the community of all living things? Is redemption complete if we give up hope for even one aspect of God's bountiful creation?

Because of Christ's resurrection, we cannot give up hope for anything that God has made. Any vision of a future redemption which gives up on even one aspect of creation is not redemption to a *better* life but a *lesser* life, because to lose even one aspect of our existence is to lose what is fundamental to life. Our hope is in the coming resurrection and new creation of *all things,* as Revelation 21 portrays so vividly. We will not escape earth and go to heaven; heaven will dwell on the earth. The glory of the Lord will cover the earth as the waters cover the sea (Hab. 2:14). It is a *new creation,* not "heaven," which is our hope.

An escapist vision of salvation neglects the concerns of social justice and the liberation of the oppressed. If we decide only to care for the salvation of "souls," then we resign ourselves to a definition of salvation incongruent with true Christian hope. The reduction of salvation to souls is a gnostic vision that disregards the social, political, and physical needs of human beings. This understanding of salvation closes us off from the liberating power of the Gospel by restricting its liberation to *another world.* Salvation is not for some isolated part of our being in another world, however; it is hope in the promised transformation of *this* world.

The Gospel proclaims liberation and justice here and now because we hope in the transformation of all things. It is in anticipation of the new creation that we work today for the liberation of the oppressed, care for the poor, and health to the sick.

An example of this reduced vision of salvation is the evangelical reaction against various liberation theologies, such as Black Liberation Theology in America (James H. Cone). While some evangelicals admit its merit, the majority reject liberation theology for its emphasis on God's liberating action here and now. Because, for evangelicals, the liberation proclaimed in the Gospel is limited to the soul's liberation from hell in the afterlife. Fighting for the liberation of oppressed people here and now is considered to be merely a *secondary* issue. This Gospel ignores the many hells that exist here and now on this earth in the form of poverty, racism, torture, rape, violence, and death. They have neglected Christ's call to proclaim the Kingdom *on the earth* and, instead, embrace an escapist vision of a pagan afterlife. This escapist vision of hope distorts the Gospel. If our Gospel message has nothing to say to the "least of these," if it is wholly unconcerned with social justice, then it is only half a Gospel at best.

Jesus did not proclaim hope in a disembodied, pagan afterlife. God's coming reign meant profound care for those who suffer in the world, not the resignation of its condition. As He declared in Luke: "The Spirit of the Lord is upon me because he has anointed me to bring good news to the poor. He has sent me to proclaim release to the captives and recovery of sight to the blind, to let the oppressed go free, to proclaim the year of the Lord's favor" (4:18). We may spiritualize this passage, but we would be reading *into* the texts our own bias rather than learning *from* them. Plainly, Jesus Christ did not proclaim the hope of *another world*; Christ proclaimed God's coming Kingdom through the liberation and transformation of *this world*. Escapism is incongruent with the Gospel.

3. CHRISTIAN HOPE: CHRIST AND HIS FUTURE

Neither utopian or escapist, Moltmann's *Theology of Hope* confronts us with a challenging vision of hope in God's promise, hope in the transformation of this world. Christian hope draws us deeper into care for the world, not escape from it. It does not lead us to trust in the progress of history, but in the faithfulness of God to the promise. In short, genuinely Christian hope is hope based on Jesus Christ and His resurrection by God. Moltmann writes, "[Christian hope] sees in the resurrection of Christ not the eternity of heaven, but the future of the very earth on which his cross stands. It sees in him the future of the very humanity for which he died" (*Theology of Hope*, 21).

The content of Christian eschatology is Christ and His future; hope springs from the resurrection of the crucified Christ. The dialectic of cross and resurrection is a defining characteristic of Moltmann's theology. We stand in the midst of the God-forsaken world of Christ's cross as we await resurrection through the faithfulness of God. We echo the groans of an unredeemed creation and hope in the promise of God's future; we await the resurrection of the very same world in which Christ was crucified. It is because Jesus is both the resurrected *and* the crucified one that our world shares in the hope of Christ's future glory. "Christian eschatology speaks of Jesus Christ and his future" (ibid., 17). Therefore, "Hope is nothing else than the expectation of those things which faith has believed to have been truly promised by God. [...] [F]aith is the foundation upon which hope rests, hope nourishes and sustains faith" (ibid., 20). We believe in Jesus Christ and His resurrection, and from this basis, we have hope in the coming Kingdom of God on this earth. This hope orients the entirety of our lives so that we rightly say: *Christianity is hope.*

ANTICIPATION

The promise of God's Kingdom calls us to take up God's mission on the earth in anticipation of Christ's future. By emphasizing forward-looking hope, Moltmann does not neglect the need for revolutionary action. The opposite is true. It is *because* of God's coming Kingdom that we take part in God's mission by working to change the world, to fight for liberation and social justice. Hope does not leave us passive. Hope spurs us to action as we anticipate God's Kingdom on this earth. Hope in God's future pushes the Church out of the comfortable safety of its reclusive culture and into the public sphere. The political and social responsibility of the Church arises from its hope.

Hope is the spark of a revolutionary Christianity. It was this hope that drove the martyrs to give their lives freely for the cause of Christ. It is this same hope which today inspires us to fight against injustice and oppression wherever it may be, because "when freedom is near the chains begin to chafe" (*Jesus Christ for Today's World*, 70). Without hope, we would blindly accept the status quo and live indifferent to its evils. Hope drives liberation. A forward-looking hope *is* a revolutionary hope. "Those who hope in Christ," Moltmann writes, "can no longer put up with reality as it is, but begin to suffer under it, to contradict it" (*Theology of Hope*, 21). Hope in the Kingdom puts us at odds with the unredeemed present and makes us critical of every system of injustice and oppression.

Anticipation is a vital element of Christian hope. God's Kingdom is not of this world; it belongs to the new creation and Christ's *parousia* (arrival). The Kingdom does not come through human efforts. When the Kingdom comes, it will be wholly and entirely God's sovereign work of grace. Does this mean revolutionary action for the transformation of the world is superfluous? Certainly not. On the contrary, reliance on God's grace and trust in God's faithfulness *strengthens* revolutionary action. It is in the assurance of a better world that we are set free from the fear of death and failure and filled with the courage to act selflessly in God's mission. Every liberating act *anticipates* the imminent success of the coming Kingdom.

Distinguishing the historical anticipation of the Kingdom from its arrival in the culmination of all things protects Christian hope from its naturally utopian tendencies. This principle also guards us against complacency, because it means we must keep our eyes open to suffering and death in the world. The principle of anticipation stands between the cross and resurrection: we are realistic about the way things are, and therefore we resist utopian hope, but the expectation of God's imminent Kingdom fills our hearts, and thus we work to transform this world. We remember the cross by concerning ourselves with suffering on this earth, by refusing to shut our eyes to the horrors of the present unredeemed world, yet we expect the resurrection whenever we fight for liberation and justice. We cannot mistake even the most peaceful human kingdom for God's Kingdom, but in the midst of this unredeemed world, hope pulls us onwards in the assurance of the success of God's mission. Martin Luther King, Jr. popularized the statement, "The arc of the moral universe is long, but it bends toward justice" (credited initially to Theodore Parker). That is only true because God will be faithful to the promise.

Hope spurs the Church forward, so that faith and action come together. In the assurance of God's faithfulness to the promise, we fight for the liberation of the oppressed in the cause of justice. Hope awakens us to see the darkness of history in the light of God's future, *to see the world is evil and rise to change it.*

REVELATION AND PROMISE

A helpful insight to show how Moltmann applies this eschatological orientation is in the way he understands divine revelation and the phrase, "Jesus is Lord." Moltmann particularly has Karl Barth in mind, but not exclusively. He essentially argues that Barth neglects the eschatological dimensions of both doctrines. Moltmann thinks Barth's emphasis on revelation is more closely akin to Greek "epiphany" than Jewish hope in the promise. In contrast, Moltmann interprets the knowledge of God *eschatologically*: God makes Godself known through the harmony of promise and fulfillment. Thus, God's faithfulness to the promise *is* God's revelation; God's essential nature is faithfulness. Likewise, for Barth, "Jesus is Lord" is a *realized* description. However, a realized understanding of Christ's lordship overlooks its eschatological connotations. For Barth, "Jesus is Lord" is a *perfect tense* phrase, but Moltmann stresses its *future tense* implications. For Moltmann, that "Jesus is Lord" is a truth still to come even in its anticipation here and now. Truly, Jesus *is* the Lord, but this implies both a declaration (present tense) *and a promise* (future tense). We say "Jesus is Lord" in *anticipation* of the reign of God's Kingdom on the earth, in the expectant hope of the day in which God will be "all in all." Thus, both revelation and the lordship of Christ are eschatologically reimagined in Moltmann's theology.

God is called the God "who is, who was, and who is to come" in Revelation 1:8. Why is God the God *"who is to come"* and not the God "who will be?" We would expect God simply to "be," if God is timeless and without a future, but Moltmann contests this notion. Instead, God has a future which draws the present towards itself. Better yet, as Moltmann writes:

The God spoken of [in the New Testament] is no intra-worldly or extra-worldly God, but the 'God of hope' (Rom. 15:13), a God with 'future as his essential nature' (as E. Bloch puts it), as made known in Exodus and in Israelite prophecy, the God whom we therefore cannot really have in us or over us but always only before us, who encounters us in his promises for the future, and whom we therefore cannot 'have' either, but can only await in active hope.

— THEOLOGY OF HOPE, 16

Revelation as "epiphany" says too much. It attempts to "have" God in the intersection of time and eternity. God is and *is to come*. Moltmann's theology is Christocentric (like Barth), but (unlike Barth) Christ is essentially the eschatological Messiah "on the way" (an image we will explore in chapter 7). Therefore, as Moltmann writes, "[A]ll statements and judgements about him [Christ] must at once imply something about the future which is to be expected from him" (ibid., 17). "Jesus is Lord" means lordship in anticipation of the coming reign of God, which here and now remains an incomplete lordship. That does not mean what we say about God is false, that Jesus is *not* Lord, but that all these statements have the character of anticipation. Thus, the knowledge of God is in the harmony of promise and its fulfillment. We await the fulfillment of God's promises, and therefore the knowledge of God is eschatologically conditioned. We *begin* with the future of God in our understanding of God's nature.

Moltmann writes:

Christian theology speaks of 'revelation', when on the ground of the Easter appearances of the risen Lord it perceives and proclaims the identity of the risen one with the crucified one. Jesus is recognized in the Easter appearances as what he really was. That is the ground of faith's 'historical' remembrance of the life and work, claims and sufferings of Jesus of Nazareth. But the messianic titles, in which this identity of Jesus in cross and resurrection is claimed and described, all anticipate at the same time the not yet apparent future of the risen Lord. This means that the Easter appearances and revelations of the risen Lord are manifestly understood as foretaste and promise of his still future glory and lordship. Jesus is recognized in the Easter appearances as what he really will be. The 'vital point' for a Christian view of revelation accordingly lies [...] in the fact that in all the qualitative difference of cross and resurrection

Jesus is the same. This identity in infinite contradiction is theologically understood as an event of identification, an act of the faithfulness of God. It is this that forms the ground of the promise of the still outstanding future of Jesus Christ. It is this that is the ground of the hope which carries faith through the trials of the god-forsaken world and of death.

— THEOLOGY OF HOPE, 84-5

We live in a world groaning for redemption; this is the world of Christ's cross. However, we also live in anticipation of God's future glory and the reign of God's Kingdom; this is our hope in the resurrection. It is in God's faithfulness to Christ in His resurrection that we recognize God to be the God who is and will be faithful. Because our world is the same world in which Christ's cross stands, so it is not a world without hope. We have the promise of a new creation. God reveals Godself as the faithful God in the resurrection of Christ, and God will be faithful to this old creation with the new creation.

Richard Bauckham identifies two points we should draw from this understanding of revelation. First, "God's self-revelation here does not abstract from history, but actually makes history" (*Moltmann*, 31). God's self-revelation invites us into God's ongoing history with the world; it spurs us into revolutionary action. Second, "[T]he knowledge of God through this revelation has to be a knowledge which draws the knower into expectant trust. In the openness of history, God is known as the one who has proved faithful in the past and is trusted for the future" (ibid.). God's future draws us into a shared history and mission in which we dependently trust in God's faithfulness to the promise. Revelation draws us forward by the remembrance of Christ and His promised future. Moltmann articulates this further, writing:

In human history God reveals himself through the consonance of promise and fulfilment, for in that consonance his faithfulness is revealed, and faithfulness is his essential nature. God identifies himself with his promises, and in doing so shows himself as the one who is dependable, steadfast and worthy of trust. 'God is faithful. He cannot deny himself' (2 Tim. 2:13). According to the New Testament, the raising of the crucified Christ is the final and eschatological proof of God's essential faithfulness, since this act overcomes the power of death. So with the raising of Christ, the revelation of God's glory begins, the glory which overcomes the force of time, together with the power of death, and which will bring about the eternal creation.

— EXPERIENCES IN THEOLOGY, 63

Moltmann argues against the excessive use of "revelation" in theology because its role in Scripture is minimal. Revelation "plays no central role in the language of the Bible"; so Moltmann prefers instead to say with the Reformers that "the correlative to Christian faith is actually God's promise" (ibid., 61). It is the *promise,* not revelation, which is central. An epiphany doctrine of revelation is too Greek-minded, whereas the Jewish understanding of God centers around the promise and its fulfillment. Therefore, "The God who makes himself dependable through his covenant promises is fundamentally differentiated from the moods and caprice of other gods or forces of destiny. His essential nature is his faithfulness" (ibid., 97). God's revelation is thus a "word of promise" rather than the epiphany of eternal truth. "Thus knowledge of Christ becomes anticipatory, provisional and fragmentary knowledge of his future, namely, of what he will be. All the titles of Christ point messianically forward in this sense" (*Theology of Hope,* 203). The knowledge of God points ahead to its fulfillment, and therefore it depends on God's faithfulness.

The promise draws us into God's history with the world, a history marked with the dialectic of suffering and hope. The Church is on the side of the poor and weak because in their midst we discover the co-suffering love of Christ. As the fellowship of Christ, we suffer with those who suffer and bring hope to the hopeless. Thus, Moltmann writes:

> To know God is to suffer God, says an old adage. But to suffer means to be changed and transformed. Knowledge of God is then an anticipatory knowledge of the future of God, a knowledge of the faithfulness of God which is upheld by the hopes that are called to life by his promises. Knowledge of God is then a knowledge that draws us onwards—not upwards—into situations that are not yet finalized but still outstanding.

It is a knowledge not of the looks of past history, but of the outlooks involved in the past promises and past faithfulness of God. Knowledge of God will then anticipate the promised future of God in constant remembrance of the past emergence of God's election, his covenant, his promises and his faithfulness. It is a knowledge that oversteps our bounds and moves within the horizon of remembrance and expectation opened up by the promise, for to know about God is always at the same time to know ourselves called in history by God.

— THEOLOGY OF HOPE, 118

This insight is consistent with what we have said about the theology of exodus—that we are pilgrims on the way, not of settlers in the home-land (chapter 1). Revelation is not a complete and perfect reality we obtain through epiphany, as if we have arrived at the home country and see God face to face, but the knowledge of God *is* itself the invitation to trust in God's promises and journey together in God's history with the world. Hope sets us on a forward-looking and forward-moving *journey*, as we trust in the promise which pulls us ahead towards the coming Kingdom.

SIDEBAR: PEACE WITH GOD

"Mission is hope in action," as Moltmann declared in an early sermon (*The Gospel of Liberation*, 32). Hope in God's coming does not leave us passive and merely "hoping for the best," because hope is the fuel of action. The Church has far too often been silent in the midst of a world full of death, injustice, and oppression. But hope condemns our silent complicity. A Church gripped by hope will be a "constant disturbance" in the world, as Moltmann writes:

> Those who hope in Christ can no longer put up with reality as it is, but begin to suffer under it, to contradict it. Peace with God means conflict with the world, for the goad of the promised future stabs inexorably into the flesh of every unfulfilled present. If we had before our eyes only what we see, then we should cheerfully or reluctantly reconcile ourselves with things as they happen to be. That we do not reconcile ourselves, that there is no pleasant harmony between us and reality, is due to our unquenchable hope. This hope keeps man unreconciled, until the great day of the fulfilment of all the promises of God. It keeps him in *statu viatoris* [on a pilgrimage], in that unresolved openness to world questions which has its origin in the promise of God in the resurrection of Christ and can therefore be resolved only when the

same God fulfils his promise. This hope makes the Christian Church a constant disturbance in human society, seeking as the latter does to stabilize itself into a 'continuing city'. It makes the Church the source of continual new impulses towards the realization of righteousness, freedom and humanity here in the light of the promised future that is to come. This Church is committed to 'answer for the hope' that is in it (1 Peter 3:15). It is called in question 'on account of the hope and resurrection of the dead' (Acts 23:6). Wherever that happens, Christianity embraces its true nature and becomes a witness of the future of Christ.

— THEOLOGY OF HOPE, 21-2

The Church of hope is a politically and socially *destabilizing* Church; it always stands up against the oppressive status quo. The Church of hope refuses to give up its birthright for a bowl of soup; it refuses to stay silent before the face of injustice and oppression. Hope in the coming of God's Kingdom places us in sharp conflict with every kingdom and ruler of the earth. The Church cannot live peacefully with an oppressive political system or an unjust social norm.

"Peacemaking" has been the cloak under which we exchanged the calling of our hope for silent complicity in an oppressive norm. Under the false guise of wisdom, radical hope fades for the sake of avoiding conflict. But peace is not the absence of conflict; it is the success of justice. We cannot be at peace with injustice. We are often silent as the poor and weak suffer. We are complicit in their oppression whenever we forgo our radical hope and live "at peace" with the systems of oppression that rule this world. Inaction *is* action when the status quo is oppressive. To be silent is to take the side of the oppressor against the oppressed. Hope denies the Church this possibility.

The de-radicalization of our hope has a lot to do with the very concept of eschatology. When defined as the doctrine of "last things," hope is pushed into *another* world, and therefore it has little relevance for *this* world. We hide in monastic reclusion and await the last things, while the poor and weak suffer from our silence. By "relegating [...] these events to the 'last day,'" Moltmann writes, we have "robbed them of their directive, uplifting and critical significance for all the days which are spent here, this side of the end, in history" (ibid., 15). We have robbed hope of its drastic significance for the world today by pushing eschatology to the sidelines of our faith in Christ.

That Christianity *is* hope means taking up eschatological *unrest* and *impatience*. Hope which expects God's reign is *hope in protest*, hope that resists the oppressive systems of this world. We are restless for God's coming, and in our restlessness, we refuse to accept things as they are. We hasten the day that is to come, working in anticipation of how things will be in the Kingdom. We stand up against oppression, fight for the liberation of the enslaved, pursue radical equality, and preserve human dignity.

Let hope spur us to action, disregarding every voice of caution as we race to meet the coming of God's Kingdom. In the safety of resurrection hope, let us give ourselves freely for the sake of the Kingdom, for the sake of the "least of these" to which it belongs, and for the sake of the poor and oppressed. And when this hope grabs ahold of our hearts, may the Church become a revolutionary agent of change, so that the world once again says of us, "These people who have been turning the world upside down have come here also" (Acts 17:6).

SIDEBAR: ECONOMIC INEQUALITY

WHAT DOES REVOLUTIONARY HOPE LOOK LIKE IN A WORLD OF EVER-INCREASING ECONOMIC INEQUALITY AND INJUSTICE?

We are living in the midst of radical economic inequality the likes of which the world has never seen before. In the final months of 2017, the three wealthiest men in America (Bill Gates, Warren Buffett, and Jeff Bezos) held more wealth in their bank accounts than the combined total of the bottom 50% of the country (according to a report published by the Institute for Policy Studies). Another report by Credit Suisse found that the world's wealthiest 1% own 50.1% of the total wealth of the entire planet. There have always been rich and poor people in the world, but the divide has never been this extreme.

At the same time, more than 3 billion people live on less than $2.50 a day, and 1.3 billion live in "extreme poverty" with less than $1.25 a day. 80% of the entire world lives on less than $10 a day. According to UNICEF, 22,000 children will die *every single day* because of poverty. Hunger is the number one leading cause of death in the world, even though there is more than enough food to meet the needs of every human being. The industrialized world wastes roughly $680 billion worth of food every year, which is nearly a third of all food production. All in all, it has been estimated that it would take just $60 billion to solve world poverty *and* world hunger (according to Oxfam). To put things in perspective, the United States alone spends an estimate of $500-600 billion every year on its military and defense budgets. A mere tenth of that budget, instead of supplying weapons of death and war, could single-handedly end world poverty and hunger. America's citizens are not without poverty since recent estimates have found that nearly 20 million Americans live in extreme poverty (Philip Alston).

There is more than enough for everyone. No person should die from unmet needs, only because of the greed of a few who hoard more than their share of the world's resources—but that is precisely what happens every day for thousands of people. That is the heart-breaking reality of severe global inequality. The hoarding of wealth in the top tiers of society is unethical. To celebrate the "success" of the 1% is to miss the point. The systems which allowed for such radical inequality to thrive cannot continue any longer; it is frankly unsustainable. Unregulated capitalism has shown itself to be morally corrupt. It is unethical to continue down the same path and expect a different result. When billions suffer from the greed of a few, it is the responsibility of the privileged to fight the system that permitted this injustice.

(Unsourced statistics can be verified by A. Shah: "Poverty Facts and Statistics"; see "Works Cited.")

Christian hope refuses to be "at peace" with these statistics. A better world is possible and necessary. The Church must take a stand for social justice, and rise in defense of the poor and oppressed. Sadly, we have often been content to live "at peace," and thus remain silent, in the face of economic injustice. In America especially, a "cult of success" has flourished, in which your bank account and profitability defines your worth. Even in the Church, "prosperity Gospel" preachers have become, in their way, members of the elite super-rich. An unchecked capitalist system has redefined the worth of human beings so that the exploitation of labor defines human value. The Church must stand up and defend the dignity of human beings, no matter their economic worth. We must stand up for the poor and disabled, those who cannot contribute to the economy but who are nevertheless loved and treasured by God. *To forsake the poor is to renounce Christ.*

The god of mammon is alive and well, and the Church must resist its charms. We need creativity and wisdom in the Spirit to learn how to navigate the systems of this world so that social justice becomes a priority. A good political system is always the one which values humanity above profitability or corporate greed. We are obligated in the name of Christ to prioritize the needs of the poor and weak. In hope and unrest, resisting every temptation to shut our eyes to the sufferings of this world, we must act in Christ's name and with the hope of Kingdom come.

3

THE CRUCIFIED GOD

SUMMARY: What does the cross mean *for God?* The cross is iconoclasm against every idolatrous image of God; it is the refutation of any apathetic, indifferent God who cannot suffer. God voluntarily suffers with us because God loves freely—because God is *this* God, the crucified God.

IN MOLTMANN'S OWN WORDS:

To know God in the cross of Christ is a crucifying form of knowledge, because it shatters everything to which a man can hold and on which he can build, both his works and his knowledge of reality, and precisely in so doing sets him free.

— THE CRUCIFIED GOD, 212

The death of the Son of God on the cross reaches deep into the nature of God and, above all other meanings, is an event which takes place in the innermost nature of God himself: the father-less Son and the sonless Father.

— EXPERIENCES IN THEOLOGY, 305

The Godforsaken Son of God takes the eternal death of the forsaken and the damned upon himself in order to become God of the forsaken and brother of the damned.

— THE EXPERIMENT HOPE, 79

SECONDARY SOURCES:

The central concept of *The Crucified God* is love which suffers in solidarity with those who suffer. This is love which meets the involuntary suffering of the godforsaken with another kind of suffering: voluntary fellowsuffering.

— RICHARD BAUCKHAM: THE THEOLOGY OF JÜRGEN
MOLTMANN, 11

INTRODUCTION

Moltmann's second major book turns "from the *resurrection* of the crucified Christ" to the "*cross* of the risen Christ" (*The Crucified God,* 5). An eschatological orientation does not contradict this orientation towards the suffering of God, but instead, these two points together make up the dialectic of cross and resurrection. The suffering cross of the risen Christ is the other side of hope. It is out of suffering that hope arises because the same Christ who suffered the cross was raised to new life by the faithfulness of God. That means there is no suffering or death which has not been embraced by the God of hope. It is to the God-forsaken death of Christ that Moltmann now turns.

The Crucified God is an invitation to rethink the core doctrines of our faith in the light of Christ's cross. As such, it is perhaps Moltmann's most theologically challenging book. It disrupts the status quo as radically, if not more radically than *Theology of Hope.*

The focus of this chapter will be Moltmann's argument for divine passibility (God's ability to suffer). The crucified God shatters our idols, so the theme of the "iconoclasm" of the cross is central to what we will consider. Finally, I will end by defending Moltmann against the two primary charges he faced: patripassianism and sadism. There is a lot worth examining in *The Crucified God*, and so, accordingly, this will be our longest chapter.

THE ICONOCLASM OF THE CROSS

The very essence of the Christian faith rises and falls with the cross of Christ. However, today the cross is no longer a scandal, it is no longer foolishness (1 Cor. 1). But the brutal realism of the cross remains a sharp blade ready to strike at the root of our idolatry. By its nature, the knowledge of the cross is a "crucifying form of knowledge." Moltmann's *The Crucified God* invites us to welcome this criticism of the cross.

The primary question we must ask, theologically speaking, is this:

> Is the doctrine of God *normative* for the
>   crucifixion?
>
> OR
>
> Is the crucifixion *normative* for the doctrine
>   of God?

In other words, how do we reconcile the doctrine of God and the horrors of the cross? We will either determine the cross according to our doctrine of God or establish our doctrine of God according to the cross. Theology has often chosen the former, to subdue the cross under a presupposed image of God. That is, it has decided to *disarm* the scandal and foolishness of the cross. The cross, then, is not the *center* of our thinking about God, but a mysterious paradox with little to no effect on God's essential being. That was the route taken by Cyril of Alexandria and many others after him. Here God was a God of "passible impassibility," a God unaffected by the crucifixion. Why must theology speak in such a paradoxical way? Does the cross mean anything *for God?* Why de-radicalize the foolishness of the cross under a metaphysical image of God? It is because theology has chosen to uphold its doctrine of God *in spite of* the crucifixion. That is precisely what Moltmann refuses to do.

What if the cross determined the doctrine of God, rather than the doctrine of God the cross? Rather than presupposing an image of God based on the abstract metaphysics of classical theism (impassible, immutable, omnipotent, omnipresent, etc.), Moltmann *begins* with the cross where Christ died abandoned by God. The book's subtitle makes this clear: "The Cross of Christ as the Foundation and Criticism of Christian Theology." The cross critically dismantles all of our idolatrous images of God, so that it might become the firm foundation of the Christian faith once again.

Moltmann challenges the status quo by refusing to *romanticize* the cross and thus allows the crucifixion to be grappled with in all its brutal realism. His iconic first paragraph illustrates this intent:

> The cross is not and cannot be loved. Yet only the crucified Christ can bring the freedom which changes the world because it is no longer afraid of death. In his time the crucified Christ was regarded as a scandal and as foolishness. Today, too, it is considered old-fashioned to put him in the centre of Christian faith and of theology. Yet only when men are reminded of him, however untimely this may be, can they be set free from the power of the facts of the present time, and from the laws and compulsions of history, and be offered a future which will never grow dark again. Today the church and theology must turn to the crucified Christ in order to show the world the freedom he offers. This is essential if they wish to become what they assert they are: the church of Christ, and Christian theology.
>
> — THE CRUCIFIED GOD, 1

By refusing to romanticize the cross, Moltmann is free to wrestle with its scandalous contradictions, which have often been dismantled or downplayed in theology. Christ's death was a cursed death, according to Paul in Galatians 3. How could the Son of God, the one in whom the Father is well pleased (Mt. 3:17), die such a horrific, God-forsaken death? The cross is like a bomb at the base of our idolatrous images of God: either we work to defuse it (and thus romanticize and de-radicalize the cross), or we will watch it go off and freely surrender our idols to the flame. Either God stands aloof in an impenetrable fortress of divine impassibility or *God suffers*. Either *we* determine the cross in the light of our idolatrous images of God or the cross determines the nature of God. "Either Jesus who was abandoned by God is the end of all theology or he is the beginning of a specifically Christian, and therefore critical and liberating, theology and life" (ibid., 4). The way forward is clear: "[A] truly Christian theology has to make Jesus' experience of God on the cross the centre of all our ideas about God" (ibid., x).

The cross, in all its brutal realism, is the permanent *iconoclasm* of God, as Moltmann writes, "I am arguing for an iconoclasm of the crucified Christ, because in him, not only the first but also the second commandment seems to be fulfilled" (ibid., 108 n. 13). The cross shatters every idea of God we imagine by way of metaphysical speculation. Ryan Neal summarizes this well: "[T]he overriding image of God in [*The Crucified God*], both implicit and explicit, is that the crucified one is the highest form of iconoclasm, destroying all other images of God" (*Theology as Hope,* 47).

Moltmann once said to Ernst Bloch, "Only a Christian can be a good atheist" (*The Crucified God,* 195), which is a clever reversal of Bloch's claim that, "Only an atheist can be a good Christian." What does Moltmann mean? A doctrine of God which takes Christ's atheistical shout of abandonment ("My God, my God...") seriously is a theology founded on a particular kind of atheism, *atheism for God's sake.* More precisely, Moltmann writes, "'For Christ's sake I am an atheist,' an atheist in respect of the gods of the world and world history" (ibid.). It is a passionate *No* against all the idols we have fashioned of God, but it is a *No* for the sake of saying *Yes* to the God who was in Christ, to the cross as the foundation of a genuinely *Christian* doctrine of God. Moltmann writes, "Jesus died crying out to God, 'My God, why hast thou forsaken me?' All Christian theology and all Christian life is basically an answer to the question which Jesus asked as he died" (ibid., 4). The iconoclasm of the cross is atheism against the idolatry of a God fashioned in our image.

THE IDOL OF SUCCESS

In a culture that prioritizes success and achievement, it would be no stretch of the imagination to say that we have fashioned God in our image as *the God of success.* The Western tendency towards optimism and progress is so ingrained in our minds that we assume its validity without so much of a second thought. Our heroes, the people that inspire us, are the *winners,* the so-called successful people of the world. In turn, we have baptized the God and Father of Jesus Christ in the name of this cult of success. We have fashioned an idol of God as the ultimate heavenly winner, turning Jesus's life into a cosmic success story. We have romanticized the horrors of calvary.

An interesting illustration of this comes from Kurt Vonnegut's book, *Slaughterhouse-Five*. A character tells of an alien species who decided to study Christianity, but they ultimately concluded that the Gospel gives off the wrong message:

> The visitor from outer space made a serious study of Christianity, to learn, if he could, why Christians found it so easy to be cruel. He concluded that at least part of the trouble was slipshod storytelling in the New Testament. He supposed that the intent of the Gospels was to teach people, among other things, to be merciful, even to the lowest of the low.
>
> But the Gospels actually taught this:
> *Before you kill someone, make absolutely sure he isn't well connected.* So it goes.
>
> The flaw in the Christ stories, said the visitor from outer space, was that Christ, who didn't look like much, was actually the Son of the Most Powerful Being in the Universe. Readers understood that, so when they came to the crucifixion, they naturally thought[...]:
> *Oh, boy—they sure picked the wrong guy to lynch that time!*
> And that thought had a brother: '*There are* right people *to lynch.*' Who? People not well connected. So it goes.
>
> — SLAUGHTERHOUSE-FIVE, 108-9

We strip the cross of its revolutionary effect whenever we romanticize it. It is inaccurate to say, as Vonnegut does, that this is a problem with the New Testament itself, but it is not unfair to say this is a problem with the way we *read* the New Testament. He is correct to point out how we tend to baptize God in the name of our culture of success, and by doing so, we miss the point. The crucifixion must become once again a stumbling block, an offense, and a foolish scandal.

In the eyes of Jewish messianism, Jesus was an utter failure. He died not as a theocratic king but as a mocked and abandoned revolutionary who failed to inspire lasting change. However, it is precisely this act which established God's Kingdom on this earth. At the center of the Christian confession you will not find a triumphant winner-God who stands above suffering, but the *crucified God*. We do not see a high and mighty king who overcomes evil by force, but the helpless Christ who suffers and dies as an outcast. Moltmann writes:

> At the core of Christianity we find [...] the God who humiliated himself, who became man, who took upon himself the suffering of inhumanity, and who died in the Godforsakenness of the cross. [...] The God of success and the apathetic man of action completely contradict what we find at the core of Christianity: the suffering God and the loving, vulnerable man. On the other hand, the crucified God contradicts the God of success and his idol-worshipers all the more totally. He contradicts the officially optimistic society.
>
> — THE EXPERIMENT HOPE, 70-1

Taken at face value, a theology of hope seems to fit well within the cult of success. But this was not the purpose of Moltmann's *Theology of Hope,* which stands in shark contrast against utopian and chiliastic hopes. A theology of hope *is* a theology of the cross and vice versa. There is no contradiction between the two orientations, as Moltmann writes, "[T]here is no true *theology of hope* which is not first of all a *theology of the cross*" (ibid., 72). Moltmann's theology of hope is not empty optimism, nor does it give into the idol of success. Fundamental to Moltmann's theology of hope is the dialectic of the rising of the *crucified* Christ.

Moltmann was in America for a conference on his theology of hope when the news came through that Dr. Martin Luther King Jr. had been shot and killed (April 4, 1968). It spurred Moltmann on to write *The Crucified God,* to emphasize the other side of hope against the cult of success. Moltmann writes:

> In a culture which glorifies success and happiness and which is blind to the suffering of others, the remembrance that at the centre of the Christian faith is an unsuccessful, suffering Christ dying in shame can open people's eyes for the truth.
>
> — A BROAD PLACE, 144 N.10

It would be a mistake to think the theology of hope is in line with the cult of success. In fact, it is a fierce *criticism* of the idol of success. That is because hope refuses to shut its eyes to the sufferings of this world; it refuses to forget the cross.

WHERE IS GOD?

In the wake of human tragedies, we often ask, "If God is good and all-powerful, then why is there suffering in the world?" But those who suffer seldom ask these sorts of questions. These are the philosopher's questions, asked from the safety of their privileged lives. In contrast, those who suffer cry out in agony, *"Where is God?"* It is the terror of abandonment, of being unseen and forsaken in the midst of suffering, which is the real suffering *in* suffering. Only those who stand apart from suffering in privileged indifference ask philosophical questions. Those who suffer themselves face the brutal despair of God's absence.

Moltmann came face to face with the question of God's absence during Operation Gomorrah, the bombing raid that took the life of his childhood friend and 42,000 others. "My question was not, 'Why does God allow this to happen?' but, 'My God, where are you?'" (*A Broad Place,* 17). In the aftermath of a brutal and dehumanizing war, many others were asking the same question. One deeply moving account comes from the work of Elie Wiesel, a Jewish holocaust survivor. Wiesel's book, *Night,* offers a heart-wrenching account of his experiences. The question he asked was also not philosophical, but rather, "Where is God?" It is the brutal indifference and silence of God that eclipses every horror. This brutality of a "silent sky," the sting of God's absence, is expressed powerfully in Wiesel's poem:

> Never shall I forget that night, the first night in
>   camp, that turned my life into one long night
>   seven times sealed.
> Never shall I forget that smoke.
> Never shall I forget the small faces of the children
>   whose bodies I saw transformed into smoke
>   under a silent sky.

Never shall I forget those flames that consumed
    my faith forever.
Never shall I forget the nocturnal silence that
    deprived me for all eternity of the desire
    to live.
Never shall I forget those moments that murdered
    my God and my soul and turned my dreams
    to ashes.
Never shall I forget those things, even were I
    condemned to live as long as God Himself.
Never.

— Night, 34

What would we dare to say to this? Can a philosophical or theological answer offer any real solace in suffering?

A particularly horrific account from Wiesel's book tells of a young boy who was killed by hanging:

The SS hanged two Jewish men and a youth in front of the whole camp. The men died quickly, but the death throes of the youth lasted for half an hour. 'Where is God? Where is he?' someone asked behind me. As the youth still hung in torment in the noose after a long time, I heard the man call again, 'Where is God now?' And I heard a voice in myself answer: 'Where is he? He is here. He is hanging there on the gallows…'

— Night, 75

To this Moltmann responds:

Any other answer would be blasphemy. There cannot be any other Christian answer to the question of this torment. To speak here of a God who could not suffer would make God a demon. To speak here of an absolute God would make God an annihilating nothingness. To speak here of an indifferent God would condemn men to indifference.

— The Crucified God, 274

The only response Christian theology could dare to make in the face of these horrors, if it is a theology that remains faithful to the crucified Christ, is to speak of *God's suffering*. An indifferent God, a "silent sky" God, would be a monster—morally repugnant and much to be pitied. God either causes pain, is indifferent to suffering, or God suffers with us in our suffering. The first and second possibilities result in an apathetic monster-god, but the third is the *crucified God,* the God revealed in Christ's cross. The suffering God alone is our solace; only the crucified Christ has anything to offer humanity in the midst of suffering and death.

Moltmann discovered a brother in suffering when he read, in a Scottish prison camp, Christ's cry of God-forsakenness. He recalls this experience, writing:

> I read Mark's Gospel as a whole and came to the story of the passion; when I heard Jesus' death cry, 'My God, why have you forsaken me?' I felt growing within me the conviction: this is someone who understands you completely, who is with you in your cry to God and has felt the same forsakenness you are living in now. I began to understand the assailed, forsaken Christ because I knew that he understood me. The divine brother in need, the companion on the way, who goes with you through this 'valley of the shadow of death', the fellow-sufferer who carries you, with your suffering. I summoned up the courage to live again, and I was slowly but surely seized by a great hope for the resurrection into God's 'wide space where there is no more cramping'. [...]
>
> This early companionship with Jesus, the brother in suffering and the companion on the road to the land of freedom, has never left me ever since, and I became more and more assured of it. [...] I am certain that then, in 1945, and there, in the Scottish prisoner of war camp, in the dark pit of my soul, Jesus sought me and found me. 'He came to seek that which was lost,' and so he came to me when I was lost. There is a medieval picture which shows Christ descending into hell and opening the gate for someone who points to himself as if he were saying, 'And are you coming to me?' That is how I have always felt. Jesus' God-forsakenness on the cross showed me where God is present —where he was in my experiences of death, and where he is going to be in whatever comes. Whenever I read the Bible again with the searching

eyes of the God-forsaken prisoner I was, I am always assured of its divine truth.

— A BROAD PLACE, 30-1

There is no suffering which is not met by the suffering of God. God in Christ has taken up solidarity with a suffering and oppressed humanity so that it is no longer possible to say God cannot or will not suffer. No one suffers or dies alone. Christ has entered into our darkness and estrangement, into the hell of our hopelessness and despair, so that no man or woman is ever alone in their suffering. The crucified Christ suffers with the pains of humanity.

With this account, the stark contrast between the apathetic God of philosophy and the God and Father of Jesus Christ is made abundantly clear. There can be no reconciliation between outdated Greek concepts of divine impassibility (the inability to suffer) and the cross of Christ. Indeed, to speak in the face of suffering about a God who could not suffer "would make God a demon," in Moltmann's profound words. This is the height of the iconoclasm of the cross. Here the line is forcefully drawn between the two ways of thinking. Either we hold fast to a metaphysical and speculative image of a God who cannot suffer, or the cross radically changes our understanding of God. In the face of human tragedies, we cannot remain content with our safe, romantic images of the crucifixion, or with an idea of the God who stands aloof from suffering.

The possibility of a theology "after Auschwitz" arises from the existence of theology *in* Auschwitz, as Moltmann notes, "Anyone who later comes up against insoluble problems and despair must remember that the *Shema* of Israel and the Lord's Prayer were prayed in Auschwitz" (ibid., 278). If we take the presence of God in the concentration camps seriously, we must recognize, with Wiesel, that God hung in the gallows, that starvation and torture killed God together with the prisoners of the camps. Which finally means that God is not only in suffering, but that suffering itself is *in God*. Moltmann writes, "If that is taken seriously [that God hung on the gallows in Auschwitz], it must also be said that, like the cross of Christ, even Auschwitz is in God himself. Even Auschwitz is taken up into the grief of the Father, the surrender of the Son and the power of the Spirit" (ibid.).

What does this mean for those who suffer? For Moltmann, it means that the suffering *in* suffering, which is its loneliness and God-forsaken-ness, is met with the co-suffering solidarity of Christ. No one suffers alone. That is neither an attempt to *explain* suffering or to *justify* its existence. Indeed, our pain remains an *open wound,* but it is now also *God's* open wound as much as it is ours.

But in hope, we have the promise that justice and righteousness will prevail; evil will not have the final word. Ultimately, the question of theodicy, of *why* there is suffering, is a question that God will answer in the new creation. It is God's burden to do justice, that is, to make right the wrongs of history. Moltmann writes, "God weeps with us so that we may one day laugh with him." Suffering is *God's* problem just as it is our's because suffering is taken up into God's being. God shares in the history of all who suffer. The perpetrators of injustice will not have the final word, because God will make all things new. No horrid scream before a "silent sky" will remain unanswered. Nothing will be lost or forgotten.

A moving story from Moltmann's life illustrates this hope. He writes:

> The most deeply emotional experience was to walk through the Maidaneck concentration and death camp, near Lublin. The plank beds in the barracks were the last resting places of starving and tormented men, women, and children. Behind glass lay the little shoes of the murdered Jewish children, and hair that had been cut off from the gassed women. We saw the pits in which more than 10,000 people had been shot on a single day. At the time I wanted to sink into the ground for shame, and would have suffocated in the presence of the mass murder, if on one of the roads through the camp I had not suddenly had a vision. I looked into the world of the resurrection and saw all these dead men, women, and children coming towards me. Since then I have known that God's history with Auschwitz and Maidanek has not been broken off, but that it goes further with the victims and with the perpetrators. Without hope for the 'new earth in which righteousness dwells' (2 Peter 3:13), this earth, which has suffered Treblinka and Maidanek, would be unendurable.

> — A BROAD PLACE, 84

The stories of the victims of injustice are also *God's* story, and it is still being written. God has taken our stories of suffering and pain, our darkness, and our sorrow, and God has made our stories part of God's own story. No one suffers or dies abandoned because God has invaded every God-forsaken space on the cross. God's story and our's remains unfinished in the expectation of a new creation.

GOD'S *PATHOS* LOVE

Moltmann is rejecting the classical doctrine known as divine impassibility, which means the inability of God to suffer or be affected by passions (from the Latin: *in*: "not" + *passibilis*: "capable of suffering"). For many theologians, this an essential attribute of God. The Westminster Confession says God is "without body, parts, or passions [emotions], immutable [unchanging]" (II.1), and Augustine writes, "Whatever is changeable is not the most high God" (*City of God*, 8.6). The significance of Moltmann's rejection of divine impassibility should not be understated; with his theology of the cross, he is challenging one of the essential definitions of God taught by classical theism.

It is vital to be clear about what precisely Moltmann means when asserting that God suffers and suffering is in God. A helpful explanation is Moltmann's claim that a God who cannot suffer *cannot love*. It is thus a defense of God's essential being as love that results in the rejection of divine impassibility. "A *Deus impassibilis* [impassible God] is neither capable of love nor capable of feeling," Moltmann writes, in response to critics who remained fixated on the doctrine of divine impassibility (*A Broad Place*, 197).

But what precisely is the doctrine of divine impassibility, and where does it come from? What has caused so many to hold onto it as an absolute fact?

The idea originates from the Greek notion of divine *apatheia*, or apathy. It means that God cannot be *affected* by anything externally, that outside forces cannot change God. God is perfect, self-sustaining, self-determining, and independent of all created things. *Apatheia* thus excludes the possibility of God's suffering or weakness, because this would imply a God who is acted upon and changed against God's own will and self-determination. Such a God would be merely a passive object of the swaying tides of emotional response, no more self-sufficient than any created being. If God is perfect, then God cannot change (i.e., God is immutable), because to change would imply a prior deficiency. God could not change Godself either, because God could only change from being perfect to being less than perfect. (This was Plato's argument for divine immutability in *Republic*, book II.)

The net result is that God must be unable to suffer, to feel, to have emotions, or, in the extreme sense, to have empathy or compassion. All these things would make God a passive subject acted on by others, no different from human beings, instead of the self-sufficient and independent God of infinite perfection. It was essential for the Greeks to strictly hold onto God's apathy because this is what sets God apart from humanity; this is what makes God *God*.

Here we see that Moltmann is not only refuting one classical doctrine of theism—impassibility—but is striking at the root of the entire definition of God according to Greek metaphysics. Included in divine impassibility is no less than the whole Greek philosophical image of God, together with God's immutability and apathy. But the cross forces us to recognize that such a God is an *idol* we have fashioned for ourselves, an idol shattered in the light of the crucified Christ. That is the full scope of the iconoclasm of the cross. The whole enterprise of presupposing an image of God *before* the cross is faulty, because, for Moltmann, the crucified Christ *is* the image of the invisible God. Moltmann writes:

When the crucified Jesus is called the 'image of the invisible God', the meaning is that *this* is God, and God is like *this*. God is not greater than he is in this humiliation. God is not more glorious than he is in this self-surrender. God is not more powerful than he is in this helplessness. God is not more divine than he is in this humanity. The nucleus of everything that Christian theology says about 'God' is to be found in this Christ event. The Christ event on the cross is a God event. And conversely, the God event takes place on the cross of the risen Christ. Here God has not just acted externally, in his unattainable glory and eternity. Here he has acted in himself and has gone on to suffer in himself. Here he himself is love with all his being. So the new christology which tries to think of the 'death of Jesus as the death of God', must take up the elements of truth which are to be found in *kenoticism* (the doctrine of God's emptying of himself).

— THE CRUCIFIED GOD, 205

Instead of presupposing divine impassibility, immutability, or apathy, Christian theology must begin with the crucified Christ as the image of the invisible God. Speculation is useless and leads us down the wrong path. If we want to know what God is like, we should look no further than to the cross.

The Greek notion of God does not deserve our reverence, but indeed only our pity. An apathetic God is without love, and a God without love is a demon. We should pity the Greek gods, not revere them. Moltmann writes:

[A] God who cannot suffer is poorer than any man. For a God who is incapable of suffering is a being who cannot be involved. Suffering and injustice do not affect him. And because he is so completely insensitive, he cannot be affected or shaken by anything. He cannot weep, for he has no tears. But the one who cannot suffer cannot love either. So he is also a loveless being. Aristotle's God cannot love; he can only be loved by all non-divine beings by virtue of his perfection and beauty, and in this way draw them to him. The 'unmoved Mover' is a 'loveless Beloved'.

— IBID., 222

There is a third way between the alternatives presented in Greek philosophy. For them, either God is impassible and therefore eternal, changeless, and self-sufficient, or God is not God. This argument relies on a metaphysical projection of *our* highest values onto God. However, Moltmann is right to criticize the horrid deficiency of love in such a God, which distances this image of God with the God and Father of Jesus Christ. Those who wish to retain divine impassibility cannot do so while holding a consistent doctrine of God's essential being as *love*. What is eternal perfection without love? But the Christian God does not merely *love* (as a verb) but *is love*, according to 1 John 4:8. The two images (Greek and Christian) are unreconcilable.

There is, however, a distinction to consider. The Greeks were right to say that God cannot suffer change *like humans* suffer change, that is, God cannot bend to foreign wills other than God's own will. *However,* what they failed to recognize, and what Moltmann argues, is that while God can and does suffer change, God does not suffer and change *in the same way that humans suffer change.* We are powerless in our suffering and against the effects of change. We are subjected to death and pain whether we like it or not. We have no freedom against it. But this is *not* the kind of suffering Moltmann has in mind when he emphasizes God's suffering. God does not suffer out of a *deficiency* of being, but precisely because of the *freedom* of God's love. It is out of the perfection of God's nature that God suffers. It is *because* God is God that God can choose, in the freedom of love, to *voluntarily* lay Godself open to being affected by that which is not God. That is, God is free to be vulnerable.

Moltmann's ultimate concern is to emphasize the divine *pathos.* Following Abraham Heschel (see *The Prophets*), the influential Jewish theologian, Moltmann reclaims the Hebraic notion of the *pathos* of God. Moltmann summarized the divine *pathos* well, writing:

In his *pathos* the Almighty goes out of himself, entering into the people whom he has chosen. He makes himself a partner in a covenant with his people. In this *pathos*, this feeling for the people which bears his name and upholds his honour in the world, the Almighty is himself ultimately affected by Israel's experience, its acts, its sins and its sufferings. In the fellowship of his covenant with Israel, God becomes capable of suffering. His existence and the history of the people are linked together through the divine pathos. Creation, liberation, covenant, history and redemption spring from the pathos of God. This therefore has nothing to do with the passions of the moody, envious or heroic gods belonging to the mythical world of the sagas. Those gods are subject to destiny because of their passions. But the divine passion about which the Old Testament tells us is God's freedom. It is the free relationship of passionate participation. The eternal God takes men and women seriously to the point of suffering with them in their struggles and of being wounded in his love because of their sins.

— THE TRINITY AND THE KINGDOM, 25-6

The notion of God's *pathos* originates from the Old Testament but finds its culmination in the crucified and risen Christ. It is God's going "out of himself" for the sake of God's chosen people. We would only have to take a cursory glance through the Scriptures to find that God's *pathos* is a central theme, but the influence of Greek thought has downplayed it. One of the many examples comes from Isaiah 63:9, "In all their affliction, He [God] was afflicted / And the angel of His presence saved them; / In His love and in His mercy He redeemed them, / And He lifted them and carried them all the days of old" (NASB). It can also be seen in the themes of exile and promise, of God's Shekinah, in the centrality of the temple, and as a significant theme in the prophetic literature. The Bible does not present a God reserved or trapped in an impenetrable prison of aloof deity, but the God who risks and goes out of Godself in compassionate love.

Moltmann writes:

> We must drop the philosophical axioms about the nature of God. God is *not unchangeable*, if to be unchangeable means that he could not in the freedom of his love open himself to the changeable history of his creation. God is *not incapable of suffering* if this means that in the freedom of his love he would not be receptive to suffering over the contradiction of man and the self-destruction of his creation. God is *not invulnerable* if this means that he could not open himself to the pain of the cross. God is *not perfect* if this means that he did not in the craving of his love want his creation to be necessary to his perfection.
>
> — THE CHURCH IN THE POWER OF THE SPIRIT, 62

The iconoclasm of the cross draws a line in the sand between these two images of God. Either we subdue the cross to a Greek metaphysical doctrine of divinity, or we discover what God is actually like through the cross. We cannot take the latter path and retain the doctrines of divine impassibility, immutability, and apathy. In the light of the cross, we must confess: God suffers, God changes, and God is passionate.

Two objections

Anyone who offers such a radical reimagining of age-old beliefs will be subject to criticism and misunderstanding. Moltmann has had his fair share of both. While I do not intend to answer every objection leveled against his work, there are two significant misunderstandings which seem to be the most common. Clarifying these issues will help us better understand Moltmann's intention.

The first is the charge of patripassianism, an early modalist heresy. The second is the charge of a sadistic God, or of "God against God," which was primarily leveled by the feminist theologian Dorothee Sölle. Both of these charges are addressed by Moltmann directly, and we should take his rejection of them seriously if we want to understand him correctly.

Patripassianism

Patripassianism was a modalist heresy that falls under the broader umbrella of Sabellianism. (Modalism is another name for Sabellianism.) Modalism is the notion that God is not *inherently* Father, Son, and Holy Spirit, but only *appears* to us in these three modes of being. In modalism, there is only one monadic God with three modes or aspects. Father, Son, and Spirit are *masks* God wears, underneath which there is the "real" essence of a monadic God.

That led Sabellius to conclude that when the Word became flesh, it was not the Son but the Father that became a human being. That is where the heresy gets its name. Since the Father became incarnate, then *the Father* suffered and died on the cross. The term breaks down into two parts: *Patri-*, meaning "Father" + *passio-*, meaning "suffering." Patripassianism is then the charge of applying the suffering and death of the Son to the Father.

The logic of bringing this critique against Moltmann is apparent since Moltmann asserts that God is not only *in* suffering, but suffering is *in* God. However, this fails to recognize the nuance of Moltmann's position. First of all, modalism is absent from Moltmann's theology. His Trinitarian theology strongly affirms the three persons of God. If anything, his thought has been (wrongly) charged with *tritheism,* which is on the opposite side of the spectrum (see chapter 5 and the sidebar, "Tritheism").

Second, when Moltmann speaks about God in suffering and suffering in God, when he places the cross at the center of the Trinity, he cautiously distinguishes between the persons of the Trinity. He does not apply the Son's death to the Father, but rather recognizes the Father's involvement in, though distinction from, the sufferings of Christ's cross. Moltmann clarifies at length:

> If we ask what the cross of Christ means for God himself, we discover the Trinitarian mystery of God. If Christ dies with a cry of God-forsakenness, then God the Father must have had a correspondingly deep experience of forsakenness by his beloved Son. But this cannot be the same pain. Jesus suffers his dying on the cross, but the Father suffers the death of the Son, for he has to survive it. We can make this clear to ourselves from our own experience: at the end of my life I experience my dying but not my death, for I shall not survive it on earth. But in the people I love, I experience death when they die, for I have to live with their death. So Jesus experiences dying, and God, whom he calls 'Father', experiences his death. Here it becomes clear how deeply Christ's death reaches into the Godness of God, and in the depth of the Godhead is an event between the Father and the Son. Is what we see on Golgotha a fatherless Son on the cross, and a sonless Father in heaven? 'One of the Trinity suffered,' said the church father Cyril. This is loosely called the 'theopaschite formula', yet today it is generally accepted. But I would add: where 'one of the Trinity suffers', the others suffer, too, each in his own way. Seen in this way, Christ's death on the cross is an event within God before it takes on a salvific significance for the world.
>
> It is the mystery within God of God's giving of himself for the redemption of the world. The pain of the Father and the suffering of the Son manifest a single movement of the triune God: the Father in his pain surrenders the Son (Rom. 8:32), and the Son surrenders himself (Gal. 2:20). The Greek word for 'forsake' is the same as the word for 'surrender': *paradidonai*. Through his self-surrender to annihilation on the cross, Jesus brings the light of fellowship with God into the abysses of annihilating God-forsakenness. That is the wonder of God's love, the God who gives himself in order to embrace those who have been given up. The Son of man who came to seek that which was lost must himself take their lostness on himself in order to find them. God 'gave him up'

so that he might become the brother and redeemer of those who have
been given up (Romans 1).

— A BROAD PLACE, 194-5

Moltmann's insight here is profound. He stresses that, "The grief of
the Father here is just as important as the death of the Son" (*The Crucified
God,* 243). A faulty, unitarian paradigm often determines how we understand the cross; the Father and the Spirit are barely involved as if the Son
was not intrinsically *bound* to the Father and Spirit. But how can the Son
suffer and the Father and Spirit remain wholly *indifferent* to His suffering?
Moltmann's thinking is thoroughly Trinitarian, as he recognizes the love
of the Father, Son, and Holy Spirit in the event of the cross.

The Son *alone* died on the cross, but Christ's death profoundly
affected the Father and the Spirit. It is profound to think of this, even if it
is perhaps a bit more speculative than we would like. Imagine the eternal
being of God, the inseparable fellowship of Father, Son, and Holy Spirit
suffering such a severe rupture. The words "suffering" and "grief" are
indeed far too weak to express what a painful experience God took up by
surrendering His Son to death on the cross. The loss of the Son disrupted
the eternal bond of love and fellowship in God's Self. We must recognize
this as real pain and grief, as shared suffering. Moltmann's emphasis on
God's Triune suffering protects him from the charge of patripassianism.
Indeed, the agony of the Father and Spirit over the death of the Son is a
significant insight, even if the Son alone dies His own death. The careful
nuance of Moltmann's approach is glossed over by this critique, yet upon
further investigation, patripassianism is indeed a mistaken claim.

SADISTIC GOD—OR GOD AGAINST GOD

In the year following the publication of *The Crucified God* (1972),
Dorothee Sölle's book *Suffering* (1973) criticized Moltmann fiercely by
labeling his doctrine of God "sadistic." Sölle was a prominent feminist
theologian, and many feminists have blindly followed her critique
without adequately reading Moltmann for themselves. That is a large part
why her analysis remains in circulation, even though it is a mistaken claim
upon a closer reading of his work.

The essential problem Sölle had with Moltmann's work was that she found in it the claim that God killed His own Son. She took Moltmann's account of Christ's God-forsakenness on the cross as God's sadistic abandonment of the Son to be executed by the Romans. With this also came the notion of "God against God," which has often plagued Moltmann's theology of the cross, but it is likewise mistaken. In the above section, we examined Moltmann's insightful recognition of the grief of the Father and the Spirit over the death of the Son. It is quite a leap to ignore these remarks and imagine that Moltmann is presenting a vision of the sadistic victimization of the Son at the hands of His own Father. It ignores all of Moltmann's emphasis on the unity of decision in self-surrender between the Father and Son. The Son was not forced to die but freely gave Himself in one accord with the Father.

Moltmann responded to this argument in his autobiography, writing:

Whoever wanted to say something critical about me took it over from Dorothee Sölle. I have consequently called talk about my 'sadistic God' a kind of 'migratory legend'. It appears in secondary literature on secondary literature. Apparently, critics no longer look back at what they criticize. Otherwise it could hardly have escaped them that stress on the difference in the suffering and pain of Jesus and of the God whom he called Abba, dear Father, is only the other side of the unity of the Father and the Son in their self-surrender, and hence the other side of the love of God from which 'nothing can separate us'. It is the precise opposite of cruelty and sadistic pleasure in torment. One cannot well suppress this side of what I have written in order to criticize the other side. Anyone who cannot recognize in the God 'who did not spare his own Son but gave him up for us all' the love which surmounts every suffering, every eclipse of God, and even hell, and who sees only a 'sadistic God who makes us suffer'—that person is on the way to abandoning the heart of the Christian assurance of faith; he has never sensed it or has never taken it seriously.

— A BROAD PLACE, 199

It is a sad fact that few consult the primary sources of great writers, but still feel free to criticize them so ignorantly. I can only think here not only of the various critics of Moltmann, but Barth, Schleiermacher, or any significant figure who fall into this trap, which Kierkegaard so prophetically recognized: "If you label me, you negate me." (The accuracy of applying this quote to Kierkegaard is questionable, but the point remains.)

Moltmann does seem hopeful, however, that in Sölle's later writings she appears to share in the same conviction of his theology of the cross, namely in the "God who is a co-sufferer in the pains and grief of the suffering people." He thus remarks that the "fierce conflict of earlier years can probably be laid to rest" (ibid., 199-200).

The love of the Father and the Son for lost and broken humanity is the uniting point even in their separation. It is not accurate to characterize Moltmann's theology of the cross as a "God against God" theology since the Father and the Son are in *one accord* in their love for humanity. The Father gives up the Son and suffers the grief of the Son's death, and the Son suffers God-forsakenness. The will of the Triune God was united in the event of self-surrender. The Father did not force the Son to suffer; the Father did not kill the Son but gave Him up to death for the love of lost humanity. The Son freely entered into our death and darkness to reach us in our suffering and shame. There are no traces of a "sadistic God" in Moltmann's theology, and to read as much into him is to misunderstand his essential point: God suffers because *God is love*.

Moltmann makes all this clear when he writes:

> There is no remoteness from God which the Son in his forsakenness did not suffer, or into which his self-giving did not reach. The doctrine of Christ's descent into hell seeks to make it clear that his self-giving reaches and opens every hell. The Father gives up his own Son, the Son of his eternal love, in order to receive those who have been given up and so that he may be there for them. The Son is given over to this death and this hell so that he may become the lord of the dead and the living. That is why the Father suffers with his Son in his passion. The Son dies in abandonment, suffering the death of sin, curse, wrath and hell. But the Father suffers the death of the Son in the unending pain of love. In his pain he participates in the Son's death. The Son is given over to the power of this death, a power contrary to God. In his abandonment by the Father he experiences the fate of the godless and takes it upon

himself for them. But as he is surrendered by the Father, so he surrenders himself as well in his limitless love. Thus, even though Jesus' dying cry reveals his total abandonment by the Father, he is at the same time entirely one with the Father, and the Father with him, in this event of self-surrender, which sunders the two so far from one another that heaven and hell are included in its grasp, and all men can live in it. As the Gethsemane story aims to show, Christ's giving of himself to death on the cross unites the Son with the Father at the very point where the separation and mutual abandonment is at its deepest. The Son offers himself through the Spirit (Heb. 9:14). The power which leads him into abandonment by the Father is the power which at the same time unites him with the Father.

— THE CHURCH IN THE POWER OF THE SPIRIT, 95

I would hope that this quotation puts to rest the notion of "God against God" in Moltmann's theology of the cross. Moltmann understands the cross as a unified movement of God's selfless love for the outcasted and the weak, for those who suffer in loneliness. We find no trace, contrary to Sölle's charge, of a sadistic God.

SIDEBAR: POLITICAL RELIGION

A Christianity which is completely 'in line' with the state of the world and the rule of 'other lords' is a Christianity without the remembrance of 'Christ crucified', and is therefore a Christianity without Christ.

— Experiences in Theology, 177

'The cross alone is our theology,' said Luther. Likewise, we contend that the dangerous memory of the cross is our political iconoclasm: the cross is our hope for the politics of liberation. The liberating memory of the crucified Jesus compels Christians to a critical political theology.

— The Experiment Hope, 118

Political religion is the religious sanctification of political systems or powers. It is when a system justifies its actions, particularly its use of violence, through religious legitimization. When a Catholic priest blessed the atomic bombs which later fell on Hiroshima and Nagasaki, killing thousands of innocents—it was political religion. When Nazi soldiers wore the slogan "Gott mit uns," meaning "God with us," on their belts—it was political religion. When the Christian Crusades adopted the motto "Deus lo vult," meaning "God wills it," as they slaughtered thousands—it was political religion. Political religion is the unholy alliance of Christian faith with political power. But like water and oil, faith in Christ and allegiance to political power does not mix.

The iconoclasm of the crucified Christ extends beyond shattering theological idols and into the public sphere where it smashes political and social idols with equal force. Political religion is idolatry, and the cross is a permanent iconoclasm against it. Unfortunately, many Christians fail to take the political implications of the cross seriously, and they gravely err by supporting political religion and thereby legitimizing systems of oppression in the name of Christ.

Christian allegiance to a political ideology is nothing less than idolatry. In the United States, this is perhaps most clearly seen whenever a political party is misidentified as *the* Christian party. To call a person an "evangelical" in America has become less of a theological designation as it has become a *political* voting block. Entire campaigns are structured around catering to these individuals. That is political religion. But, in truth, there is simply no such thing as a "Christian" political system under the cross of Christ. Christ died an outsider at the hands of political insiders, and the Church must carefully reject the temptation of trading their allegiance to Christ with loyalty to political powers.

That is not to imply that there can be no ethically Christian choice in politics. However, the moment a political party becomes *the* Christian party, then the conversation is over, and anything goes. The party is baptized in the name of Christ. Ethical and theological reflection is no longer our responsibility. A "Christian" political party can do whatever it wants because it is free to justify its actions in the name of God. But the Church must not be *bound* to a party or system, and thereby give up its allegiance to Christ. The Church can and must act politically for Christ's sake, but sanctioning a particular system is incongruent with the crucified Christ. When we recognized that our Lord was crucified by "the powers that be," we will resist every urge to lend our allegiance to these powers as they exist today.

Moltmann writes:

Glory no longer rests upon the heads of the mighty. For believers, Christ crucified was made the righteousness of God, and for them political authority was deprived of its religious sanctions. Christ, crucified in powerlessness and shame, has become their highest authority. Consequently, they no longer believe in religiopolitical authority, for the anxiety and fear that demanded it has been eliminated.

— "The Cross and Civil Religon," 35; cited in
Bauckham: Moltmann, 74

What is a Christian's role in politics? Are we to resign ourselves to silence? No, because this will only make us complicit in an oppressive status quo. We are obligated, for Christ's sake, to stand up for the rights of the poor and oppressed. When the remembrance of Christ's cross takes a central role in politics, then a new political theology arises. It is not the *politicization* of Christianity, but the *Christianization* of politics. "The new political theology is not concerned with the dissolution of the church into left-wing or right-wing politics, but with the Christianization of its political situation and function in terms of the freedom of Christ" (*The Crucified God*, 327). A successful Christianization of politics will be identified by its care for the poor—because this is where Christ is: not among the mighty but the weak.

This new political theology arises from a recognition of the political dimensions of Christ's life, death, and resurrection. A purely religious Christ is impossible. We must recognize that "the death of Christ was the death of a political offender" (ibid.). The glory of God is not among the mighty, rich, and powerful, but with the weak, poor, and powerless. "The authority of God is then no longer represented directly by those in high positions, the powerful and the rich, but by the outcast Son of Man, who died between two wretches. The rule and the kingdom of God are no longer reflected in political rule and world kingdoms, but in the service of Christ, who humiliated himself to the point of death on the cross" (ibid.).

A Christian does not enter the political sphere for their own sake *but for Christ's sake*. In practical terms, a Christianization of politics results in political concern for the "least of these" (Mt. 25: 31-46). A selfish concern to protect our privileges, to limit care for the poor and further their oppression, is a politicization of Christianity not a Christianization of politics; it is political religion and idolatry. Political action for Christ's sake means prioritizing what liberation theologians have called God's "preferential option for the poor."

Think, for example, of a tax bill which proposes to cut spending on medical assistance and welfare benefits for the impoverished and give those funds to wealthy corporations. Political action for Christ's sake means prioritizing the poor even against our comforts. As a Christian in the political sphere, I am responsible for recognizing Christ in the poor and oppressed, and therefore to consistently stand up for their rights. Even if it comes at the cost of higher taxes for me personally, it would be against the cause of Christ to support any law that neglects the poor. A selfish person enters politics to further their privileges, but a Christian enters politics for Christ's sake—and therefore unselfishly for the sake of the less privileged. The same is true for the rights of the homeless, of prisoners, of foreigners, and of oppressed minorities. Political action for Christ's sake recognizes Christ in the least of these and stands up for their rights at all costs. Political action for Christ's sake means standing up in defense of those who have no voice. In remembrance of Christ's death and resurrection, a new political theology draws political conclusions from its theological reflection on the life and teachings of Christ. Therefore, it is necessarily a political theology which prioritizes care for the poor, liberation for the oppressed, and health for the sick.

Some may argue that God does not take sides, that preferential care for the poor presents a biased image of God. "God helps those who help themselves" is a common phrase, but it is not a Christian one. While it is true that God is classless and stateless, God has *already* taken sides in Jesus Christ. He did not come to the rich but the poor; He did not serve the religious insiders but sinners. God is "the God of the poor, the oppressed and the humiliated," writes Moltmann (ibid., 329). To have a neutral God, a God who does not take sides, is to have a God that legitimizes the oppression of the poor and weak. That is not the God and Father of Jesus Christ, but the God of the empire, the God of political religion. A genuinely *Christian* political theology recognizes God's preference for the poor and oppressed on account of Christ's solidarity with the weak.

In all areas of life, a Christianization of politics means preferential care for the poor and oppressed. This Christianization of politics rejects all

SIDEBAR: THE DEATH PENALTY AND TORTURE

Should Christians support the death penalty?

In America today, 31 out of 50 States allow the death penalty. Does faith in Christ align with supporting the death penalty? For Moltmann, the answer is simple, "The resurrection of the Crucified Christ is God's no to the Death Penalty" (Houtz: "Moltmann at 90"). In an even sharper statement, Moltmann declares: "As Christians, we receive our salvation from the justifying righteousness of God. We reject all forms of retributive justice. We reject the death penalty in the name of God" (Winright: "Jürgen Moltmann on Capital Punishment").

This conviction has long since been a part of Moltmann's thought. In an early collection of sermons, Moltmann strongly criticized the death penalty, writing, "[A]nyone who kills another human being murders God too" (*The Power of the Powerless*, 9). It is "preposterous" to Moltmann that anyone would attempt to justify the death penalty with an appeal to the Bible. It is for *Christ's* sake that we condemn the death penalty, because "after the capital punishment that Jesus suffered, there can be [...] no justification for capital punishment" (Merritt: "Protest Hope").

This conviction became personal for Moltmann after befriending an American death-row inmate, Kelly Gissendaner. Gissendaner was sentenced to death for persuading her boyfriend to kill her husband in

1998. While in prison, she had a radical conversion experience. Kelly was a changed woman. She ministered to other women in prison, and even studied and graduated from a theology program run by Emory University. She was attracted to the works of Dietrich Bonhoeffer, Rowan Williams, and Jürgen Moltmann. She sent one of her papers on Bonhoeffer to Moltmann directly, and it impressed him. After that, they regularly corresponded and became friends. Over a period of four years, they exchanged some twenty or thirty letters.

Her ministry efforts in prison became well known, and many passionate calls for clemency emerged as her execution drew near. Many came forward offering proof of clear reform. Fellow inmates shared videos online to express how her ministry changed their lives. She even saved a woman's life once by talking her out of suicide. News of her faith reached as far as Pope Francis, and on his behalf, Archbishop Carlo Maria Viganò urged the State of Georgia to spare her life. In spite of all this, she was executed on September 30, 2015. A university professor, who would often visit and teach Gissendaner in prison, witnessed the execution and called it "pure evil wrapped in this respectability and law" (McBride, quoted in The New York Times: "A Death Row Inmate…").

Moltmann, a year later, publicly reflected on his friendship with Gissendaner:

> I followed the execution of Kelly Gissendaner very carefully. What theology do these prisoners develop? I myself was a prisoner in Scotland. What happens there in prison with human beings? Kelly was confined to silence, solidarity, isolation, and celibacy. She couldn't even shake hands longer than thirty seconds. She spent years not knowing if this day was her last, and this is cruel and unusual punishment. People after five years in solitary confinement go crazy and are stripped of humanity. John of the Cross described this as the dark night of the soul. Kelly sang songs and prayed prayers to survive death row. Jesus, the Spirit of Life, will visit you in your prison cell. Kelly said do not allow prison to rob you of your dreams and dignity. A miracle occurs and our life is redeemed and not wasted. Kelly Gissendaner sang Amazing Grace as she was executed and was the only free person in prison.

The sin of the middle class is indifference. Get out and live and the spirit will bless you.

— HOUTZ: "MOLTMANN AT 90"

Moltmann is right: the sin of the middle class *is* indifference, but the cross of the passionate God forbids apathy in the face of inhumane suffering. The way of Jesus Christ sets us free from the apathetic chains of indifference and paralysis; Christ compels us to take a stand against injustice. God suffered and died at the hands of the Georgia State executioners together with Kelly Gissendaner; God suffered her psychological torments and was with her in the loneliness of prison—just as God suffered and died in her husband's death, the death she was in jail for orchestrating. Violence will not put an end to the vicious cycles of violence, only suffering love will. The cross is a call to resist all forms of violence and counter-violence.

The death penalty is cruel, and there is no Christian justification for it. It is a symptom of the cycles of violence we are called to reject in the name of Christ. Retributive justice is not God's justice; God's justice heals and saves. "We reject the death penalty in the name of God" (Winright: "Jürgen Moltmann on Capital Punishment").

WHAT ABOUT TORTURE?

Another form of state-sanctioned violence is torture. In America, the best example is the inhumanity of the Guantanamo Bay detention camp. This facility holds inmates *indefinitely* and *without trial.* It has been widely deemed a breach of human rights and has been liberal in its use of torture to obtain information. Guantanamo Bay has been justified under the guise of anti-terrorism, playing on the fears of Americans in the aftermath of 9/11. But it is not only in Guantanamo Bay that the State has sanctioned torture. Journalists have uncovered proof that the CIA has used torture as an interrogation strategy, in spite of its proven ineffectiveness (Foster: "US Torture Report"). Torture is cruel, unnecessary, and it should never be considered acceptable.

Torture is a crime and a human injustice in every circumstance, but it is especially grievous when sanctioned by the state. When torture is a politically sanctioned act, no one is held accountable. Bob Dylan sang, in one of his many great songs of protest, "The executioner's face is always well hidden" ("A Hard Rain's A-Gonna Fall"). When acts of violence are committed anonymously, no one is held responsible, and nothing changes. When the state ordains violence, it hides its brutality under the false guise of legality.

The crucified Christ delegitimizes all such abuses of state power. Moltmann notes that those who torture in the name of their country are in fact "destroying it, not protecting it" (*Jesus Christ for Today's World*, 63). Ultimately, torture is an offense against Christ, who was tortured and killed at the hands of politically sanctioned violence. We must remember that Christ's death was a *legal* death, a death sanctioned and legitimized by the powers that be.

But Christ is among the tortured, as Moltmann writes:

> He is among them as their brother, as a sign that God shares in our suffering and takes our pain on himself. Among all the un-numbered and un-named tortured men and women, that 'Suffering Servant of God' is always to be found. They are his companions in his suffering, because he has become their companion in theirs. The tortured Christ looks at us with the eyes of tortured men and women.
>
> — IBID., 65

For Christ's sake, there can be no legitimate politically sanctioned acts of violence. In the name of God, we reject war, police militarization and brutality, torture, and Guantanamo Bay. When we see Christ in the eyes of all those who suffer violence, we reject violence unequivocally. A Christianity that remains silent in the face of state-sanctioned violence is complicit in the suffering of Christ in the victims of oppression.

4

THE CHURCH IN THE POWER OF THE SPIRIT

SUMMARY: The one, holy, catholic, apostolic Church discovers its unity in freedom, its holiness in poverty, its catholicity in partiality to the poor, and its apostolicity in suffering. As the Church of *Jesus Christ,* it is found among those whom Christ took up solidarity with, namely, the poor, homeless, oppressed, and persecuted. As the Church in the power of the Spirit, it is structured "from below" in the shared ministry and gifts of all believers. As the Church of the Kingdom, it is active in the public sphere for Christ's sake.

IN MOLTMANN'S OWN WORDS:

"The one holy, catholic and apostolic church is the church of Jesus Christ. Fellowship with Christ is its secret. [...] Unity in freedom, holiness in poverty, catholicity in partisan support for the weak, and apostolate in suffering are the marks by which it is known in the world."

— THE CHURCH IN THE POWER OF THE SPIRIT, 361

The church will become the church of the poor for Christ's sake, for in the poor we find Christ's real presence.

— GOD WILL BE ALL IN ALL, 287

'Birds of a feather flock together' is nothing other than the social form adopted by self-righteousness. It is an expression of fear.

— THE POWER OF THE POWERLESS, 101

SECONDARY QUOTES:

[Moltmann's] vision of the church is rooted theologically in its relationship to the trinitarian history of God. The hierarchical, authoritarian and clerically managed church depends, according to Moltmann, on a monarchical image of God as power and rule: fundamentally 'monotheistic' (i.e. in Moltmann's usage, unitarian) doctrine of God. Clerical rule in the church is then legitimated by a descending authority structure in which 'the people' are subjects to be ruled and administered. But this thinking is non-trinitarian. It neglects Jesus' transformation of the notion of rule into liberating service, his open friendship and identification with 'the people', and his cross, which smashes all idols of religious power. [...] God in his trinitarian history is not a justification for clerical rule, but is the vulnerable and liberating love which makes possible open fellowship in freedom and responsibility [...]. In this trinitarian context ecclesiology cannot be reduced to 'hierarchology', preoccupied with the authority of the ministry, but must begin with the fact that every believer is a responsible member of the messianic fellowship.

— RICHARD BACUKHAM: THE THEOLOGY OF JÜRGEN
MOLTMANN, 139

INTRODUCTION

While *Theology of Hope* and *The Crucified God* are among Moltmann's most frequently discussed works, his third major book, *The Church in the Power of the Spirit*, is no less radical in its re-orienting scope. When I first read the book, I was amazed by the breadth of its vision, but I was also surprised by how little attention it has received. Moltmann offers a radical vision for Church reform in this book, and we should consider it as seriously as his first two. The iconoclasm of the cross and Moltmann's profound vision of Christian hope may be the more *theologically* radical proposals, but his approach to Church reform is just as important.

For Moltmann, the Church is *essentially missionary* in the fellowship of *dialectical hope*. These two definitions make up a broader description of the Church, favored by Moltmann, as the *messianic fellowship*. It is the Church "in the power of the Spirit," the Church freely endowed with the Spirit's *charisma* or gifts. Thus, one of the critical implications of this vision is Moltmann's argument for a grass-roots Church against its current hierarchical structure. We will begin this chapter by grasping an overview of Moltmann's proposal through the classic fourfold definition of the Church as "one, holy, catholic, apostolic." Then we will examine more closely this grass-roots structure. Finally, we will discuss what it means for the Church to be active in the political sphere.

ONE, HOLY, CATHOLIC, APOSTOLIC

This classic definition of the Church is a *statement of faith*. It is not automatic that the Church is one, holy, catholic and apostolic merely by calling itself the Church; it is because of *the Lord* of the Church that these are valid. It is Christ who gathers together the divided Church in His unity, Christ who deems her holy in His holiness, Christ who enacts her universality, and Christ who joins her with the first witnesses and their proclamation of the Gospel. As a statement of faith, this fourfold definition is also a *statement of hope*. It is in *anticipation* of becoming the one, holy, catholic, and apostolic Church that we confess this identity. It reflects the eschatological orientation of the Church, the Church *on the way* towards God's future.

Therefore, as statements of *hope* and *faith*, these are at once statements of *action*, of *love*—definitions of a *missionary* Church. The Church is one, holy, catholic, and apostolic whenever it acts according to God's mission and history on the earth. These definitions affirm the essential missionary nature of the Church. The Church is not the Church of Christ in static isolation, but only as it goes out in the mission of Christ to the "least of these."

The Church is what is it because of Christ, because of God's future, and because of God's mission. If the Church is the one, holy, catholic, and apostolic Church, then these terms reflect its *faith, hope,* and *love*.

With this in mind, we will begin to examine what these terms mean for Moltmann. He offers a helpful summary:

> The church's unity is its *unity in freedom.* The church's holiness is its *holiness in poverty.* The church's apostolicity bears *the sign of the cross,* and its catholicity is linked with its *partisan support for the oppressed.*
>
> — THE CHURCH IN THE POWER OF THE SPIRIT, 341

A missionary Church is involved in social and political concerns. There is no apolitical Church, no neutral Church. The Church is not indeed the Church when it is shut in on itself, concerned only with its own affairs. The true Church is *open* to the world. In the Church's openness to the world, Moltmann arrives at his summary by reflecting on the mission of the Church:

- "What form is to be taken by the *one* church in Christ in a world of hostility?" Answer: *unity in freedom.*
- What form is to be taken by "the church made *holy* in the Spirit in a world of poverty?" Answer: *holiness in poverty.*
- What form is to be taken by "the *catholic* church as it testifies to the kingdom in a world of violence?" Answer: *partisan support for the oppressed.*
- What form is to be taken by "the *apostolic* church in the world of the cross?" Answer: *the sign of the cross.* (See ibid., 341-2.)

These definitions express the form a missionary Church takes in its openness to the world. Rightly, Moltmann asks, "Is the situation in which the church finds itself in this society not bound to stamp it with the signs of poverty, suffering, liberation and partisanship?" (ibid., 341). If the Church falls back upon an introspective, self-centered definition, then it is "forsaking the cross of its Lord" (ibid.). Christ's Church is where Christ is in the world: among the poor, the homeless, the weak, and the oppressed. The Church's mission *is* its identity, in this sense.

In this context, we will now explore Moltmann's description of the Church regarding its "unity in freedom," "catholicity in partisanship," "holiness in poverty," and "apostolicity in suffering."

What is unity without freedom? The Church is not bound together by its conformity, unanimity, or uniformity of perception. The unity of the Church *is* its freedom. That is, the Church is united in the liberty of its diversity. Unity without freedom is control and domination. Hierarchal forms of leadership have often abused a rigid definition of unity. It has often become an excuse for an iron-fisted rule, or for the exclusive triumphalism of "correct doctrine" against all other perspectives. In the name of Church unity, many essential views have been excluded and marginalized. Real unity is not conformity to a single perspective, but freedom: freedom for disagreement, for dialogue, for shared discovery. It is true that empty pluralism will kill freedom as quickly as uniformity, but the Church tends to err on the side of uniformity; it is the greater danger.

The *charisma* of the Spirit is a central element in this unity. There are many gifts but one Spirit, as Paul explained in 1 Corinthians 12, which leads to a grassroots understanding of the Church. It is therefore united not by a hierarchal structure from above but from below in the congregation. The Church finds its essential unity in the one Spirit who gives many gifts.

Thus, Moltmann writes:

> The all-important thing is therefore to present and organize the fellowship between local churches not from above but from below. [...] The open friendship of Jesus, which is experienced and lived in the gathered congregation, and 'the unity of the Spirit in the bond of peace', cannot be surpassed.
>
> — THE CHURCH IN THE POWER OF THE SPIRIT, 344-5

The priesthood of all believers and the *charisma* of the Spirit affirms a Church "from below" against a Church "from above." It calls for a renewed organizational structure in the Church today so that everything takes on this congregational center rather than a pastoral or top-down center. It is a radical proposal because it means re-constructing two millennia of hierarchal leadership. We will return to this in more detail below. But it is vital to recognize how this "from below" organization is a logical implication of the *charisma* of the Spirit; every believer is responsible for the life of the Church because of their gifting.

So far we have only examined the *internal* freedom in unity of the Church, the Church in itself, but we must also consider how the Church becomes a unifying force by its missionary involvement in the world. Moltmann writes, the Church as the "messianic people of Christ" is a "unifying force [...] [unity] is the church's task in the world as well [as its attribute]" (ibid.). What does it look like when the Church goes outside of itself and enters a world of disunity? For Moltmann, it means fellowship with the *other,* with those who are "oppressed, humiliated, and forsaken" in society (ibid.). A united Church stands in a world of disunity as the Church in the fellowship of sinners and outcasts. The Church follows Christ into solidarity with strangers. Moltmann writes:

> The church would not witness to the whole Christ if it were not a fellowship of believers with the poor, a fellowship of the hopeful with the sick, and a fellowship of the loving with the oppressed. Its unity would no longer be a 'predicate of the time of salvation' if it were not to achieve liberation for the downtrodden, justice for those without rights, and peace in social conflicts. It is not 'one' for itself; it is one for the peace of divided mankind in the coming kingdom of God.
>
> — IBID.

The Church is united *for* the world, not for its own sake. The Church is fundamentally the *fellowship of Christ*; its unity is *Christ's* unity. Where is Christ to be found on the earth? Christ is in the midst of the forsaken, the poor, the oppressed, and the suffering. Patrick Oden thus offers a challenging insight in this connection, writing:

> [F]ellowship with Christ does not simply encourage including the poor in our services or reaching out to them or giving them what we think they require, acting in paternal ways. Rather, this fellowship insists on involving ourselves in true solidarity, seeing them not as objects to fix but as people included in our fellowship, the fellowship of Christ.
>
> Indeed, it might even be said that it is not our choice to include

them in our fellowship with Christ but to seek their fellowship so as to
be included with Christ who is already with them

— THE TRANSFORMATIVE CHURCH, KINDLE LOC. 1584

Fellowship with Christ means fellowship with the poor. As Moltmann
writes, "Fellowship with the crucified Jesus is practiced where Christians
in solidarity enter the brotherhood of those who, in their society, are
visibly living in the shadow of the cross; the poor, the handicapped, the
people society has rejected, the prisoners and the persecuted" (*The Church
and the Power of the Spirit,* 97). The Church as a messianic fellowship
stands with the oppressed, the poor, and the marginalized. That is the
responsibility of every Church which bears the name of the crucified
Christ. It is the unity of the Church.

CATHOLICITY IN PARTISANSHIP

Catholicity describes the Church's universality. "Catholicity in partisanship" then seems like a contradiction, at first glance. How can the
catholicity of the Church include partisanship? Does the universal
Church take sides?

It is essential first to recognize that the Church's catholicity is not
related to an abstract idea of universality but specifically to the catholicity
of Jesus Christ. It is only in and through Christ that the Church is
universal and all-embracing. Its catholicity derives from the universal lordship of Christ. Therefore, in Moltmann's eschatological orientation
(chapter 2), this means lordship *anticipated* in the promise. Thus, it is an
eschatological catholicity. It describes the *hope* of the Church, as promised
in the coming Kingdom of God. Moltmann writes:

Thanks to its hope it cannot surrender any individual person or any part
of creation. 'Catholic' is therefore not an adjective describing the
church's state; it is an attribute describing its movement, its mission and
its hope. [...] The church is related in a missionary way to the whole of
mankind, because its resurrection hope and its eucharistic prayer include

everyone. 'Catholic' is therefore an eminently eschatological definition of the church.

— The Church in the Power of the Spirit, 349

This hope describes the Church's *mission*. Our mission excludes no one and overlooks no aspect of creation. The partisanship of the Church is thus *provisional* partisanship which anticipates the eschatological goal of catholicity. Moltmann points out that a *realized* (non-eschatological) concept of catholicity has led to a Church which is no longer adequately concerned with its mission. That is to say, if the Church is *already* considered catholic, then the mission of God's Kingdom is only a secondary issue. The ecclesiastical glory of the Church and its hierarchical structure becomes the central issue, and thus it downplays its mission. That is why we must qualify the catholicity of the Church as an eschatological *hope* rather than a realized fact.

The eschatological catholicity of the Church spurs the Church into the world for the sake of God's mission. God's purpose is specific, it is *first* to the poor and oppressed, as Jesus' life and preaching reveal. Jesus was not universally focused but showed partisanship towards the marginalized. Of course, Jesus came *for the world*, but this manifested itself in His partiality for the poor. That brings up an important point. Partisanship is always *for the sake of catholicity*. The Church is on the side of the poor also *for the sake of the rich*, on the side of the oppressed also *for the sake of the oppressors*. God's preferential option for the poor is never *against* the rich and privileged, but *for* their salvation. God's liberating movement begins with the least of these, without excluding the high and mighty. "The last will be first, and the first will be last" (Mt. 20:16, NRSV). With this in mind, Moltmann writes:

> Christian partisan support for the oppressed is intentional and its goal is to save the oppressor also. [...] The rich and the mighty are not rejected out of revenge but in order to save them. Masters are rejected because of their oppression, so that they may experience the fullness of the common humanity, of which they are depriving themselves and others.

— The Church in the Power of the Spirit, 352

Liberation for the oppressed includes the liberation of their oppressors. Acts of oppression and violence against fellow human beings have a dehumanizing effect on both the oppressor and the oppressed. Freeing the oppressed *is* at once a step towards liberating their oppressors. The oppressed are liberated from their oppression and the oppressor from their acts of cruelty. As history has shown, the oppressed often *become* oppressors themselves, so that today's oppressors were often yesterday's oppressed. It is a vicious cycle. Only the preferential treatment of the poor together with repentance and forgiveness for their oppressors will end the cycle. Freedom for both sides of the spectrum is the goal of the Church. Thus, partisanship is the historical manifestation of the Church's eschatological hope for catholicity. Wherever oppression exists, the Church must take sides with the least of these. Wherever there is poverty and injustice; wherever the strong steal the rights of the weak, the Church will take sides with the weak and the poor. That is its catholicity.

HOLINESS IN POVERTY

The Church is holy because Christ is holy. It is sanctified by Him and by His Spirit. Moltmann emphasizes the fact that the Church's holiness is directly related to "Christ's activity in and on it." He then proposes that holiness "consists of *being made holy*, in sanctification, the subject of the activity being God (1 Thess. 5:23; 2 Thess. 2:13)" (*The Church in the Power of the Spirit*, 353; emphasis mine). It is a "verbal noun" understanding of holiness, in which we do not possess holiness but receive it continually by the grace of the Spirit called *Holy.* It is a *dependent* form of holiness so that we never *own* holiness but receive it continuously as a gift. Therefore, the Church is at once the communion of saints *and* sinners, according to Luther's formula: *simul justus et peccator*—at once justified and sinful.

Moltmann writes, "The church is holy because God shows himself to be holy in the grace of the crucified Christ acting on it. The revelation of his holiness means redemption" (ibid., 354). That implies an ongoing renewal of the Church; it is at once holy *and* being made holy by the Spirit. Moltmann thinks the Church's sanctification is in its service to and solidarity with the weak and lowly. He writes:

The church is therefore sanctified wherever it participates in the lowliness, helplessness, poverty and suffering of Christ. Its glory is manifest through the sign of poverty. When believers take up their cross, the kingdom of God is manifested to the world. In this sense we can say that the church is sanctified in this 'perverse world' through the signs of poverty, suffering and oppression. These are the birth pangs of the new creation in the midst of the creation that is still enslaved.

— Ibid., 355-6

That follows Paul's logic in 2 Corinthians 12:9, which states that God's "strength is made perfect in weakness." The very fact that the Church is the fellowship of Christ necessitates that the Church is partial towards the poor. It has a unique calling to recognize the Kingdom of God in the small and weak things of this world. The secret of the universe, which the Church knows by Christ's life and teachings, is that the weak things *are* strong and the strong things *are* weak. Our Lord does not rule by might, but by the suffering love of the cross. Whomever the world rejects will find friendship in the community of Christ because Christ's glory is among the poor and weak.

Moltmann relates this to the eschatological hope of God's coming Kingdom, writing, "Christian poverty therefore means the fellowship of the poor and fellowship with the poor—but as the fellowship of the messianic mission and the hope for the kingdom. In this sense Christian poverty, as 'an expression of love is solidarity with the poor and is a protest against poverty'" (ibid., 356). Poverty itself is not the goal, and the Church's fellowship *of* the poor and *with* the poor is its resistance *against* poverty. But it is in solidarity with the poor that the Church stands for their liberation, in anticipation of the Kingdom. Herein is the Church's holiness: holiness in poverty.

APOSTOLICITY IN SUFFERING

The apostolicity of the Church is its dependence upon the apostolic witness. Accordingly, Moltmann thinks this aspect of the Church will come to an end with the new creation; that is, it is a description with a temporal limit. It is a "forerunner of what is to come" (*The Church in the*

Power of the Spirit, 357). The Church's dependence upon the apostolic witness to Christ will end when we stand "face to face" with God, and before that day, the apostolic witness stands in the place of this direct encounter. Moltmann then concludes, "The expression 'apostolic' therefore denotes both the church's foundation and its commission" (ibid., 358).

But why does this description take the form of the Church's suffering, according to Moltmann? Because the mission and proclamation of the Church brings it into conflict with the violent powers of this world. The Kingdom we proclaim threatens every earthly kingdom. "Participation in the apostolic mission of Christ therefore leads inescapably into tribulation, contradiction and suffering. The apostolate is carried out in the weakness and poverty of Christ, not through force or the strategies of force" (ibid., 361). Suffering in the world is the sign of the Church's apostolicity. That was Paul's sign of his apostleship (2 Cor. 6-7), and Church history is overflowing with stories of martyrdom and persecution, even up to the present day. Moltmann writes:

> The church is apostolic when it takes up its cross. It then witnesses to the glory of the risen Christ in its fellowship with those who suffer, and his future in its fellowship with the imprisoned. In our godless and inhuman world 'the church under the cross' shows itself to be the true apostolic church. Its apostolic succession is the succession of the passion of Christ.
>
> — Ibid.

The true Church is not glorified in its strength, in ecclesial glory, but in its weakness and suffering. In tribulation, the Church witnesses to its crucified and risen Lord; it proclaims hope in the new creation.

REIMAGINING THE CHURCH "FROM BELOW"

Perhaps the most radical proposal of Moltmann's ecclesiology is the call to organize the Church from below rather than from above. The Reformation merely established yet another form of hierarchy, but perhaps we need another reformation to disavow hierarchy altogether. This proposal is attractive to me on a personal level. At a young age, I became involved in the so-called house Church movement. I grew up in a charismatic environment (technically Methodist with a charismatic focus), which was a natural breeding ground for recognizing the diverse gifts of the Spirit and the priesthood of all believers. It was not a far leap for me to then question the hierarchal structure of the Church. The house Church model empowered myself and others to come together, form small house churches, and practice the gifts of the Holy Spirit. George Barna's popular book, *Pagan Christianity*, radicalized this resolve because it placed a large question-mark against the way the Church operates. While that particular book is not one I would wholly endorse today, I mention my own experiences with this kind of Church because it explains why I feel so drawn to Moltmann's proposal. You may not find it as compelling as I have, but I hope you still see some benefit from allowing further reflection on this idea.

The point is not to end every form of leadership in the Church, but to move away from leadership *over* the congregation to the leadership *of* the congregation. In other words, leadership as *service* instead of the leadership of *control*. One of the reasons often cited for the lack of engagement with Moltmann's proposal is its lack of concrete details. That is true, but it could also be an invitation for creative leaders to experiment with a new kind of leadership based on Moltmann's theological convictions.

Instead of discussing the details of what this kind of Church organization could look like, here we will outline why Moltmann finds reform necessary. He first makes a connection between the doctrine of the Trinity and the Church "from below," writing:

> Throughout, my purpose was to understand the triune God as the God who is community, who calls community into life and who invites men and women into sociality with him. The community of Christ is permitted to see itself as an earthly reflection of the divine Triunity.
>
> — THE CHURCH IN THE POWER OF THE SPIRIT, xv

We will turn in the next chapter to examine Moltmann's doctrine of the Trinity, but this is a necessary connection to recognize. It is a *Trinitarian* doctrine of the Church that Moltmann argues we must adopt, against a *unitarian* doctrine of hierarchal leadership. A doctrine of God which highlights the Oneness of God over the Threeness of God implies a hierarchy of Church order, while a doctrine of God which emphasizes the community of the Three in One means a Church that is primarily *fellowship*. In the next chapter, we will explain why Moltmann finds the first definition problematic, but for now, this distinction will be enough as we continue.

With this Trinitarian intention in mind, Moltmann calls the "practical intention" of his book the desire "to point away from the pastoral church, that looks after the people, to the people's own communal church among the people" (ibid., xx). This shift is the only way Moltmann thinks that the Church can fulfill its purpose: "There is no other way for the church to exercise its office, its charge and its ministry, [except] in the congregation, with the congregation and through the congregation" (ibid.). It is not the people who make up the *pastor's* Church, but it is the *people's* Church that the pastor supports. Therefore, the mission of the Church is beyond our grasp if we remain trapped in a hierarchal structure, which binds the congregation rather than frees it to fulfill its mission on the earth.

As we have seen above, the fellowship of the Church is not a fellowship for its own sake but for the sake of its mission in the world. The Church that is first and foremost a loving fellowship within itself acts as a missionary Church when it takes up fellowship with sinners. The Church has often imagined its mission within the context of "us against them," but the fellowship of Christ rejects this false dichotomy. Our mission is not to objectify people as lost "souls" to win, but in fellowship, the Church extends the circle of its love to embrace the whole world. We become friends with sinners and tax collectors, as Christ did, because of the Spirit of fellowship within us.

Open friendship is how we might describe the relationship we enjoy with God in the Spirit, and as such it is our joy to make friends for Christ's sake. Moltmann writes, "The *congregatio sanctorum*, the community of brethren, is really the fellowship of friends who live in the friendship of Jesus and spread friendliness in the fellowship, by meeting the forsaken with affection and the despised with respect" (ibid., 316).

Members of the Church become lifeless and apathetic towards one another in a hierarchal model. They, in turn, become apathetic to the world, reclusive and uninvolved in the fellowship of those who suffer.

Friendship and fellowship must become the new center of the Church of Jesus Christ. Fellowship is of so little importance to us that we seldom engage one another in friendship, except perhaps at the yearly Church potluck. A Church from below prioritizes active involvement and care for one another. The congregation is not in the care of the pastor; the congregation shares in the care of its members, as the pastor offers support. The ministry of all believers prioritizes the shared responsibility of every believer in the congregation. We cannot see ourselves as passive subjects, but instead, must learn to be active participants in the mission and care of the Church.

In a Church from below, genuine friendship can flourish. In the hierarchal Church, friendship is prostituted as an evangelism strategy, in which we objectify "outsiders" and hide our real agenda of conversion. Christ was called the friend of sinners, but the Church is yet to earn this title.

The Spirit in all believers, which gives diverse gifts for the edification of the body (1 Cor. 14), is the primary reason why we should adopt this model. The Church is full of believers who have gifts for the Church given by the Holy Spirit, but when we exclude those gifts which do not fit within a hierarchal model, the Church suffers. The hierarchal Church restricts which gifts it will accept, and it has therefore rejected some of the Spirit's essential gifts. Only talented preachers, pastors, theologians, singers, or musicians benefit from seeing the spotlight shine on their gifts. There is a whole body of believers with diverse gifts that do not fit within traditional categories. The Church is *rejecting* these gifts and their Source by operating in a top-down model rather than from below.

The Holy Spirit is, according to Paul, the power of the resurrection (Rom. 8:11), and therefore the "divine power of creation and new creation," according to Moltmann (*The Church in the Power of the Spirit*, 295). The Spirit is the power of an "eschatological new thing" (ibid.). The gifts of the Spirit are foretastes of the new creation; these gifts are then as diverse and abundant as the new creation itself. The *charisma* of the Spirit necessitates the free organization of the Church since it presupposes the active involvement of all believers. The Holy Spirit is the orchestrator of the gifts (1 Cor. 12). Leadership under the Spirit is therefore empowering and not restricting.

Pneumatology is at the heart of Moltmann's vision for the Church "from below," so that the Church from below is the same as the Church "in the power of the Spirit." It is an offense to the Spirit that gives gifts to the Church whenever we exclude the participation of all believers in Church life. We reject a hierarchal Church structure for the sake of the Holy Spirit.

POLITICAL CHURCH

"A missionary church cannot be apolitical" (*The Church in the Power of the Spirit*, 15). It is important to recognize that this is a decisive break from Moltmann's context. The German Churches had decided on a policy of political neutrality. What Moltmann rightly identified, however, is that the Church cannot escape its political dimension. Either the Church stands in support of an oppressive status quo, or the Church stands up for the cause of the poor and weak. There is no middle ground. In its silence, an apolitical Church is complicit in the oppression of the less-privileged. With its voice, the Church must be an advocate for the voiceless.

As an American, I have sometimes wondered how it was possible that slavery went on for as long as it did. But the answer is quite simple: those who benefited from slavery, the privileged white Americans, were silent. Their silence supported slavery. It does not matter if they were for or against it. While the privileged white Church remained neutral, an oppressive status quo enslaved, brutalized, and murdered thousands upon thousands of black slaves. The slave owners were allowed to perpetuate this injustice only *because* of the silence of the privileged. Is it any different today? Will the Church remain silent in its privilege or will we stand up for those who have no voice?

Not every American supported slavery, but the majority benefited from it. Remaining silent was in the best interest of the privileged. That is how it always works, even today. If you have to wonder whether or not you are among the privileged, you probably are. By failing to recognize and renounce our privilege, the Church stands complicit to the injustices of history.

In our silence, we perpetuate oppression. When will we stand up against the systemic racism that still exists in America today? When will we fight for the rights of the poor and disabled? When will we be a voice for the foreigners and refugees in need?

Slavery, too, has not been eradicated from this earth. There are millions of slaves all around the world, mostly working as forced laborers. In America, we benefit from inexpensive clothing, food, and other material goods. *We benefit from slavery.* How does this fact make you feel, knowing that your silence supports the oppression of another human being? There is a test you can take online that estimates how many slaves work for you based on your spending habits (slaveryfootprint.org). For those of us in the first world living in prosperity and happiness, we must recognize that our privilege comes at the expense of creating a "hell on earth" in the third world. Dorothee Sölle once provocatively said, "The third world is a permanent Auschwitz." We cannot be a Church that remains indifferent to the cries of those who suffer. Ours is an unethical privilege we must recognize and reject. To stay silent and do nothing is to be complicit in injustice, to condone *slavery.* It will always come at a cost, but the liberation of men and women from such injustices is the cause of Christ. It is, therefore, the mission of the Church. We no longer have to ask ourselves what we would do if we lived in a time of slavery—*we are alive in such a time.* What will we do about it?

The Church of Jesus Christ must be on the forefront of the fight for social justice. The Church must become a voice for the voiceless, for the weak, poor, oppressed, and outcasted. There is no apolitical Church: we are either silently complicit in injustice or actively involved in the cause of Christ.

Moltmann writes:

> Historically, the church has always had a political dimension. Whether it likes it or not, it represents a political factor. It is hence only a question of how it presents itself as a political factor. [...] [T]he acknowledgment of the sole lordship of Christ plunges the church into political conflict. A logical and consistent Christian discipleship always has logical political consequences.
>
> — The Church in the Power of the Spirit, 15

That is not a "politicizing of the Church," but rather, "a Christianization of the church's politics according to 'the yardstick and plumbline of Christ'" (ibid.). The Church in the power of the Spirit is the Church of liberation. Forgoing our privilege and rejecting the oppressive status quo is the task of a liberating Church. Concretely, Moltmann emphasized, "Working for liberation means taking sides with the oppressed and humiliated" (ibid., 17).

Political silence is a privilege we must reject. In the comfort of our cushy lifestyles, it is easy to become complacent and shut our eyes to the sufferings of this world; but these are the *sufferings of Christ*. We must learn to see Christ in the eyes of the oppressed, and rise to their defense. That is where the true Church is in the world. To be a Christian (to follow Christ) is to stand up for the rights and dignity of the poor and the oppressed. We who are privileged in the first world are responsible because of our status. Privilege necessitates responsibility for the less-privileged. That is the cause of Christ in the world today, and as such, it is the cause of His Church.

SIDEBAR: THE SACRAMENTS

Traditionally, the Lord's Supper is a closed meal restricted to believers, while baptism is open to all as an entrance to faith. Moltmann thinks this is an error and argues the opposite: an open table and a closed baptism. We will explore the reasons why in this section.

A story from Moltmann's travels in England and Scotland will help establish some context:

> In October 1968 I had two different eucharistic experiences which made me think, and later put their stamp on my doctrine of the Lord's Supper. On 25 October I flew to London, where I met Paul Oestreicher [...]. He invited me to an anti-Vietnam demonstration that was to take place in the streets of London. A motley collection of Protestant and Catholic Christians, together with people from 'the highways and byways', met in the offices of the Catholic publisher Sheed & Ward, and with a celebration of the Lord's Supper, sitting on the floor, we prepared ourselves for the demonstration by agreeing to renounce violence; for in the previous demonstration many people had been hurt. Bread and wine passed from hand to hand in a small circle, and we felt the bodily presence of Jesus among us. The next morning we sprang through Fleet Street and Trafalgar Square, shouting, 'Ho Ho Chi

Min.' It all passed off without any violence or obscenities, and everyone was happy. [...]

[In Edinburgh,] I preached in St Giles, John Knox's church. After the sermon, those who stayed behind were served the Lord's Supper on silver trays by servers clad in black. The participants sat separate from one another, scattered here and there in the great church. There was no sense of community, and I went out of the beautiful church depressed. Where does Jesus' feast belong? On the streets of the poor who follow Jesus, or in the church of the baptized, the confirmed and established? I decided for the feast that is open to all, and to which the weary and heavy-laden are invited. Baptism, on the other hand, should be reserved for believers. That certainly contradicts the practice of our mainline churches, but it is in conformity with Jesus according to the Synoptic Gospels. Jesus' Supper is not a church meal for people who belong to one's own denomination. It is the feast of the crucified Christ, whose hands are stretched out to everyone. [...] The Eucharist is in Jesus' literal sense 'catholic', that is to say all-embracing, exclusive of no one but inclusive of all.

— A Broad Place, 163-4

The contrast between these two experiences could not be more profound.

The Lord's Supper is an open invitation because it is *Christ's* meal, not a religious ritual under the Church's control. The Church has no authority to turn aside those whom Christ has called and wills to have at His table. Whenever the Church limits the Lord's Supper, it is standing in the way of Christ's all-embracing invitation. That is clear if we remember that the Church is subject to the Supper, not the Supper to the Church, as Moltmann writes:

The church owes its life to the Lord and its fellowship to his supper, not the other way round. Its invitation goes out to all whom he is sent to invite. If a church were to limit the openness of his invitation of its own accord, it would be turning the Lord's supper into the church's supper and putting its own fellowship at the centre, not fellowship with him. By using the expression 'the Lord's supper' we are therefore stressing the pre-eminence of Christ above his earthly church and are calling in question every denominationally limited 'church supper'. [...]

The Lord's supper takes place on the basis of an invitation which is as open as the outstretched arms of Christ on the cross. Because he died for the reconciliation of 'the world', the world is invited to reconciliation in the supper. It is not the openness of this invitation, it is the restrictive measures of the churches which have to be justified before the face of the crucified Jesus. But which of us can justify them in his sight? The openness of the crucified Lord's invitation to his supper and his fellowship reaches beyond the frontiers of the different denominations. It even reaches beyond the frontiers of Christianity; for it is addressed to 'all nations' and to 'tax-collectors and sinners' first of all. Consequently we understand Christ's invitation as being open, not merely to the churches but to the whole world.

— IBID., 244-6

The Lord's Supper is thus a harsh criticism against any ecclesiastical model which uses this meal to *restrict* fellowship rather than to *open* itself up to an all-embracing community. Because it is not a meal that belongs to the Church—it is the *Lord's* Supper—it is a meal that stands in judgment against every divided and elitist Church. Just as the cross is both the foundation and *criticism* of the Church, so the Lord's Supper, as an image of Christ's death and coming Kingdom, stands in critical opposition to the Church's exclusive tendencies.

The Lord's Supper is an open meal because it is *Christ's* meal. Moltmann asked above where this meal belongs: among the poor and weak, or the high and mighty? It should be clear. Just as Christ did not come to the high ecclesiastical order with its endless restrictions and limitations, so the meal of Christ is an open invitation for the weak and the outsiders; it is the meal of Jesus, the friend of sinners, not a ritual of exclusion.

Turning to baptism, Moltmann thinks that a strong sense of missionary responsibility should be bound together with baptism. Moltmann writes:

It is a missionary sign. Through a baptism of this kind, the meaning of one's own life is comprehended in the wider framework of God's history with the world. Baptism joins a fragmentary and incomplete human life with the fullness of life and the perfect glory of God.

— THE CHURCH IN THE POWER OF THE SPIRIT, 241

In baptism, we join our story with God's great story and take up responsibility for God's mission in the world. It is not merely the sign of Church membership, but of participation in the Church's mission as it takes part in God's history with the world.

Naturally then, Moltmann rejects infant baptism and suggests we restrict the sacrament to adults who can freely decide. But Moltmann is well aware that years of tradition will not change overnight. So he proposes the blessing of children instead of baptism, and that there should be no obligation for parents or clergy to baptize children. Baptism is a call to freedom, yet it is a freedom bound in responsibility to the mission of the Church. Therefore, it should be a social sacrament in which the whole community takes responsibility for the baptized individual as they join the fellowship of believers. Instead of perceiving baptism as a kind of exchange performed by the Church hierarchy, the whole congregation should recognize its role as active subjects in the baptismal sign. The baptized individual is not alone in their commitment to God's mission in the world, but together with them, the whole congregation takes part in God's mission.

5

THE TRINITY AND THE KINGDOM

SUMMARY: The Triune God is not best defined speculatively as an absolute subject or unitarian monad, but only according to the biblical history of Jesus Christ. It is in the *perichoretic* fellowship of the Father, Son, and Holy Spirit that we discover their essential unity. The biblical narrative portrays a God whose very being is in this communion. And this fellowship is open to history and the world so that the self-giving love that God is in Godself extends to all creation.

IN MOLTMANN'S OWN WORDS:

God is not a solitary Lord of heaven, who subjugates everything, as earthly despots have always done in his name. Nor is God a cold, silent force of destiny, which determines everything and is touched by nothing. The triune God is a God in community, rich in inner and outward relationships. It is only of him that we can say 'God is love', for love is not solitary, but presupposes those who are different, joins those who are different, and distinguishes those who are joined. If 'the Father and the Son and the Holy Spirit' are joined together through eternal love, then their one-ness is in their *concord* with each other. They form their unique, divine community through their self-giving to one another.

— EXPERIENCES IN THEOLOGY, 309-10

The New Testament talks about God by proclaiming in narrative the relationships of the Father, the Son and the Spirit, which are relationships of fellowship and are open to the world.

— EXPERIENCES IN THEOLOGY, 144

SECONDARY QUOTES:

[Three points on Moltmann's social doctrine of the Trinity:] First, it is in their relationships to each other that the three are persons. [...] Second, since the unity of God is thus defined in terms of love, as perichoresis, it is a unity which can open itself to and include the world within itself. The goal of the trinitarian history of God is the uniting of all things with God and in God: a trinitarian and eschatological panentheism. [Third:] In himself God is not rule but a fellowship of love; in his relationship with the world it is not so much lordship as loving fellowship which he seeks; and in his kingdom [...] it is relationships of free friendship which most adequately reflect and participate in the trinitarian life.

— RICHARD BACUKHAM: THE THEOLOGY OF JÜRGEN
MOLTMANN, 17

INTRODUCTION

The first book in Moltmann's "systematic contributions to theology" opens up a robust critique of traditional Trinitarian thinking. In retrospect, Moltmann states his intention: "[To] perceive the relationships of sociality in God and to practise a new 'Trinitarian thinking'. By that I meant thinking in relationships, in communities, and in transitions. I wanted to put an end to the old thinking in terms of substances and determining subjects, a method which cannot work without dividing and isolating its objects" (*A Broad Place*, 187). That results in "a *social doctrine of the Trinity*, according to which God is a community of Father, Son and Spirit, whose unity is constituted by mutual indwelling and reciprocal interpenetration" (*The Trinity and the Kingdom*, viii).

This doctrine will be the primary focus of this chapter. First, we will explore the differences in how Moltmann and Barth arrive at a doctrine of the Trinity. Second, we will then explain why Moltmann makes such a sharp break from Barth. And finally, we will discuss its social and political implications.

Moltmann's social trinitarianism is controversial in many respects, but here I primarily aim to show the logic behind its development. If we can arrive at an understanding of *why* Moltmann argues for this, then perhaps we will be in a better position to appreciate his conclusions and thus avoid rash judgments. In a sidebar to this chapter, I will address one of the primary criticisms leveled against Moltmann, that of tritheism, but we must first recognize the way he develops this insight before defending it.

DIFFERENCES WITH BARTH: GOD THE LORD OR THE FATHER OF JESUS CHRIST?

Karl Barth is often credited with revitalizing the doctrine of the Trinity in modern theology—and rightly so since his *Church Dogmatics* is profoundly Trinitarian in structure and logic. Moltmann, however, brings some sharp criticisms against how Barth developed his doctrine of the Trinity (particularly in *Church Dogmatics* I/1), and to correctly understand Moltmann's focus in developing his doctrine of the Trinity, we will begin by noting their differences.

For Barth, that "God reveals Himself as the Lord" is the "root" of the doctrine of the Trinity (*Church Dogmatics* I/1, 307). In other words, this is the foundation from which the Christian doctrine of the Triune God develops. Barth explains:

> Revelation is the revelation of lordship and therewith it is the revelation of God. For the Godhead of God, what man does not know and God must reveal to him, and according to the witness of Scripture does reveal to him, is lordship. Lordship is present in revelation because its reality and truth are so fully self-grounded, because it does not need any other actualisation or validation than that of its actual occurrence, because it is revelation through itself and not in relation to something else, because it is that self-contained *novum* [new thing]. Lordship means freedom.
>
> — IBID., 306

Accordingly, Barth develops what Moltmann terms a "monotheistic" doctrine of the Trinity by emphasizing the God's lordship in revelation (though "unitarian" is a more apt term for what Moltmann has in mind). In the summary heading of §9, Barth writes, "The God who reveals Himself according to Scripture is One in three distinctive modes of being subsisting in their mutual relations: Father, Son, and Holy Spirit. It is thus that He is the Lord, i.e., the Thou who meets man's I and unites Himself to this I as the indissoluble Subject and thereby and therein reveals Himself to him as his God" (ibid., 348).

Barth's doctrine of the Trinity is highly creative, and his placement of the Trinity within the dogmatic prolegomena (introduction) is revolutionary; it results in giving the Trinity a controlling center in the whole of his theology. The importance of his doctrine of the Trinity, therefore, should not be understated, even if we must consider some of Moltmann's objections to it.

The primary issue Moltmann has with Barth's logic is this attempt to root the Trinity in God's lordship. Barth connects God's self-revelation with God's lordship and even goes so far as to claim that the very "Godhead of God [...] *is Lordship*" (*Church Dogmatics* I/1, 306; emphasis mine). Beginning with divine lordship is problematic because it results in God as the absolute subject in self-differentiation. In other words, for Barth, the lordship of God determines what it means for God to be Triune. Should it not be the reverse? Moltmann writes: "Unlike Karl Barth, we have started from the assumption that the unity of the triune God is not to be found initially in his subjectivity and the sovereignty of his rule; it is already to be discovered in the unique, perfect, perichoretic fellowship of the Father, the Son and the Holy Spirit" (*God in Creation*, 258). In other words, Moltmann does not begin with the presupposed lordship of God, of God's unity, but with the perichoretic fellowship of the Father, Son, and Holy Spirit. Only by *first* considering God's self-giving fellowship in the history of Jesus can we rightly understand God's Lordship.

The issue with Barth's doctrine of the Trinity could be summarized (roughly) as beginning with the *oneness* of God (God's lordship) and only then considering the *threeness* of God (God's fellowship), rather than beginning with the *threeness* and only then arriving at God's *oneness*. For Moltmann, this is incongruent with the biblical narrative of the Triune

God. Thus, he thinks Barth begins with a "non-trinitarian concept of the unity of the one God—that is to say, the concept of the identical subject" (*The Trinity and the Kingdom*, 143). By beginning with a non-trinitarian concept of God's unity, Moltmann thinks that Barth works from an improper doctrine of God's sovereignty (lordship) and only then interprets the Trinity in the light of his own presupposed definition. It would be better, Moltmann argues, to begin with God's Triunity and *then* come to a conclusion about God's sovereignty. Moltmann writes:

> It is of decisive importance for the doctrine of God whether we start from the Trinity in order to understand the sovereignty of God as the sovereignty of the Father, the Son and the Spirit, or whether we think in the reverse direction, proceeding from the sovereignty of God in order to secure this as being the sovereignty of the One God by means of the doctrine of the Trinity. If we start from the sovereignty of God, then our premise is God as the identical subject of his rule. The doctrine of the Trinity can then only be presented as 'Christian monotheism'. It is nothing other than a development of the recognition that God is Lord. This was the starting point Karl Barth chose.
>
> — Ibid., 140

Moltmann notes that this is a typically "Western" way of developing the doctrine, which traces back to Augustine, Aquinas, and, in modern times, Hegel. That is, it is not only Barth's mistake to operate in this way. In this Western procedure, God is the "absolute subject" who "identifies himself with himself," and therefore "His unity is a unity dialectically differentiated in itself" (*Sun of Righteousness, Arise!*, 150). Though not directly referring to Barth, Moltmann calls this method of developing the doctrine of the Trinity a kind of "philosophical monotheism" (*The Trinity and the Kingdom*, 130). Holding onto a monotheistic (unitarian) image of God as our primary definition is severely problematic, as Moltmann writes, "Strict monotheism obliges us to think of God without Christ, and consequently to think of Christ without God as well. The questions whether God exists and how one can be a Christian then become two unrelated questions" (ibid., 131). Moltmann is ultimately pursuing a "Christianization of the concept of God" (ibid., 132).

How can the doctrine of the Trinity move away from philosophical monotheism and rediscover a more Christ-like God? Moltmann writes:

> After considering all this, it seems to make more sense theologically to start from the biblical history, and therefore to make the unity of the three divine Persons the problem, rather than to take the reverse method —to start from the philosophical postulate of absolute unity, in order then to find the problem in the biblical testimony. The unity of the Father, the Son and the Spirit is then the eschatological question about the consummation of the trinitarian history of God. The unity of the three Persons of this history must consequently be understood as a communicable unity and as an open, inviting unity, capable of integration.
>
> — IBID., 149

Moltmann asks a critical question against Barth's assertion that we begin with the lordship of God: "But is this the God whom Jesus addressed in so intimate and familiar a way as 'Abba' and taught his followers to call upon?" (*History and the Triune God*, 7). Is God "the Lord" truly the same God and Father of Jesus Christ?

Historically speaking, Moltmann thinks that a Roman, monarchical concept of God has infected how the West developed its doctrine of God. Here "God the Lord" and "God the Father" merged into one, but this is to ignore the fact that the New Testament only ever refers to *Christ* as the "Lord." As a result of this Roman influence, theology adopted a patriarchal and hierarchal notion of the Godhead. That is, they adopted an image of God as the one ruler, the first cause, or the absolute subject of history. The one God is then mirrored on earth by the rulership of the one king. The lordship of God was therefore used to validate the rule of the emperor (see Moltmann's argument: ibid., 4-10).

A profound contrast is evident between God as the one Lord and the God whom Jesus addressed as His dear "Abba." Moltmann notes, "God is called 'Father' 11 times in the Old Testament, but according to the New Testament he is addressed as 'Father' by Jesus himself 170 times. With exception of his dying cry on the cross, [...] Jesus always addressed God only as 'Abba', and spoke of him always only as 'my Father'" (ibid., 10).

This distinction is at the heart of the issue. Whenever the doctrine of the Trinity centers on God as "the Lord," rather than Jesus' testimony of the God He called "Abba, Father," *then we are not Trinitarian in the same way the New Testament is Trinitarian.* The Scriptures speak about the Trinity within the context of the fellowship of the Son with the Father and in the Spirit. Thus, the Father is not once called "the Lord," but is always the "Father of Jesus Christ." The Son is not properly called the "second person of the Trinity" but the "Son of the Father." That is, fellowship is essential to the very identity of God so that the Father is not properly Father without the Son or the Son without the Father. Likewise, we often speak of the Holy Spirit in abstract and impersonal terms, but the New Testament regularly speaks of the Spirit relationally as the "Spirit of Christ" (Rom. 8:9). To be Trinitarian in the same way that the New Testament is Trinitarian means to speak of the fellowship of Father, Son, and Spirit *first* before arriving at a notion of their unity. If we begin with a speculative concept of divine unity, we fail to correctly recognize the way God has revealed Godself in the history of Jesus Christ.

Connecting this insight with the suffering of God on the cross, Moltmann writes:

> When [the Father] is understood as 'Lord God' in heaven, the Father cannot suffer, since all things come from him and he is dependent on no one. But understood as 'Father of the Son', the Father is passionately involved in the fate of the Son: where the Son is, there too is the Father; when the Son suffers, the Father suffers with him; when the Son rejoices, the Father also rejoices: the Son is from him, but he is also dependent on the Son, for they are one in their mutual love. Thus neither can be without the other, for the Father is in the Son and the Son is in the Father (John 14:10f.), and so by virtue of their mutual indwelling they are 'one', as the Gospel of John puts it.

> — History and the Triune God, 19-20

Notice particularly this final phrase: "by virtue of their mutual indwelling they are one." It is not "by virtue of their oneness they are three in self-distinction," but in the mutual indwelling of the Father, Son, and Holy Spirit, God is one. The former method constructs the Trinity according to philosophical monotheism (unitarianism), but the latter describes the Trinity according to the narrative history of Jesus in the New Testament. That is the genius of Moltmann's doctrine of the Trinity. Richard Bauckham summarizes it well: "The basis of the doctrine of the Trinity is the history of Jesus Christ, which the New Testament tells as a narrative of relationships between three divine Persons" (*The Theology of Jürgen Moltmann*, 173).

Moltmann is not arguing from a philosophical standpoint, but from the desire to be genuinely *Christian* in his Trinitarian thinking and thus to be faithful to the way the New Testament narrates God's Triunity. Jesus Christ did not proclaim God "the Lord" but His dear "Abba." That is the only "root" of the Trinity Moltmann is interested in. Here it is the *love* of God which is essential, not lordship.

Perichoresis and God's history

The Bible, Moltmann writes, is "the testimony to the history of the Trinity's relations of fellowship, which are open to men and women, and open to the world" (*Trinity and the Kingdom*, 19). At the core of Moltmann's social doctrine of the Trinity is his emphasis on a doctrine known as the divine *perichoresis*: the inter-Trinitarian fellowship of mutual indwelling and love. *Perichoresis* is the shared love and joy of the Father, Son, and Holy Spirit in their interrelatedness. An image is sometimes used to describe this mutual indwelling: three cups of wine simultaneously pouring out and being poured into, in a continuous circle of total self-giving love and fellowship. The identity of each cup is in its self-giving, in being for another. While no image adequately reflects the great mystery of God, this one can be helpful in describing *something* of what the divine *perichoresis* means.

Others have used the image of dance to help explain the movement of God's mutual indwelling. (C. S. Lewis: "[I]n Christianity God is not a static thing—not even a person—but a dynamic, pulsating activity, a life, almost a kind of drama. Almost, if you will not think me irreverent, a kind of dance" [*Mere Christianity*, 175].) We will never fully comprehend this mystery, but we can perhaps have some indication of what it means. In this regard, such images are useful. For our context, however, it is essential to recognize the centrality of the divine *perichoresis* in Moltmann's Trinitarian theology.

Perhaps Jesus described the divine *perichoresis* best in John 17:

> As you, Father, are in me and I am in you, may they also be in us, so that the world may believe that you have sent me. The glory that you have given me I have given them, so that they may be one, as we are one, I in them and you in me, that they may become completely one, so that the world may know that you have sent me and have loved them even as you have loved me. Father, I desire that those also, whom you have given me, may be with me where I am, to see my glory, which you have given me because you loved me before the foundation of the world.
>
> — JOHN 17:21-24, NRSV

There are two things we should notice about this text, which correspond well to Moltmann's social doctrine of the Trinity. The first is to recognize the *source* of the Trinitarian unity, and the second is to acknowledge the essential *openness* of that unity. The unity of the Trinity is not in the hierarchy of divine lordship, but in the unity of mutual indwelling. Only in this mutual-indwelling does Christ describe Himself as being "one" with the Father. The second point highlights Moltmann's concept of the "open Trinity," which expresses God's desire to include humanity in the Triune fellowship of love. In Jesus' prayer, he expresses this by opening up the mutual indwelling of the Trinity to include love for human beings (both God's love for us and our love for each other). Thus, Moltmann writes that this openness implies that the Trinity is a soteriological (saving) doctrine: "The union of the divine Trinity is open for the uniting of the whole creation with itself and in itself. So the unity of the Trinity is not merely a theological term; at its heart, it is a soteriological one as well" (*The Trinity and the Kingdom*, 96). The Triune God of love is *open* to human history. The divine *pathos* implied this already (chapter 3), in God's going out of Godself vulnerably to the world.

AN IMAGE IN SUMMARY

Moltmann's doctrine of the Trinity forces us to think of God in a new way by recognizing God as essentially *fellowship* and *communion* and not as divine ruler or hierarchy. While writing, Moltmann had before him Andrei Rublev's famous icon of the Holy Trinity:

Moltmann writes about its significance:

> Here too, as in other theological work, there has been a picture in front of me. It is Andrei Rublev's wonderful fifteenth-century Russian icon of the Holy Trinity. Through their tenderly intimate inclination towards one another, the three Persons show the profound unity joining them, in which they are one. The chalice on the table points to the surrender of the Son on Golgotha. Just as the chalice stands at the centre of the table round which the three Persons are sitting, so the cross of the Son stands

from eternity in the centre of the Trinity. Anyone who grasps the truth of this picture understands that it is only in the unity with one another which springs from the self-giving of the Son 'for many' that men and women are in conformity with the triune God. He understands that people only arrive at their own truth in their free and loving inclination towards one another. It is to this 'social' understanding of the doctrine of the Trinity that this book is an invitation.

— THE TRINITY AND THE KINGDOM, XVI

This image summarizes some of the core insights in Moltmann's doctrine of the Trinity.

The passion of the crucified Christ is central, represented by the cup, but it involves the whole Godhead as God goes outside of Godself in open vulnerability and suffering in and for the world (*pathos*). "For through his Shekinah God participates in man's destiny, making the sufferings of his people his own" (ibid., 118). "The cross is at the centre of the Trinity" (ibid., 83).

The Triunity of God is in their mutual indwelling and interpenetration; it is a unity not found in a hierarchal monarchy or a philosophical one subject, but unity in Tri-unity. The image does not show any priority of status among the persons, but a shared equality. "Jesus did not proclaim the kingdom of God *the Lord,* but the kingdom of God *his Father*" (ibid., 70).

God is a *fellowship* in Godself—God is love—and therefore salvation means participation in God's Triune life of love. "The history of salvation is the history of the eternally living, triune God who draws us into and includes us in his eternal triune life with all the fullness of its relationships. It is the love story of the God whose very life is the eternal process of engendering, responding and blissful love. God loves the world with the very same love which he is in himself" (ibid., 157).

The openness of the Trinity is thus an invitation for us and for all creation to take part in the fellowship of God's loving communion. The stance of the three persons in this icon represents this. They are not closed in on themselves and focused on their own fellowship, but open to the world. "[T]he triunity is open in such a way that the whole creation can be united with it and can be one within it" (ibid., 96).

The unity of the Triune God, in openness to the whole world, reflects God's eschatological goal. "In eschatological thinking, on the other hand, the unity of God is the final, eschatological goal, and this unity contains in itself the whole union of the world with God and in God" (*The Future of Creation*, 91). In the new creation, God's presence will be unmediated; therefore, God will be "all in all." We look ahead in hope for the cosmic incarnation of God. God is not at rest until God has found rest in and with creation.

POLITICAL AND SOCIAL IMPLICATIONS

As we briefly considered in the last chapter, a social doctrine of the Trinity has direct implications for the structure of the Church. Understanding the doctrine of God's Triunity as the fellowship of persons leads to rejecting hierarchy in the Church, the state, and in society. We should strive towards a community free from hierarchy and patriarchy, an open fellowship of equals. Leadership will remain necessary, just as the lordship of Christ and sovereignty of God remain essential aspects of God's nature, but leadership in a non-hierarchal system will become less about control and more about supporting and protecting the fundamental equality of persons. We need a new definition of leadership. Thus, Moltmann's Trinitarian theology is one of the best allies for the cause of modern feminism (of which his wife, Elisabeth, was an influential voice), as well as for liberation theologies such Black Theology in America (Cone) or Latin American Liberation Theology (Gutiérrez). While some feminist theologians have criticized the doctrine of the Trinity for supporting patriarchal thinking, Moltmann shows that a social doctrine of the Trinity is the best argument *against* a patriarchal system (more on this in the following sidebar).

We must reimagine every aspect of society in the light of the Triunity of God. The monarchy of the Father used to represent the lordship of rulers, but a social doctrine of the Trinity is the ultimate democratization of politics and society. In the realms of economics, education, and social-welfare, the implications of God's sociality can have a profound effect. Moltmann approvingly quotes Nicholas Fedorov, who writes, "The Trinity is our social programme" (cited in *Experiences in Theology*, 332).

The very notion of what it means to be "persons," for example, should be reimagined. We are persons not in isolation from others but only in fellowship. That is what it means for humans to be in the image of God: we discover our identity in relationships, first with God and then with one another. The modern world has promoted an individualized image of personhood, but this is not in line with the Triunity of God. We tend to divide ourselves from our fellow human beings and perceive them as the enemies of our success. They are our "competition" in an increasingly utilitarian age, in which only the useful and the successful may survive. But a social doctrine of the Trinity allows us to recognize the essential interrelatedness of our humanity. Every human being has value irrespective of their profitability or their success. A moving aspect of Moltmann's thought is how passionate he was about including the disabled into society: "The disabled are not a burden, nor are they a threat to the non-disabled; they are an enrichment for human society" (*A Broad Place*, 89). It is not hard to see that this is a necessary implication of his doctrine of the Trinity.

The same is true for every marginalized people group or class in society. We need to recognize our essential *dependence* upon those who are not like us, who have nothing that we can exploit for profit or status, who stand with us merely in their humanity as those whom God loves. We desperately need a society in which *shared humanity* is the only criteria for acceptance, inclusion, and fellowship. It can begin in the Church, as we come to grips with the practical implications of the Triunity of God, but then it should spread to the world. A social doctrine of God's Triunity invalidates racism, sexism, ageism, nationalism, or any other form of social exclusion.

If we only fellowship with people like us, we engage in a kind of *social self-justification*. "'Birds of a feather flock together': that is nothing other than the social form of self-justification and the expression of anxiety" (*The Passion for Life*, 30). Salvation by grace alone extends to this social form of sin, so that grace in our lives looks like the inclusion of those who are unlike us. Loving our enemies is not a suggestion for the Christian life; it is a sign of God's grace.

We have restricted God's acceptance of us by grace to personal sin only, with no implications on social life, but this is a mistake. God's grace towards us is how we are called to live towards one another. We often exclude others by their works rather than including those who are unlike us simply because they are loved by God, because of grace. But this is the way of Jesus Christ in our world: to accept the outcast, to embrace the stranger, to welcome the foreigner. Though how many times have you seen *Christians* look at the homeless on their city streets and complain they just need to "get a job?" We cannot proclaim God's salvation by grace alone and then turn to our neighbor and demand their performance to earn our acceptance of them. That is pure hypocrisy. Are we any better than the self-righteous Pharisees of Jesus' parable (Lk. 18:9-14)? Grace necessitates the renunciation of our social self-justification because we are sinners justified only by grace. God's very being and nature is in the open fellowship of Father, Son, and Holy Spirit, so our lives must become known for the inclusion of others and the self-giving love we have for strangers.

If the Gospel we profess has nothing to say against racism, for example, then it is not the same Gospel Jesus proclaimed. Justification by God's grace alone spurs us forward to create a society of free equals and open friendship. Paul calls us to "accept one another" in the same way that "Christ has accepted you" (Rom. 15:7). If the Gospel we proclaim fails to condemn social exclusion, then it is not Jesus' Gospel; it is the Gospel of justification by merit, the Gospel of the Pharisees. Christ's acceptance of sinners forces us out of our closed circles of self-justification and into open friendship with the "least of these." We have not adequately learned the message of grace until we actively make friends with those who are different from us. The Gospel in today's world means overcoming social exclusion in all its forms. That does not mean collapsing the Gospel into its social effect, but we can no longer accept a Gospel that has nothing to say to our concrete social situations. The hope of the Gospel is not for *another* world, but for the transformation of *this* world. The social doctrine of the Trinity reminds us that we are not yet who we were created to be until we live in harmony and fellowship with our brothers and sisters, with outsiders.

A CLARIFICATION IN CLOSING

Theology is never neutral. There are always political and social implications to theology. While some would prefer to keep theology and politics separate, this is an impossibility. We cannot speak of God on the one hand and ignore God's mission on the other. God is not an object we may describe abstractly, but the living God, the God of liberation and justice.

Moltmann is concerned for political and social change *because* of his theological convictions, not in spite of them. Whenever a theologian draws out the political or social implications of theology, however, there is a tendency to criticize them for politicizing God. Thus, Moltmann writes:

> At this point I should like to repudiate a hasty and stereotyped criticism. Whenever one draws practical conclusions from a theological insight, one is suspected of doing so in the interests of some political option. In this case, the assumption is that, first being convinced of the need for a classless and casteless society, one has then constructed a social doctrine of the Trinity in order to substantiate it. This reproach is nonsense and rebounds on the critic, since it could equally well suggest that he is against a social doctrine of the Trinity because he is in favour of a class and caste society and wants to defend it.
>
> — A Broad Place, 292

Theology cannot escape its political and social dimensions. Theology must be a constant voice of criticism in the world. Drawing out the political implications of theological thought is not only necessary but essential.

SIDEBAR: GOD, HIS & HERS

The Church has not received the feminist movement very well. While some have begun whole-heartedly embracing its cause, there are still many who reject it and actively resist the egalitarian revolution it inspires. For example, a famous American reformed theologian—not merely a fringe thinker, but a man who has sold *millions* of books—once said, "When somebody mentions they have a female pastor of their church, I immediately reply that they do not have a pastor and they do not have a church." That was put forward by John MacArthur, and it has become a standard phrase repeated among the reformed. John Piper, another well-known reformed author, has recently expressed his opinion that women cannot be professors in seminary. Both men have been outspoken in their desire to exclude women from Church leadership.

But men like Piper and MacArthur are dying out, and their views are becoming the minority opinion. They may still have a strong following, but it is diminishing. The wave of feminist thought and its effect on the Church has only increased with time, and the Church cannot ignore it any longer.

Elisabeth Moltmann-Wendel, Moltmann's wife, was a significant figure in early German feminist theology. She wrote several books, with *The Women Around Jesus* being one of the most well known. Her influence is felt still today.

Moltmann's thinking was profoundly impacted by Elisabeth's theology, as he writes:

> Personally, the discussions with Elisabeth about a joint theology taught me to say 'I' and to withdraw my seemingly objective professorial language—'this is the way it is'—reducing it to my own conviction. Whatever we see and perceive is limited by the conditions of the place where we stand. If we want to communicate our perception to other people, we must be aware of our perspectives. Male and female existence in their respective socio-cultural forms are part of these conditions for possible perceptions. This does not at all mean putting what has been perceived down to existential conditions, as Feuerbach and Marx thought. Not every objective perception is 'nothing other than' a self-perception, but every perception is a link between the perceiver and the perceived, and creates community between the two. Consequently, the subjective perception of one's self belongs to every perception of God, even if this leads to a self-forgetting astonishment. I have learnt to introduce theological questions and perceptions into the context of the life in which I myself am living together with others. For this path 'out of ideas into life' I have to thank Elisabeth and her feminist theology.
>
> — A Broad Place, 330-1

It will be beneficial for us to take note of Elisabeth's feminist theology, and of feminist theology more generally, because Moltmann's doctrine of the Trinity lends support to its cause. A hierarchal and patriarchal image of God has legitimized much of the sexist and elitist structures that exist today in the Church. God as the supreme Lord above all, often spoken of with masculine traits and in male pronouns, means a Church and community structured under the dominion of the male. Even Barth fell into this pattern, and it is clear that it impacted his social understanding when he reinforced patriarchal gender roles between men and women (see *Church Dogmatics*, III/4 §54.1). A patriarchal and hierarchical understanding of the Church and society, however, can be overcome by a more robust doctrine of the Triunity of God.

Moltmann's social doctrine of the Trinity is a strong argument *against* the patriarchy. We disavow patriarchy *because* we can no longer think of God according to the one Lord over all but as the God of communion. Moltmann's theology provides a sound *theological* reason for the Church today to embrace the feminist movement and its critique of patriarchal culture. The fellowship of Jesus is not the fellowship of masters and slaves but of friends in the Holy Spirit. No individual stands "over" another, whether male or female. The Triunity of God is no hierarchy; it is a fellowship of mutual love and compassion. The old structure in which the one God validates the authority of an individual above all (such as one pope or one king) is no longer valid in the light of God's Triunity. The idea of men alone as pastors or in leadership roles, either in the Church or the family, is deemed faulty in the light of God's being-in-community.

There is a rich history in the Church of using feminine images to express something of God's nature, and a rediscovery of these would be a step towards celebrating female voices in the Church. We have lived for too long under the image of a "male" God, but it is time we rediscover those traits which might be deemed feminine in God. Of course, God is neither male nor female, but there are masculine and feminine *traits* in God. When only the male traits are deemed valid, then we miss out on a rich tradition. For example, the male image of God the "almighty" is often a clear matter of Church doctrine, but what about God the comforter? What about God's *pathos*—or co-suffering love—which Molt-mann has expressed so well (chapter 3)? That, too, might be called a "feminine" image of God, because vulnerability is seldom considered masculine (albeit wrongly).

Here will we consider a few historical examples. Count Zinzendorf, the founder of the Moravian Brethren, once emphasized the "Motherly ministry of the Holy Spirit" in a 1741 sermon in Pennsylvania. He borrowed this image from the homilies of pseudo-Makarios (Symeon of Mesopotamia). Here the motherly ministry of the Holy Spirit was argued from two perspectives. First, the *comfort* of the Holy Spirit (the Paraclete) in John 14:26, and second, the *new birth* by the Spirit in the New Testament. Early Pietism after Zinzendorf took up this tradition; the Brethren even made it a part of Church doctrine. As a result, this image captivated the mind of John Wesley, the founder of the Methodist movement. In this tradition, the idea of calling God "Mother" took hold long before the feminist movement did the same. (However, it should be noted that this designation of God as "mother" is not an ontological one, but pictorial.) The motherly care of the Holy Spirit is an apt description of the Spirit's role in the life of the believer, but we miss this whenever we force a strictly masculine definition of God. Feminist theology is thus *freeing*, not restricting, by helping us discover the roots of our tradition.

Even further back, historians have discovered ancient icons in Ethiopia which portray the Trinity by depicting the Spirit as Mother. The ancient Greek Church held a similar image by presenting the first family (Adam, Eve, and Seth) as an image of the Triune God, thus deeming the Holy Spirit to be a mother like Eve. This image was so typical in the early Church that Augustine wrote against it in his great work, *On the Trinity*. Rightly, he criticizes the model for its anthropomorphism, but this still reveals that a keen awareness of the feminine characteristics of God was present in the early Church.

The point here is *not* that "God is a man" or "God is a woman" or even "both," but that God is a *community*. Replacing patriarchy with matriarchy is not the goal since both systems are hierarchical by nature. The entire hierarchal and patriarchal structure of the Church, as promoted by MacArthur and Piper and many others, is based on a faulty doctrine of the Trinity. (It also might be traced back to their rigid fundamentalism, which reduces biblical texts to infallible statements.) Moltmann's doctrine of the Trinity is a compelling argument in favor of feminist theology and its vision of an egalitarian Church.

Is Feminism against Men?

Clarifying this common misconception regarding feminist theology will be helpful. Much of the fear the term inspires, especially among men, comes from the misguided notion that feminism is *against* men, that it hates men and wants to create a matriarchy in the place of patriarchy. That is entirely false. Perhaps a fringe of bitter feminists have these extremist views, but by far the majority of feminist thinkers are not interested in reversing the hierarchical order but merely seek equal status. Replacing one kind of hierarchy with another is not justice but yet another type of oppression.

In fact, feminism works towards the liberation of both women *and men*, because *both* men and women are dehumanized in a patriarchal system—though certainly not in the same way. In systems of oppression, there are always two sides, and an oppressive order dehumanizes both the oppressors and the oppressed.

Moltmann writes at length:

> Oppression always has two sides: on the one hand the master, on the other the slave; on the one hand the ruling man, on the other the serving woman. But oppressions of this kind destroy humanity on both sides. The oppressed are robbed of their human dignity, and the oppressors lose their humanity. Both are alienated from their true being; it is just that the one side suffers under the fact, while the other side is quite content with the situation. But if the oppressors were also to recognize themselves for what they are, they would discover how much their dominating position cheats them of their true human happiness. How are children brought up to be 'men'? In my generation the process was undoubtedly extreme. We were turned into soldiers in order to die for our country as sacrificial victims. In other generations, too, boys are brought up to be men after the pattern of their fathers. They have to learn to control themselves in order one day to be able to control others. For this they are made to live in constant fear of being a nonentity, who 'has to make something of himself'. The patriarchy halved the man and elevated him into a determining subject of understanding and will (with which he had to identify himself), and degraded him to an object of heart, feeling, and needs (from which he had to detach himself). This distorted relationship to himself was then reflected in his distorted relationship to the woman and to nature. When today women set out to break out of the roles assigned to them in the patriarchy and to 'be persons in their own right', men are also freed to shake off the repressions assigned to them, which cut them off from true life, and are able to become true human beings. The way to a 'new community of women and men' is still a long journey, for men too. [...] 'The master in the man must die so that the brother prepared for open friendship can be born.'

> — A BROAD PLACE, 328-9

Feminism is not against men; it is against the patriarchal system which keeps both women *and* men enslaved. The former by the dehumanization of oppression and the latter by the dehumanization of control. In America, especially, there is a cult of false-masculinity that enslaves men. Men are cut off from their emotions; they are told to "man up" and alienate themselves from every sensitive aspect of their nature. I do not mean to overemphasize the struggles of men, because certainly in comparison with women we have it easy. But I merely point this out to show that the goal of feminism, which is simply equality, would also mean the liberation of men from self-alienation and self-dehumanization. The goal of feminism is to rediscover men as brothers "prepared for open friendship." The freedom of women *includes* the freedom of men. But it will require men to step back and listen to women, to give up their false-masculinity, which in truth is nothing less than insecurity. Men must become humble and listen to the experiences and struggles of women, and give space for them as partners and friends. The entire structure of society, but also in the Church, must be rethought and reorganized into a community of free men and women.

The Church should be on the forefront of this movement, but it has often resisted it. If we open our eyes to the feminist dimensions of Christ's life and teachings, then we can begin to discover how the Gospel might have a revolutionary role to play in the modern feminist movement. Jesus was extraordinarily inclusive of women, and there is evidence the early Church also placed women in leadership roles. Elisabeth often highlighted the fact that there would be *no* Church today if it were not for the testimony of women. She writes, "What would have happened had women in fact kept silent in the church? There would be no church" (*God, His & Hers*, 45). Women were the first to proclaim the resurrection. We would be nothing if the disciples had rejected their testimony.

We need to listen to the voices of women in the Church today and prioritize their essential contribution, even though we have attempted to live without it for far too long. Jürgen Moltmann writes about the need for feminine voices in the Church:

For too long we have heard only half the gospel, with the male half of humankind. It is important today to understand it completely in the fullness of the female and male creation of humankind and with the fullness of the Spirit that comes upon sons and daughters. It therefore goes without saying that men and women confess their faith together and interpret the gospel together.

— IBID., 40

Feminist theology is not going away anytime soon, as much as some would like to ignore it or exclude it from the Church. It is, in fact, not primarily a human movement at all: it is part of *God's* liberating action. The power enacting revolutionary change in the form of this feminist movement is not the power of human beings—it is God's Spirit, as Elisabeth writes:

The power which is now bringing women to life in the face of patriarchal structures, which is making them free to stand upright like the woman who was bent over, and who was healed by Jesus, which is making them discover sisters, is the power of the Holy Spirit.

— GOD, HIS & HERS, 14

The Spirit is always doing a new thing in the Church, and those who resist it will find themselves fighting against the mission of the Triune God. Elisabeth rightly recognizes the historical importance of women for the Church; we would not even have a Church today if women were forbidden by Jesus to have a voice. The way of Jesus is the way of liberation. The feminist cause is a liberating movement in the power of the Spirit, and those who oppose it will find themselves fighting against God. It is the work of the Triune history of God towards the Kingdom of freedom. Thus, in its vision of total freedom and equality, feminism is an anticipation of the Kingdom of God on this earth.

SIDEBAR: TRITHEISM

George Hunsinger, among others, has fiercely charged Moltmann with the Trinitarian heresy of tritheism, even against his explicit denial of it. It will be worth examining why this critique is made and explore the ways Moltmann defends himself against it.

Tri-theism is explained by its name. It is plainly: *tri,* meaning "three" + *theism,* meaning "God." Therefore, tritheism is the charge of holding to *three Gods* or divine entities, and more specifically, in the Christian sense, it is the belief that the Father, Son, and Holy Spirit are each their own distinct Gods. Hunsinger claims, "*The Trinity and the Kingdom* is about the closest thing to tritheism that any of us are ever likely to see. That Moltmann has finally succumbed to the tritheistic temptation long latent in his theology can be seen not only from his constructive proposals, but also from the drift of his polemics" ("Review of Jürgen Moltmann," 131).

The issue arises from Moltmann's argument against thinking of God as "one, identical divine subject" (*The Trinity and the Kingdom,* 18). He argues this under the broader rejection of monotheism (or unitarianism). Moltmann's perichoretic notion of divine personhood, however, necessitates three divine subjects who nevertheless share a common divine being. The unity of God is found then not in the solitariness of a single divine subject but the *fellowship* of the three subjects.

Moltmann argues there are only two paths for developing the doctrine of the Trinity, "[T]he metaphysical one and the biblical one" (*Experiences in Theology*, 321). The metaphysical starting point arrives at God as *one substance* in self-differentiation, whereas the biblical starting point develops from the divine history and only then arrives at the perichoretical unity of Father, Son, and Holy Spirit. Moltmann prefers the second method over the first, writing, "[I]t seems to make more sense theologically to start from the biblical history, and therefore to make the unity of the three divine Persons the problem, rather than to take the reverse method—to start from the philosophical postulate of absolute unity, in order then to find the problem in the biblical testimony" (*The Trinity and the Kingdom*, 149).

Richard Bauckham argues that the charge of tritheism ultimately fails upon a "careful reading of [Moltmann's] later trinitarian work" (*The Theology of Jürgen Moltmann*, 25). In fact, Bauckham thinks Moltmann is far more in line with the "mainstream Christian tradition" than critics allow. Moltmann argues the same point. It is because critics have failed to carefully understand his perichoretic notion of divine personhood that Moltmann insists the charge of tritheism simply does not stick. Moltmann writes, "This perichoretic form of unity is the only conceivable *trinitarian concept of the unity* of the triune God, because it combines threeness and oneness in such a way that they cannot be reduced to each other, so that both the danger of modalism and the danger of 'tritheism' are excluded" (*Experiences in Theology*, 322). Moltmann is interested in developing a genuinely Trinitarian concept of unity against a *philosophical* concept of unity, and this is the crucial role his perichoretic notion of personhood plays in the doctrine of the Trinity. Without recognizing the importance of the divine *perichoresis*, it could be easy to judge Moltmann to be a tritheist. But careful readers who perceive the centrality of God's perichoretic unity will not make this mistake.

In fact, Moltmann goes on to argue that the charge of tritheism is a false one, a ruse of sorts that monotheistic (unitarian) doctrines often hide behind. In other words, when someone levels the objection of tritheism, it is nothing less than shadow-boxing, arguing against a phantom that does not exist. There have never been Christian tritheists, as Moltmann writes:

> In the discussions about trinitarian theology, the charge of tritheism has no objective foundation, because there has never

been a Christian theologian who maintained a doctrine of three gods. It is an ancient, first Arian and then Islamic, charge levelled at orthodox Christianity. Later it became a charge directed by the Western church at the theology of the Eastern church. Today it serves to conceal one's own modern modalism. But from the perspective of Islamic monotheism, all Christian theologians— whether it be Augustine or Aquinas, Barth or Rahner, Pannenberg or Greshake, or whoever—are 'tritheists' as long as they adhere to the divine Sonship of Christ and call God 'the Father of Jesus Christ'. It therefore seems to me eccentric when Greshake [...] thinks that he can show that I have a 'tritheistic understanding of Person', while overlooking the perichoretic understanding of Person which I have in fact developed.

— IBID., N. 30.

Tritheism was a false charge assailed against Christianity by Islamic and Arian theologies. Even Barth, in his long argument against tritheism (*Church Dogmatics* I/1 §9), cannot name any specific tritheists. History openly names modalists or other heretical individuals, but the fact that there has never been a genuine tritheist in the Church should be a sign that it is a false charge with little to no meaning. For Moltmann, God's unity is genuinely Trinitarian if it is understood, not philosophically, but *perichoretically*, according to the biblical history of Jesus Christ and the Spirit. To call this tritheism relies on rash judgments and unwarranted heresy-hunting.

The charge is plainly unmerited in a closer reading of the text because Moltmann explicitly states his aversion to it. To show an example, he writes:

In their perichoresis and because of it, the trinitarian persons are not to be understood as three different individuals, who only subsequently enter into relationship with one another [...]. But they are not, either, three modes of being or three repetitions of the One God, as the modalistic interpretation suggests. The doctrine of the perichoresis links together in a brilliant way the threeness and the unity, without reducing the threeness to the unity, or dissolving the unity in the threeness. The unity of the triunity lies in the eternal perichoresis of the trinitarian persons. Interpreted perichoretically, the trinitarian persons form their own unity by themselves in the circulation of the divine life.

— THE TRINITY AND THE KINGDOM, 175

Both tritheism and modalism are ruled out in this example. For Moltmann, a genuinely *Christian* doctrine of the Trinity must begin with the biblical history of Jesus Christ, and thus it must *first* form a perichoretic notion of the divine persons before conceiving of God's unity. It is not tritheism but a more faithfully theological account of the biblical history of God, which stands sharply against the modern tendency towards philosophical unitarianism.

6

GOD IN CREATION

SUMMARY: Two insights result in a highly creative doctrine of creation. First, God's self-limitation, and therefore passion, as the first act of creation; and second, God's Sabbath as the true crown of creation. Creation is thus an eschatologically oriented doctrine and points ahead to its fulfillment in the coming of God.

IN MOLTMANN'S OWN WORDS:

Fleeting time makes people restless: the sabbath gives rest in the happiness of the presence of the Eternal One. Work allows people to exist in their own world; the sabbath rest leads them into God's creation again, and into his pleasure in them themselves. On the sabbath the future redemption of the world is celebrated, for the sabbath rest is already a foretaste of the redeemed world.

— GOD WILL BE ALL IN ALL, 280

We shall not be redeemed *from* this earth, so that we could give it up. We shall be redeemed *with* it. We shall not be redeemed *from* the body. We shall be made eternally alive *with* the body.

— THE SOURCE OF LIFE, 74

SECONDARY QUOTES:

A central metaphor which Moltmann explores to grasp the indwelling of
God in creation is the notion of 'home' (*Heimat*) or inhabitation
(*Wohnen*). His *eco*logical theology involves far more than merely taking
up the ecological crisis into his thinking. It means considering the idea
that the earth is destined to be God's home ('eco' is derived from the
Greek *oikos*, meaning 'house (hold)' or 'dwelling;' [*God in Creation*]:
xiv). By picturing creation as God's home-to-be, Moltmann holds that
creation as a whole will be liberated from the bondage to the powers of
negation and death. The 'inner secret' of creation is the eternal and final
indwelling of God amidst all his creatures [...]. Thus creation is seen in
an eschatological, *messianic* perspective; it is, potentially, the renewed
creation, the new heaven and earth, God eternal dwelling place, the
'temple' where he comes to rest ([*The Trinity and the Kingdom*]: 104).

— TON VAN PROOIJEN, LIMPING BUT BLESSED, 267

INTRODUCTION

In 1980, Moltmann received an invitation to give the esteemed Gifford
Lectures for 1984-85. Only four previous German theologians had the
honor of delivering these lectures: Barth, Tillich, Brunner, and Bultmann.
Moltmann was honored above any of his peers from Germany with the
invitation since those who gave the presentation before him all belonged
to the generation of his teachers. It is no surprise for Moltmann to
remark, "This invitation put me on cloud nine" (*A Broad Place*, 295). He
took the lectures very seriously, and it resulted in the publication of his
second systematic contribution to theology: *God in Creation*.

Continuing some of the themes of Moltmann's thought so far, *God in
Creation* presents a proposal as radical and controversial as his previous
books. Accordingly, the work is among the most innovative doctrines of
creation written in recent history.

There are several themes Moltmann addresses, and it would be impossible to summarize all of them and still given due credit to each one.
Accordingly, we will focus on the two key aspects which make it so innovative: God's self-limitation and God's Sabbath as the crown of creation.

THE ECOLOGICAL CRISIS

Before we discuss those points, we should first understand Moltmann's stated context: the ecological crisis. Moltmann writes:

> Our situation today is determined by the ecological crisis of our whole scientific and technological civilization, and by the exhaustion of nature through human beings. This crisis is deadly, and not for human beings alone. For a very long time now it has meant death for other living things and for the natural environment as well. Unless there is a radical reversal in the fundamental orientation of our human societies, and unless we succeed in finding an alternative way of living and dealing with other living things and with nature, this crisis is going to end in a wholesale catastrophe.
>
> — GOD IN CREATION, 20

The Church is not exempt from blame. In fact, it is perhaps our human-centric doctrine of creation which permits the domination of nature. The rule of human beings against the environment has led to the crisis of global warming, and the Church has done little to limit its damaging effects. However, reaching an understanding of nature as *God's creation* would be a productive step towards a new relationship with nature, as Moltmann writes:

> Interpreting the world as God's creation means precisely not viewing it as the world of human beings, and taking possession of it accordingly. If the world is God's creation, then it remains his property and cannot be claimed by men and women. It can only be accepted as a loan and administered as a trust. It has to be treated according to the standards of the divine righteousness, not according to the values that are bound up with human aggrandisement [the pursuit of increasing power and wealth].
>
> — IBID., 30-1

Knowledge, according to Francis Bacon, is power. Scientific knowledge of creation has often resulted in an attempt to increase wealth and power by turning nature into a profitable commodity. In this sense, the ecological crisis is the result of our struggle as human beings to "deify" ourselves to the status of gods. However, Moltmann argues for a new understanding of the purpose and use of knowledge. Scientific knowledge of God's creation is not focused on control and power, but on *participation*.

Not domination but participation is the proper definition of knowledge, against Bacon's famous one. This understanding of knowledge includes *love*. "Through this form of astonished, wondering and loving knowledge, we do not appropriate things. We recognize their independence and participate in their life. We do not wish to know so that we can dominate. We desire to know in order to participate" (*God in Creation*, 32). Scientific knowledge of creation can no longer be used to dominate nature but to better participate in it.

Instead of offering a doctrine of creation centered around human beings, here is a doctrine of *God's creation*, particularly of God's Sabbath rest. Human beings have the privilege of participating in God's world, *but we have no right to dominate it*. The earth must be protected *for God's sake*, as well as for our survival. We will only save the planet from the destruction we have cause when we reject every attempt to subject the earth to human domination. Theologically, we take a necessary step towards the renunciation of violence against nature when we recognize creation as *God's* creation. Creation does not belong to human beings: "The earth is the Lord's and all that is in it" (Ps. 24:1). It is this ecological concern that makes up a large part of Moltmann's work.

GOD'S SELF-LIMITATION

Moltmann already offered a brief description of the doctrine of creation at the end of *The Trinity and the Kingdom*. Here he relates creation to God's *pathos*, so that creation itself is considered an act of divine passion. The first act of creation, then, is God's act on God's Self, God's *self-limitation*. "The very first act of the infinite Being," Moltmann writes, "was therefore not a step 'outwards' but a step 'inwards', a 'self-withdrawal of God from himself into himself', as Gershom Scholem puts it; that is to say, it was a *passio Dei* [passion of God], not an *actio* [activity]" (*The Trinity and the Kingdom*, 110). As we have noted before, it is vital to be clear that Moltmann does not understand this to be a limitation by way of *deficiency*, as if God has no choice or freedom, but instead, it is the highest expression of God's sovereignty that God limits Godself in love for another. Thus, Moltmann writes:

> He creates by withdrawing himself, and because he withdraws himself. Creation in chaos and out of nothing, which is an act of power, is also a self-humiliation on God's part, a lowering of himself into his own impotence. Creation is a work of God's humility and his withdrawal into himself. God acts on himself when he acts creatively. His inward and his outward aspects therefore correspond to one another and mirror one another. His action is grounded in his passion.
>
> — IBID.

Traditionally, creation corresponds to God's infinite power. Moltmann perceives power, however, not as unrestricted force and domination, but, according to the cross of Christ, as the power which includes the freedom to be weak and limited. That is in line with the *pathos* of God, which we have seen is an essential insight for Moltmann. It is so that God might go out of Godself that God becomes self-limited: "God withdraws himself in order to go out of himself. Eternity breathes itself in, so as to breathe out the Spirit of life" (ibid., 111).

These insights are developed further in *God in Creation*. Creation describes God's free creative decision. With this decision "*God* commits *himself* to create a world" (*God in Creation*, 80). However, God's creativity is an expression of God's Self, so if we ask *why* God creates, the simple answer is because God is God; it is an expression of God's nature. Creation is not something God does once and then sets aside, but an *ongoing* process. That is important to point out because it highlights the essentially *eschatological* orientation of creation, even from its beginning. Creation, as God's self-limitation or the restriction of God's presence for the sake of another, remains *open* as it moves towards the *new creation* in which God will be "all in all." Creation and eschatology belong together. God restricts Godself for the sake of creation, and creation awaits for the day when God will *de-restrict* Godself so that "the earth will be filled with the knowledge of the glory of the Lord as the waters cover the sea" (Hab. 2:14).

Creation is *ongoing* and *unfinished*; it looks ahead towards its eschatological consummation. There are then three modes of creation: creation in the beginning (Gen. 1:1), continuous creation (Is. 43:18-9), and the new creation (Rev. 21:5). Thus, Moltmann writes, "In this respect our underlying theological premise must be that *creation is not yet finished, and has not as yet reached its end*" (*God in Creation,* 196). Moreover, he writes, "Creation is not a work once performed and then finished and done with. It is a process, extended over time and open to the future" (*The Way of Jesus Christ,* 301). We will examine this idea further when we come to the Sabbath.

Returning to the idea of God's self-limitation, here Moltmann is implementing a doctrine known as *zimzum,* which means "contraction." It is a Jewish kabbalistic doctrine, and Moltmann uses it to understand the Christian doctrine of *creatio ex nihilo,* or "creation out of nothing." Consider this question: "Where does this *nothingness* come from if God is all in all?" That is to say if before creation there was only God, then the negative space for creation, the nothing, must *first* come to "be," if creation indeed is temporal and not eternal. God's first act in creation was thus to limit Godself in passionate love, to create a Godforsaken space called nothingness, so that there may be room for creation. This is necessary if we maintain that creation is neither eternal nor equal with God. Since the Church has always affirmed the temporal nature of creation, then God must give space for creation by limiting Godself.

Moltmann writes:

> In order to create a world 'outside' himself, the infinite God must have made room beforehand for a finitude in himself. It is only a withdrawal by God into himself that can free the space into which God can act creatively. The *nihil* [nothing] for his *creatio ex nihilo* [creation out of nothing] only comes into being because—and in as far as—the omnipotent and omnipresent God withdraws his presence and restricts his power.
>
> — GOD IN CREATION, 86-7

Here God's self-limitation becomes essential because only in the restriction of God's presence may there be space for creation to come into being. God makes room for that which is not God, and this space-making is an act of God's passion and love, an act of self-limitation. God's self-humiliation reaches its culmination on the cross of Christ, but if the cross reveals the same God who created the world out of nothing, then in creation we must likewise recognize God's passion and God's suffering. If the cross reveals God's nature, then self-humiliation and passion were in God's nature even *before* creation. The *same God* who suffered on the cross creates out of self-limitation, in the self-restriction of God's omnipresence and omnipotence. In other words, creation is possible only in God's free will to suffer change and limitation. "Even in order to create heaven and earth, God emptied himself of his all-plenishing [all-filling] omnipotence, and as Creator took upon himself the form of a servant" (ibid., 88).

The result is a radical re-interpretation of the very act of creation. We often imagine creation as an act of masculine will and power, but Moltmann highlights the corresponding *feminine* elements of the creation event. Moltmann writes:

> This points to a necessary correction in the interpretation of creation: God does not create merely by calling something into existence, or by setting something afoot. In a more profound sense he 'creates' by letting-be, by making room, and by withdrawing himself. The creative making is expressed in masculine metaphors. But the creative letting-be is better brought out through motherly categories.
>
> — IBID.

It may be helpful to understand Moltmann's doctrine of creation in contrast with the two alternatives he is rejecting: pantheism and theism. Moltmann posits pan*en*theism as the genuinely Christian alternative between the two.

Pantheism identifies God with all things. God *is* creation itself; all reality is a part of God's being. When we look out at a tree or see a bird, we are seeing God. It is a typically pagan understanding of creation, although it does have some history in the Christian tradition.

Theism offers the opposite perspective by pushing God wholly outside of the world. In theism, God is not involved in creation or history. God is far removed and distant from the earth. Deism is an example, which imagined the world as a mechanical clock with God as its clockmaker. The world runs by divine causality so that the Clockmaker is not involved any longer.

Neither cosmology adequately describes the biblical account of creation. In contrast to both pantheism and theism, Moltmann argues for pan*en*theism. Notice the italics. Here it is neither God *as* the world nor God *without* the world; this is God *in* the world and the world *in* God. There is no dualistic *separation* of God's space and the space of creation, but neither is there the mistaken *identification* with God and creation. Moltmann thinks the biblical account of creation requires an understanding the self-limitation of God so that we recognize creation *in* God. The nothingness that God allows in self-limitation is not separate from God but *in* God, since God permeates all things except that which God permits in self-restriction. It is a Godforsaken space within God, which implies the suffering love of God *before* creation.

Moltmann explains at length:

> *Creatio ex nihilo* [creation out of nothing] in the beginning is the preparation and promise of the redeeming *annihilatio nihili* [annihilation of nothingness], from which the eternal being of creation proceeds. The creation of the world is itself a promise of resurrection, and the overcoming of death in the victory of eternal life (1 Cor. 15:26, 55–57). So the resurrection and the kingdom of glory are the fulfilment of the promise which creation itself represents.
>
> This brings us to a final interpretation of the statement about the *creatio ex nihilo* [creation out of nothing], from the standpoint of the cross of Christ. If God creates his creation out of nothing, if he affirms it and is faithful to it in spite of sin, and if he desires its salvation, then in the sending and surrender of his own Son he exposes himself to the annihilating Nothingness, so that he may overcome it in himself and through himself, and in that way give his creation existence, salvation and liberty. In this sense, by yielding up the Son to death in God-forsakenness on the cross, and by surrendering him to hell, the eternal God enters the Nothingness out of which he created the world. God enters that 'primordial space' which he himself conceded through his

initial self-limitation. He pervades the space of God-forsakenness with his presence. It is the presence of his self-humiliating, suffering love for his creation, in which he experiences death itself. That is why God's presence in the crucified Christ gives creation eternal life, and does not annihilate it. In the path of the Son into self-emptying and bondage, to the point of the death he died, and in the path of his exaltation and glorification by the whole creation, God becomes omnipresent. By entering into the God-forsakenness of sin and death (which is Nothingness), God overcomes it and makes it part of his eternal life: 'If I make my bed in hell, thou art there' (Ps. 139:8).

In the light of the cross of Christ, *creatio ex nihilo* [creation out of nothing] means forgiveness of sins through Christ's suffering, justification of the godless through Christ's death, and the resurrection of the dead and eternal life through the lordship of the Lamb.

— GOD IN CREATION, 90-1

Notice how carefully Moltmann ties creation, reconciliation, and redemption (eschatology) together. It is an original insight which may at first shock us, but the beauty of it and its logic should be evident. It is also a logical result of *The Crucified God* and its orientation. Understanding God in the light of the cross (and not the reverse) requires not just a change in the doctrine of God but truly a reorientation of *all* theology, including the doctrine of creation. We could even call Moltmann's proposal, "creation *in the light of the cross.*" Moreover, it is a reorientation that is necessary for the Church today. We often talk about creation in metaphysical categories, with far too much of a reliance on natural theology or logical deduction rather than on the revelation of God in Christ. On the cross, God revealed Godself as the God who loves us even when it requires self-limitation and self-humiliation for our sake. So that we might live, God goes out of Godself. So that we might come to be, God limits Godself. The same God who suffered and died on the cross is the God who created the world by restricting God's presence. It may shock us to draw these conclusions, but they are the necessary implications of what we considered in chapter three regarding the divine *pathos*.

GOD'S SABBATH: THE CROWN OF CREATION

Human beings are not the crown of God's creation; we are neither the central nor the highest point of existence. An eschatologically oriented doctrine of creation rejects any such human-centric (anthropocentric) focus. Instead, *God's Sabbath rest* is the real crown of creation. Moltmann writes:

> '[T]he crown of creation' is God's sabbath. It is for this that human beings are created—for the feast of creation, which praises the eternal, inexhaustible God, and in this hymn of praise experiences and expresses its own joy. The enduring meaning of human existence lies in its *participation* in this joyful paean of God's creation.
>
> — GOD IN CREATION, 197

We are commanded to keep the Sabbath holy in anticipation of the new creation, in which God will come and dwell in creation. Creation in the beginning has this end and purpose in mind. Creation is therefore *open* to God. Moltmann writes, "A world which has been created by God, and which continues to be created every moment, is bound to be a world *open to God*. It does not revolve within itself" (ibid., 163). That means the goal of creation is not to *return* to some primordial state of perfection. Redemption does not mean we return to the Garden of Eden, but that we look ahead to the *new* creation of heaven and earth. "Its goal is the revelation of the glory of God" (ibid., 207). In the new creation, God's unmediated presence will permeate all existence; we will see "face to face" what we see now darkly as in a mirror.

We often overlook God's Sabbath rest in our creation accounts, but this is a mistake, since "according to the biblical traditions creation and the sabbath belong together. It is impossible to understand the world properly as creation without a proper discernment of the sabbath" (ibid., 277). The Sabbath is the goal of creation. "[T]he whole work of creation was performed for the sake of the sabbath" (ibid.). The Sabbath is therefore called the "feast of creation," as Moltmann writes:

> The seventh day is rightly called the feast of creation. It is the crown of

creation. Everything that exists was created for this feast. So as not to celebrate the feast alone, God created heaven and earth, the dancing stars and the surging seas, the meadows and the woods, the animals, the plants, and last of all human beings. They are all invited to this sabbath feast. All of them are God's fellow celebrants, each in its own way. That is why God had 'pleasure' in all his works, as the psalms say. That is why the heavens declare the glory of the Eternal One. Everything that is, is created for God to rejoice over, for everything that is, comes from God's love.

— GOD FOR A SECULAR SOCIETY, 114

What is the purpose of creation and why do we exist? Wholly, for God's joy. There is no utilitarian purpose to existence; it is for the glory of God, which is the joy of God's love, that creation exists. The Sabbath rest points ahead to the future glory of God in all creation, to its eternal feast. In this sense, when we keep the Sabbath day holy, it is not as the *end* of a week but as its beginning. The Sabbath is not a reminder of the past when God rested on the seventh day, but it pulls us forward to the first day of the new creation. As such, it is a weekly reminder of the coming Kingdom of God.

The coming of God is the *Shekinah* (indwelling) of God in all creation, the de-restriction, and de-limitation of God's presence. It is the *cosmic incarnation* of God. This vision of God's coming culminates in the glorification of God, which is why Moltmann ends his eschatology, *The Coming of God,* with the phrase: *Soli Deo Gloria* ("To God alone be the glory"). God's glory is in the Sabbath rest and feast of creation, in which God will dwell with God's people. The Sabbath day looks ahead to the glory of God's unrestricted presence in creation and with humanity. Moltmann writes:

According to the New Testament, this is God's final promise: 'Behold, the dwelling of God is with men. He will dwell with them, and they shall be his people' (Rev. 21:3). Then the earth will be newly created so as to become God's dwelling place. Then human beings too will be born again, so as to find their home country in God.

— IN THE END—THE BEGINNING, 16

Moltmann draws a parallel between this insight and the doctrine of *perichoresis*. An indwelling not wholly unlike the perichoretic indwelling of God's being will come about in the new creation: God will dwell in creation and creation will dwell in God. We may be shocked by this idea, and rightly so. Moltmann, however, reminds us that this is not an idea foreign to the Christian faith since John has already described the experience of love in this way: "He who abides in love abides *in God,* and God abides *in him*" (1 John 4:16; emphasis mine). The love of God anticipates the coming indwelling of God in the new creation.

The Sabbath rest of God is the crown of creation because here God will dwell in all things and all things will take part in God. From its beginning, God orchestrated all existence towards this future glory: the Sabbath rest of God's unmediated presence, God's cosmic incarnation.

We reject the idea that creation is merely a disposable environment for human beings who will later escape it to a disembodied world of the soul. Creation is indispensable; it is not like a throwaway plastic cup. Creation will be the home of God. God will be at rest together with humanity and all the creatures of the earth. This emphasis on the Sabbath expands the vision of God's glory to include all things. In the end, *nothing will be lost.*

SIDEBAR: EVOLUTION

Moltmann's doctrine of creation readily embraces the scientific theory of evolution. That may be cause for alarm to some, but here we will explore the reasons why Moltmann embraces the theory. Beyond the simple fact that the scientific community has reached a consensus on the validity of evolution, Moltmann lists three reasons why theology is only hindering itself by rejecting evolution.

First, Moltmann points out that the biblical testimonies were never written to nullify further scientific research into nature. Plainly, the Bible is not a scientific document. It does not attempt to establish once and for all every scientific fact about nature. To read it as such is to force the Bible into a definition it never provides for itself. The opposite approach is more faithful to the biblical testimony. Rather than *hindering* research, the Scriptures actively *encourage* further investigation into nature. For Moltmann, the Scriptures are testimonies to the *history* of God with the world. Because history is *ongoing*, the Bible directs its readers to discover new experiences in and around the world. The Bible is not a restriction but an invitation for further exploration. For Moltmann, "[T]he stories of creation belong within a hermeneutical process of revision and innovation, as the result of new experiences" (*God in Creation*, 192). The Bible, rather than bearing testimony to a *complete* history with God, bears witness to an essential *openness* to the future. Scripture thus "permits no dogmatism" (ibid., 193), which means that the theory of evolution can and should be embraced and synthesized with the biblical accounts. It is contrary to the Bible's self-description and intent to reject the theory outright.

Second, Moltmann notes that the theory of evolution can free us from a limited reading of the creation accounts. He notes how the doctrine of creation became limited by the (over)reaction of those who reject the theory of evolution because it forced theologians to ignore the doctrine of *continuous* creation. To resist evolution, fundamentalist doctrines of creation became fixated on a finished and perfect creation in the beginning, so much so that they ignored the continuation of creation in history. Thus, "The doctrine of the divine 'making', the doctrine of continuous creation (*creatio continua*) and the doctrine of the new creation still to be consummated (*creatio nova*) all receded into the backround and were forgotten" (ibid.). In turn, this restricted God's relation with the world to one of pure "causality," in such a way that God is no longer an active participant in history (deism and determinism are two extreme examples). However, the doctrines of continuous creation and the eschatology future of creation are too vital to ignore.

Third, a primary reason why Moltmann thinks we actively resist the theory of evolution is because it disturbs our human-centric understanding of creation. "The unduly violent reaction of the churches and the civic community to Darwin's evolutionary theory can be explained by the anthropocentric view of the world which it assailed" (ibid., 194). We have discussed already Moltmann's movement towards a theocentric doctrine of creation (God's *Sabbath*, not humanity, is the crown of creation). In this connection, Moltmann offers insight into why we ultimately feel the need to reject evolution, despite the overwhelming scientific consensus on its validity.

Perhaps we actively resist the theory of evolution not because we think it is incongruent with belief in God, but because we fear it removes humanity from the center of the creation story. It is fundamentally threatening to our sense of security and importance. In our pride, we would much prefer to retain our status in the world. We like to imagine ourselves as the fundamental element in the whole history of creation and existence, as the crown and purpose of all things. Perhaps we reject evolution, then, not because of the reasons we explicitly state, but because, in truth, we are afraid of coming to terms with our cosmic insignificance. Because we fear the idea of a creation in which we are not the *center*, we actively resist evolution and find excuses not to take it seriously.

Moltmann's doctrine of creation displaces us from the center of the universe because he challenges our assumption that we are the crown of creation. For Moltmann, it is not human beings that are the crown of creation, but God's Sabbath rest. We often ignore the seventh day in the creation account. Genesis purposefully describes the seven days as a progression leading up to the high-point of creation. We often stop short of recognizing that it is not the sixth day, with the creation of humanity, but the *seventh* day that is the goal of creation. Evolution displaces humanity from the center of creation and helps us recognize creation as a continual work of God, and it is therefore perhaps *more* biblical than the biblicist would like to admit.

The number of valid biblical or theological reasons for resisting the theory of evolution is little to none. In the scientific community, evolution is widely considered to be the most plausible theory for human development, and in the Scriptures themselves, there is less evidence against it than we imagine. The theory of evolution may help us become *more* biblical in our thinking about creation. The synthesis may be possible if we recognize that 1) evolution is not about creation in the beginning but helps us recognize *continuous* creation in the ordering and forming of existence. 2) Theologically speaking, this means creation must be considered unfinished and eschatologically oriented. 3) Biblically speaking, the doctrine of creation is not human-centric, but dynamically forward-looking in expectation of God's final Sabbath rest (see ibid., 196-7). A synthesis between the Christian doctrine of creation and the theory of evolution is not only possible, but it is also in the best interest of Christian faith and theology.

Teilhard de Chardin

With that said, however, Moltmann cautions us not to put *too much* hope in the theory of evolution. At best we must recognize that its role remains limited to a still *unredeemed* creation. Naturally, then, he sharply criticizes Teilhard de Chardin's doctrine of *Christus Evolutor*. In this theory, Chardin essentially collapses salvation history into union with the theory of evolution, so that evolution is the very *means* of God's salvation. The incarnation of Jesus Christ marks the beginning of the deification of humanity (becoming gods), which results in a strong faith in the *progress* of human history. He even speculates the production of a superhuman arising out of the process of history. It was pushed to the extreme by Chardin when, in letters to his friends during the War, he argued they should *celebrate* the war (and its mass death) for its contribution to natural evolution. Moltmann explains how radical this vision was for Chardin:

> When the first atomic bomb was dropped on Hiroshima on 6 August 1945, Teilhard was filled with enthusiastic admiration for the scientific and technological advance which this achievement of a scientific super-brain acting in teamwork had brought humanity. He believed that the control of atomic power would promote the evolution of humanity and the human consciousness in a hitherto unheard-of way. Here Teilhard gave no thought to Hiroshima's hundred thousand dead and the people who are still dying today from radiation damage.
>
> — THE WAY OF JESUS CHRIST, 295

The difficulties with this theory should be obvious, as Moltmann writes, "A *Christus evolutor* without *Christus redemptor* is nothing other than a cruel, unfeeling *Christus selector*, a historical world-judge without compassion for the weak, and a breeder of life uninterested in the victims" (ibid., 196). It is this disregard for the weak and the lost of history that Moltmann finds so dangerous about Chardin's theory. Evolution's core mode of operation is the "survival of the fittest." However, without the redemption of Christ, this becomes the salvation of "winners" against their victims. It rewards cruelty and encourages the destruction of the weak. It is therefore wholly incompatible with the Christian faith in Jesus Christ, the friend of sinners who died helplessly forsaken on the cross.

Thus, Moltmann concludes:

> There is therefore no meaningful hope for the future of creation unless 'the tears are wiped from every eye'. But they can only be

wiped away when the dead are raised, and when the victims of evolution experience justice through the resurrection of nature. Evolution in its ambiguity has no such redemptive efficacy and therefore no salvific significance either. If Christ is to be thought of in conjunction with evolution, he must become evolution's redeemer.

— IBID., 197

Justice for the victims of suffering and oppression is an essential hope in the redemption promised by Christ's resurrection. A *Christus evolutor* has no such hope to offer victims of injustice. Instead, the Christian hope must be extended to *include* the victims of evolution.

A synthesis can and should be reached between the theory of evolution and the biblical doctrine of creation, but certainly not at the expense of Jesus' solidarity with victims. Moltmann's insistence on the biblical continuity with the theory of evolution is a step towards such a synthesis, even if he cautions us on becoming too convinced of evolution's merits in the history of salvation. Evolution itself is part of the unredeemed creation, an aspect of God's continuous act of creation, and as such, it points ahead to creation's culmination and redemption in God's coming.

SIDEBAR: ECOLOGICAL RESPONSIBILITY

I cannot recall the exact specifics of this story, nor have I been successful in tracking down its source, but it is well worth repeating in connection with Moltmann's doctrine of creation:

Moltmann was invited to speak at the annual "Karl Barth Conference" at Princeton Theological Seminary in the summer of 2015. A group of students drove to the conference center together for the morning lectures. They saw a man in a suit walking along the side of the road. In America, this is a strange sight. In his autobiography, Moltmann lamented the fact that so few people walk in America and therefore that there are almost no sidewalks for people to walk on. The students were surprised when they got closer to the walker and realized this man was, in fact, professor Moltmann. Seeing as they were all going to the same place, they slowed down to offer him a lift. As they called out from the car, Moltmann surprisingly declined. When the students asked why he preferred to walk, he simply replied, "Ecological responsibility." So the German professor walked on in solitude for the earth's sake, as a simple form of protest against an American car-culture which thinks so little about its ecological impact.

The details of this story may not be exactly right, but the general idea remains. The ecological crisis is a significant concern of Moltmann's theology as well as his life. It is a *theological* problem since we must reckon with the truth that this world does not belong to us but to God. It will be God's dwelling place (Rev. 21), and we are merely borrowing it for the time being. It is *God's* home, and we have not been respectful house guests. This story highlights a call to environmental action which we cannot ignore in Moltmann's doctrine of creation. The protection of the earth is a Christian responsibility.

Unfortunately, we have reached a point in which personal actions will not be enough to reverse the damage of global warming. Political action is necessary to enact large-scale change. Companies that are unrestricted and unpunished for damaging the earth have become the worst cause of climate change. Industrialization has resulted in the mass pollution of our earth. A political response is required. New corporate restrictions need to be developed and enforced to effect lasting change in protecting the ecology of our planet.

Companies often push the responsibility onto consumers, so that they are not held responsible themselves. They promote recycling and other personal steps we can take, but ultimately it is the companies who are by far the worst polluters. Personal action is still necessary, even if it only amounts to an act of protest, but political action is what will make a difference in the long term. It will not be until the governments of the world decide to no longer accept the destruction of our environment at the hands of corporate pollution that life on earth will survive. Systemic pollution is a political problem that requires political change.

Denmark is an excellent example of a country whose leaders take the impending danger of ecological catastrophe seriously. As I write this book, I am living in Lund, Sweden, which is just a short train ride away from the Danish capital, Copenhagen. Looking out the windows on the train as it crosses between the two countries, you will see a collection of wind turbines in the Øresund strait. Almost 30% of Denmark's energy is clean or wind-generated. 60% of electricity in Denmark is from renewable sources. By 2050, Denmark hopes to become entirely dependent on renewable energy. Denmark's production of renewable energy is so successful that it often has an energy surplus to sell to its neighboring countries.

We need to become a Christianity that fights for the earth for God's sake. Renewable energy is a viable alternative we must take seriously. Education seems to be a significant hindrance to implementing these changes, so we need to promote public concern over climate change and its effects. We also need an education on the success of renewable energy. A better world is possible, and it is *necessary* since the current rate of pollution is simply unsustainable. There is an overwhelming scientific conscious on this issue, yet Christians are often resistant to seeing climate change as a real threat. For the sake of God's coming glory and the new creation, we cannot accept the corporate abuse of our planet.

ETHICS OF THE EARTH

Moltmann appeals to Nietzsche, who writes, "I implore you, my brothers, remain true to the earth and do not believe those who talk to you about celestial hopes!" (cited in *Ethics of Hope,* 118). Christian hope is not an otherworldly hope but hope for *this* earth. Therefore, we need a Christian ethic of the earth. The earth is our home; we will not soon escape it for another world. God will come and dwell with us in the new creation. Thus, ethical responsibility to the earth is a Christian obligation.

Moltmann appeals to Bonhoeffer, who writes:

'Only the person who loves the earth and God in one can believe in the kingdom of God.' 'Christ ... does not lead people to a flight from the world into worlds behind the world; he gives the earth back to them as their faithful sons.' 'In the hour in which the church prays for the kingdom today, it pledges itself to faithfulness to the earth, to misery, to hunger, to dying.'

— CITED IBID.

There is a profound this-worldliness that is has been lost in Christian faith as we know it today. We need an ethical dedication to the earth, in place of all the escapist mentalities which have condemned the earth to suffer the violence of human pollution. When heaven is our goal, the earth is dispensable; when the Kingdom of God is our goal, the earth is indispensable. Heaven is not our goal, however. The Church today has lost sight of God's coming Kingdom, and in its place, we have fantasized about the destruction of this earth and of escaping to some other world.

The earth will outlive humanity, even if we destroy ourselves through ecological suicide. A Christian ethic of the earth is an ethic for the sake of God's future coming; the earth will one day be God's dwelling place and home. Care for the earth for humanity's sake is egotistical, but care for the earth for God's sake is Christian. It is included in the commandment to keep the Sabbath holy, as Moltmann writes:

> The celebration of the sabbath, and reverence for 'the sabbath of the earth', can become our own salvation and the salvation of earth from which we live. [...]
>
> According to the Bible, the sabbath laws are God's ecological strategy, designed to preserve the life which he has created. In its rest and its rhythmical interruption of time, the sabbath is also the strategy which can lead us out of the ecological crisis and, after the one-sided forms of progress made at the expense of nature, can show us the values of sustainable development and harmony with nature.
>
> — GOD FOR A SECULAR SOCIETY, 116

Moltmann proposes that the Church adopt an "earth day" festival to its calendar. It would be a day of profound remembrance, in which we actively pause to reflect on the devastating harm we have done to this planet. Moltmann writes:

> On 'earth day' we should bow before the earth and beg for forgiveness for the injustice we have inflicted on it, so that we may once more be accepted into community with it. On 'earth day' we should renew the covenant which God made with Noah and the earth.
>
> — IBID.

The United Nations unanimously voted to ratify the Universal Declaration of Human Rights on December 10, 1968, and to this day it strives to hold accountable any nation that fails to uphold these rights. Unfortunately, however, we have not yet declared the fundamental rights of the earth. Moltmann proposes a few ideas of what these rights might look like

(*Ethics of Hope,* 143-5), and this would be an important step in protecting the earth. We must defend the rights of the earth against capitalist exploitation of its resources and the mass pollution that goes with it.

We live in the hope that one day *this* world will become the dwelling place of God. Thus, we fight to protect the earth in the name of God.

7
___

THE WAY OF JESUS CHRIST

SUMMARY: The image of "the way" presents a more vibrant portrait of Jesus Christ than in traditional Christology. A three-dimensional, dynamic Christ thus takes the place of a static, one-sided Christ. These dimensions include Christ and His future (the messianic), Christ and His Father (the theological), and Christ, the friend of sinners (the social). Christology is Christopraxis; we cannot contemplate the doctrine of Christ apart from the discipleship of Christ.

IN MOLTMANN'S OWN WORDS:

At the centre of the Christian faith is *the passion of the passionate Christ.*

— JESUS CHRIST FOR TODAY'S WORLD, 31

Anyone who hears the message of the crucified Jesus hears the call to discipleship as well; and anyone who enters into the discipleship of Christ must be prepared to take up the cross. That is what the Gospels already tell us. Christ isn't merely a person. He is a road too. And the person who believes him takes the same road he took.

— IBID., 47

SECONDARY QUOTES:

The Way of Jesus Christ is certainly one of the finest of Moltmann's books - in my judgment the finest since *The Crucified God* - and it is probably the most important work on Christology for a decade at least. [...] It is one of the few recent christologies which is capable of reinvigorating christological thinking, expanding its horizons and realigning it with the church's task of witness to the contemporary world.

— RICHARD BAUCKHAM: THE THEOLOGY OF JÜRGEN
MOLTMANN, 199

INTRODUCTION

Moltmann's third systematic contribution, *The Way of Jesus Christ*, offers an innovative doctrine of Christ. The title might seem peculiar at first glance, but Moltmann explains what he intends with this image of "the way" (three points):

1) "The way" indicates process towards a goal. Specifically, the history of Christ's life from birth, baptism, death, and resurrection. It also implies a *continued* path that extends up to our present day, a path which anticipates the future coming of God. Thus, Christ is still "on the way." The image, therefore, aligns Christology towards a clear and definite goal, the new creation of all things. It is then also an all-inclusive image, which involves not only Christ's future but the future of all creation.

2) "The way" recognizes the historical limitations of every doctrine of Christ. Christology is a human endeavor, bound to the same limitations as any other human field of study. Therefore, Moltmann does not call this a "Christology of the home country," but a "Christology of the way." It is a Christology of faith, not sight. As such, it is open to further dialogue.

3) "The way" is an *invitation*. The way of Jesus Christ invites us to follow Him; it is inherently *ethical,* in the discipleship of Christ. We cannot resign ourselves to mere theories *about* Christ without also reflecting on the *praxis* (practice) required by Christ's life and teachings. The way of Jesus Christ invites us to follow Christ, rather than merely observe Him.

There is another characteristic of note about this volume, which provides a broader framework for the whole work. As we have seen in previous chapters, Jewish thought has had a significant influence on Moltmann's theology. Recall, for example, his debt to Ernst Bloch, Elie Wiesel, and Abraham Heschel, as well as to Jewish kabbalistic insights such as the *zimzum*. Moltmann takes Jewish thought seriously, especially here in his doctrine of Christ. It should be no surprise then to see that he places Christology within the context of the messianic hope of the Israelites. That much is clear from the book's subtitle: "Christology in Messianic Dimensions."

In traditional Christology, Jesus is frequently torn away from His historical and cultural context, but Moltmann is right to emphasize Jesus' place within Jewish messianic hope. Therefore, Moltmann writes:

> We can only truly and authentically understand Jesus if we perceive him and his history in the light of the Old Testament promises and the history of hope of Israel today.
>
> — THE WAY OF JESUS CHRIST, 1

This book gets right to the heart of Moltmann's theology, which has always been Christologically focused. However, that also means some of the insights we have already discussed reappear in this text. For brevity's sake, therefore, we will only focus on a few of its unique themes.

First, we will discuss the importance of Jewish messianism in Christology, especially in its eschatological dimension. Then we will explore the three-dimensional portrait of Christ which Moltmann proposes for the sake of a more robust Christology, in contrast with traditional doctrines. Finally, we will explore the vital connection between the *doctrine* of Christ and the *discipleship* of Christ, that Christology *is* Christopraxis. In a sidebar to this chapter, we will further explore that connection by highlighting the Christian commitment to nonviolence.

MESSIANIC HOPE

What is messianic hope? Geiko Muller-Fahrenholz provides a helpful definition:

It is the unrest which cannot be content with history as it is. With such unrest in one's heart, one thinks back and says, 'It can't have been that!' So memory seeks in the past for unsettled and unfulfilled moments; it looks for what has not yet had its future and attempts to give it a chance. But can the messianic unrest be content with what is there in the present? There must be still more life in life, it says. There must be more than everything.

— THE KINGDOM AND THE POWER, KINDLE LOC. 1877-80

Messianic hope is expectancy; it is trust in God's faithfulness and justice, which leaves us perpetually discontent with the way things are. "Therefore it consumes itself in restless expectation and only finds rest when God himself has found rest" (ibid., 1891). Accordingly, Moltmann writes, "The messianic hope was never the hope of the victors and the rulers. It was always the hope of the defeated and the ground down. The hope of the poor is nothing other than the messianic hope" (*The Way of Jesus Christ*, 13). Messianic hope is thus the restlessness of an unredeemed world.

Thinking of Christology in the context of messianic hope protects it from becoming stagnant and rigid. Moltmann writes, "Anyone who confesses Jesus as 'the Christ of God' is recognizing the Christ-in-his-becoming, the Christ on the way, the Christ in the movement of God's eschatological history; and that person enters upon this way of Christ in the discipleship of Jesus" (ibid., 33). Without recognizing the way of Christ, we will flatten out the process of Christ into a finished event. But Jewish messianism forces us to admit that it is still ongoing, that Christ is still on His way to the redemption of all things.

Therefore, the Christian "yes" to Jesus must include a consideration of the Jewish "no." The messianic hope of Israel remains unfulfilled. The "no" of Jewish hope means that the Christian "yes" to Christ is at best only *anticipatory*. The expectation of messianic hope is unfulfilled until the redemption of *all* creation. Christians say "yes" to Jesus in anticipation of God's coming Kingdom, and Israel says "no" because these things have not come to pass. Therefore, the Christian "yes" is incomplete without regard for the Jewish "no." Moltmann writes:

Even the raised Christ himself is 'not yet' the pantocrator [ruler of all]. But he is already on the way to redeem the world. The Christian 'yes' to Jesus' messiahship, which is based on believed and experienced reconciliation, will therefore accept the Jewish 'no', which is based on the experienced and suffered unredeemedness of the world; and the 'yes' will in so far adopt the 'no' as to talk about the total and universal redemption of the world only in the dimensions of a future hope, and a present contradiction of this unredeemed world. The Christian 'yes' to Jesus Christ is therefore not in itself finished and complete. It is open for the messianic future of Jesus. It is an *eschatologically anticipatory and provisional* 'yes'—'maranatha. Amen, come Lord Jesus' (Rev. 22:20). [...] The earthly Jesus was on the way to the revelation of his messiahship. This is what people call Jesus' 'messianic secret'. The risen Lord is on the way to his rule, which merely begins here, and is by no means universal, and his purpose is at the end to hand over the completed rule to God, who will then be 'all in all' (1 Cor. 15:28).

— THE WAY OF JESUS CHRIST, 32-3

Christology must avoid both the errors of a *realized* eschatology and a *chiliastic* eschatology. That is the role of the Jewish "no" against the Christian "yes." The first error claims that Christ's rule over all has already been accomplished, and thus turns a blind eye to the sufferings and injustices of history. The second error denies Israel its hope, and thus historicizes the kingdom of God, marginalizes the Jewish people, and excludes them from God's history. Both are to be rejected in Christology because both fail to reflect the messianic hope of the poor adequately. These views exclude the poor by professing faith in the triumphant of history. But that is possible only if we ignore the Jewish "no."

What is a realized eschatology? It asserts that God's work of redemption is *already* complete but remains hidden until its unveiling on the last day. Realized eschatology says: here and now Jesus is Lord of all and redemption is accomplished. Moltmann opposes this view by arguing with an eye to the still unredeemed state of the world; we have not yet arrived at the new creation. Jesus Christ is Lord only in *anticipation* of His coming reign (chapter 2). We reject realized eschatology because it ignores the Jewish "no" to Jesus, proclaimed in the light of the suffering of history. The

Jewish "no" resists a realized definition of redemption and therefore refuses to allow Christian's to turn a blind eye to the sufferings of this world.

What is a chiliastic eschatology? Here Moltmann refers to what is sometimes called historical millennialism. Chiliasm derives from the Greek word for "thousand." This eschatology places the thousand year reign of Christ *in history* and thus implies that human force and power can establish the Kingdom of God on this earth. (It is thus a form of utopian hope, as we discussed in chapter 2.) Therefore, it tends to support authoritarian and tyrannical systems such as Hitler's pseudo-messianic leadership. Moltmann experienced firsthand the horrors of what a chiliastic eschatology mixed with nationalistic pride can do.

Continued dialogue with Jewish thought is necessary if the Christian faith is to remain loyal to the messianic history of Jesus. If we refuse to recognize the Jewish "no" to Jesus, then we risk stripping Christ from His history as an Israelite in the messianic tradition. Without this dialogue, we will fundamentally misunderstand Jesus as the *Christ* ("Messiah").

In a sense, the Jewish "no" protects Christianity from becoming oppressive. Christianity is not the faith of *victors* but *martyrs*. It is the faith of the poor, the downtrodden, and the outsiders—because it is faith in the crucified Christ. The Jewish "no" is thus a call to the remembrance of Christ's cross and the unredeemed world on which it stands. Because the world is not yet redeemed, because we have not yet arrived in the new creation of God's reign, we remain "one the way" of Christ and His cross.

THREE DIMENSIONAL PERSON OF JESUS CHRIST

Every non-messianic Christology will inevitably reduce Jesus Christ down to a flat, one-sided person. Moltmann offers us a more vibrant doctrine of Christ, which we might call a *dynamic* rather than *static* Christology.

There are two classic doctrines in particular which Moltmann thinks need reworking because of this messianic focus. First, the "two natures" doctrine of Christ, and second, the "threefold office" of Christ. The first doctrine describes Jesus Christ as fully-God and fully-man. The second describes His office of priest, prophet, and king. The issue with these, for Moltmann, has more to do with their lifeless tendencies than their actual content. These doctrines tend to reduce the dynamic movement of Christ's being "on the way" into a dead, static event with neither a future nor past.

Moltmann explains:

> Jesus' personhood does not exist in isolation, *per se*; nor is it determined and fixed from eternity. It acquires its form in living relationships and reciprocities, and becomes an open identity in the course of Jesus' history. In the traditional christologies, the metaphysical concepts of nature or essence are used to elucidate the constitution of the divine-human person of Christ. But these are not helpful, because they define divinity and humanity by way of mutual negations of the characteristics of the other: finite—infinite, mortal—immortal, passible—impassible, and so forth. The definitions are not drawn from the positive interplay of these attributes. The concepts of *efficacy*, which are summed up in the Protestant doctrine of 'Christ's threefold office' as prophet, priest and king, are also one-sided, because they do not take account of the living relationships and interactions in which Christ acts as prophet, as priest or as king. In this dogmatic doctrine, the picture of the solitary man and his unique work cuts Jesus off from reality and isolates him from the community of men and women.
>
> — The Way of Jesus Christ, 136

Moltmann proposes a three-dimensional person of Jesus Christ. These dimensions include Christ 1) the messianic human being, 2) the childlike human being, and 3) the brotherly and sisterly human being. The first dimension is *eschatological*; He is Israel's Messiah and the hope of God's Kingdom. The second dimension is *theological*; this is the "Abba mystery" of Christ, His unique relationship with God the Father. The third dimension is *social*; He is a person among other persons, the "friend of sinners."

Moltmann criticizes traditional Christology for its emphasis on the "vertical" Christ while neglecting the "horizontal" Christ. That is, Moltmann thinks we often focus on the theological truth of His Sonship but forget to recognize the equally essential truths of His social and messianic personhood.

One of the most evident indications of this failure is in the Nicene and Apostles' Creeds, which have *nothing* at all to say about the life of Christ. There is simply a comma between His birth and death. It is almost as if there was nothing significant to be found between these two events. Accordingly, there has been little theological consideration given to Christ's life. There are plenty of books on the theological significance of the work of Christ, on His death and resurrection, but far less have drawn theological insights from His *history* and *relationships*.

To counteract this error, Moltmann proposes, in addition to this three-dimensional portrait of Christ, that we should add the following lines to the Nicene and Apostles' Creeds (between "born of the Virgin Mary" [Apostles'] or "was made man" [Nicene] and "crucified under Pontius Pilate"):

> Baptized by John the Baptist,
> filled with the Holy Spirit:
> to preach the kingdom of God to the poor,
> to heal the sick,
> to receive those who have been cast out,
> to revive Israel for the salvation of the nations, and
> to have mercy upon all people.
>
> — THE WAY OF JESUS CHRIST, 150

Jesus is not *only* the Son of God—He is this, but He is also the Messiah of Israel, the friend of sinners, the son of Mary, the carpenter from Nazareth, the political and religious outsider, and the man crucified on Golgotha. To ignore these dimensions and focus only on a "vertical" Christ is to present only part of His personhood. Christology must consider all three aspects. That is Moltmann's challenge to Christology, which so often relies on out-dated metaphysical categories instead of thinking about Christ in a new way.

CHRISTOPRAXIS

The Church has often treated Christ's ethical and political convictions as if they were *optional*. The Sermon on the Mount, as an example, is deemed significant only as instruction for living a good Christian life, but it has not been considered *essential* to an adequate understanding of Christ. However, we cannot discuss the doctrine of Christ without recognizing Christ's call to discipleship. Discipleship should be inseparable from Christological reflection.

We proclaim a "naked" Christ, a Christ stripped of all His ethical and political convictions, whenever we ignore discipleship in Christology. But that is a failure to recognize Christ adequately. We cannot contemplate Christ from a distance. To know Christ is to follow Christ. That is what the image of Christ's "way" indicates. We do not examine Christ like an object under a microscope in a controlled, scientific laboratory; we are *confronted by* Christ and His radical call to discipleship. Christology *is* Christopraxis; what we believe about Christ is incomplete without discipleship. What good is it to have a perfect doctrine of Christ without loving our neighbors? If we ignore the hungry, the poor, and the foreigners? Thus, all genuine Christology includes discipleship. To contemplate Christ without following Him on His way is utter hypocrisy.

Moltmann's Christology seamlessly joins together the political, ethical, and theological implications of the person of Jesus Christ. That is its genius; it is integrative. In the next section, we will consider one of the most significant practical implications found in the life and teachings of Christ: the Christian commitment to nonviolence. Christ's call to nonviolence is not optional. If we are His disciples, nonviolence is the path we must follow; it is Christ's *way*.

SIDEBAR: NONVIOLENCE

Three contemporary issues contextualize Moltmann's Christology: the crisis of global inequality, the impending threat of nuclear annihilation, and the possibility of ecological disaster. No universally valid Christology exists which can stand above the challenges of historical existence. Therefore, Christology is a time-bound discipline that must take into consideration its contemporary context.

For Moltmann, "[F]aith in Christ can no longer be separated from ethics" (*The Way of Jesus Christ,* 118). Christology is inseparable from Christopraxis, as Moltmann writes:

> There is no christology without christopraxis, no knowledge of Christ without the practice of Christ. We cannot grasp Christ merely with our heads or our hearts. We come to understand him through a total, all-embracing practice of living; and that means discipleship.
>
> — JESUS CHRIST FOR TODAY'S WORLD, 47

The common denominator of these three contemporary issues is *violence*. It is either through violence against one another (nuclear annihilation and global inequality) or against the earth (the ecological crisis). Sin is personal, but it is also social. The Church has often focused its attention so singularly on the *personal* sins of individuals that it has ignored the *social* sins of the community. However, just as the Gospel means healing for personal sin, it also includes the communal healing of social sins. That is the purpose of Christ's command to embrace nonviolence. The discipleship of Christ calls the Christian community to resist the social sin of violence and counter-violence by taking up a commitment to nonviolence. In this way, the Church participates in Christ's redemption by overcoming the endless cycle of violence through love.

Moltmann writes, "[T]he centre of the Sermon on the Mount is the liberation from violence" (*The Way of Jesus Christ*, 127). While some have read Christ's call to nonviolence as nothing more than a personal *suggestion*, Moltmann rightly recognizes its essential significance. If the Gospel has any relevance for the world today, a world on the brink of global annihilation, then redemption must involve freedom from violence. Nonviolence is the way of Jesus Christ in a world destroying itself through violence.

Above all, it is Christ's cross which demands Christian commitment to nonviolence. Brian Zahnd summarizes this well: "The cross is shock therapy for a world addicted to solving its problems through violence. The cross shocks us into the devastating realization that our system of violence murdered God" (*A Farewell to Mars*, Kindle Loc., 1021). To take up violence against another human being is to do violence to Christ.

Church history, unfortunately, has not always reflected this conviction very well. We have often given in to the temptation of violence. However, for the first few centuries of the Church, Christians were widely devoted to nonviolence, often to the point of martyrdom. Thus, the blood of the martyrs speaks more faithfully to the cross of Christ than the sins of a violent Church. The Church reflects Christ best in *weakness,* not in strength and violence. In truth, its "weakness" *is* its strength.

The early Church Fathers regularly stressed this commitment to nonviolence. In fact, it was so crucial to the early Church that they often forbid Christians from serving in the military. Here we will consider several examples of this commitment. (See "Works Cited" for unsourced quotes.)

It is absolutely forbidden to repay evil with evil.

— TERTULLIAN

Christ, in disarming Peter, disarmed every soldier.

— TERTULLIAN: ON IDOLATRY, CHAPTER 19

You cannot demand military service of Christians any more than you can of priests. We do not go forth as soldiers with the Emperor even if he demands this.

— ORIGEN

I serve Jesus Christ the eternal King. I will no longer serve your emperors... It is not right for a Christian to serve the armies of this world.

— MERCELLUS THE CENTURION

I am a soldier of Christ. I cannot fight.

— MARTIN OF TOURS, A ROMAN SOLDIER, WHO IN 336 REFUSED TO FIGHT AND WAS THROWN IN JAIL. SEE MARK KURLANSKY: NONVIOLENCE, 26-7.

A soldier of the civil authority must be taught not to kill men and to refuse to do so if he is commanded, and to refuse to take an oath. If he is unwilling to comply, he must be rejected for baptism. A military commander or civic magistrate must resign or be rejected. If a believer seeks to become a soldier, he must be rejected, for he has despised God.

— HIPPOLYTUS OF ROME

For since we, a numerous band of men as we are, have learned from His teaching and His laws that evil ought not to be requited with evil, that it is better to suffer wrong than to inflict it, that we should rather shed our own blood than stain our hands and our conscience with that of another, an ungrateful world is now for a long period enjoying a benefit from Christ, inasmuch as by His means the rage of savage ferocity has been softened, and has begun to withhold hostile hands from the blood of a fellow-creature.

— ARNOBIUS, ADVERSUS GENTES I:IV

Christians, instead of arming themselves with swords, extend their hands in prayer.

— ATHANASIUS

Any Christology that ignores the call to renounce violence is missing an essential aspect of the way of Jesus Christ and thus has failed to understand Him accurately. In America, our so-called Christian nation spends billions of dollars every year on weapons of war and death. That is only possible if we forcefully rip Jesus away from His ethical commitments. Moltmann's Christology is a vital step forward in the modern world, which no longer has an option except to embrace nonviolence or else face a catastrophic end. We do not have a proper doctrine of Jesus Christ without His ethical commitments to nonviolence. That the Church has so often circumvented Jesus' ethic and openly embraced violence is one of the greatest tragedies of Christianity, but it is, in part, a failure of Christology.

VIOLENCE AS SIN

Moltmann provocatively states, "[H]umanity's real sin is the violence that leads to death" (*The Way of Jesus Christ*, 127). It will be helpful to arrive at a new definition of sin in the light of Christ's nonviolent commitments. To say that sin *is* violence is not actually a reinterpretation of sin but rather the rediscovery of an overlooked biblical tradition. The Jewish understanding of sin has never resembled our abstract theory of "original sin." Instead, in their understanding of Genesis, it was Cain's murder of Abel which was the first act of sin. Sin's root, therefore, is *violence*. (Moltmann cites Martin Buber as an example; see Buber: *Good and Evil.*)

The texts themselves also reveal this understanding of sin. Genesis 6 describes God's disdain over the "wickedness" of the earth. What precisely was this wickedness? In verse 11, the text explicitly links *corruption* with *violence*: "Now the earth was corrupt in God's sight, and the earth was filled with violence" (NRSV). Why was the earth corrupt in God's sight? Because of its violence. Violence, therefore, is not merely a fruit of sin but is *itself* sin—perhaps even the very root of sin.

Moltmann explains further:

[T]he centre of the Sermon on the Mount is the liberation from violence; enmity is to be surmounted through the creation of peace. The presupposition here is that humanity's real sin is the violence that leads to death; and that consequently humanity's salvation is to be found in the peace that serves our common life. Compared with Christian theology's traditional doctrine of sin and grace, this is an unusual position; and we are therefore stressing it particularly.

The primaeval history told in the Priestly Writing knows nothing of the story about the Garden of Eden and the Fall, which we find in Genesis 3. This story has dominated the doctrine of sin in the Western church ever since Augustine, although the terms 'sin' and 'guilt' do not in fact occur in the story at all. According to the Priestly Writing, the sin is the rampant growth of violence on earth, to which God responds with the annihilating Flood. Jewish exegesis does not interpret the story about the Garden of Eden through a doctrine of original sin either. Jewish interpreters see sin as beginning only with Cain's murder of his brother Abel. According to Genesis 6:13, the earth was 'full of wickedness'. What does this wickedness consist of? Apparently the spread of violence and rape.

— The Way of Jesus Christ, 127-8

Moltmann does not reject the traditional doctrine of sin, but as he states, he wants to stress this notion of sin mainly because of the overemphasis on a spiritualized concept of sin in the Christian tradition. The Sermon on the Mount is often stripped of its theological content so that violence is deemed only an effect of sin and not sin itself. But the Bible presents a clear link between sin and violence, and to spiritualize sin and ignore God's disdain for violence is a grave error with devastating results.

Violence is a *cycle*. Nonviolence is the only way to end its neverending parade of death and destruction. Nonviolence is thus the redemption of communities from the cycle of violence. Moltmann writes:

> Violence committed by people against other people, and by human beings against weaker creatures, is sin, and a crime against life. Violence always has two sides: on the one side is the person who commits the act, and on the other is his victim. On the one side the master sets himself up as superior, on the other the slave is humiliated. On the one side the exploiter wins, on the other the exploited person loses.
>
> An act of violence destroys life on both sides, but in different ways—on the one hand through the evil committed, on the other through the suffering. The person who commits the act becomes inhumane and unjust, the victim is dehumanized and deprived of his or her rights. Because violence has these two sides, the road to freedom and justice has to begin with both: the liberation of the oppressed from the suffering of oppression requires the liberation of the oppressor from the injustice of oppression. Otherwise there is no liberation and no justice that can create peace.
>
> — The Spirit of Life, 132

The vicious cycle of violence is overcome only by nonviolence. Through nonviolence both the oppressed victims and their oppressive assailants are set free from the cycle of violence. We have often stressed the saving effects of Christ's *death,* but there are soteriological implications to be discovered in Christ's teachings, too. Freedom from the cycle of violence is a social aspect of the Gospel of peace. Therefore, nonviolence is essential to the Gospel we proclaim.

What would the world look like if we proclaimed the Gospel of peace, which includes Christ's commitment to nonviolence, and not just the Gospel of salvation from hell? I have no doubt the world would be a better place to live, and that fewer Christians would be comfortable condoning acts of violence. The call of peace, however, has slipped through our fingers because we would much rather *escape* the world than *change* it (see chapter 2).

In the Church, we have permitted violence, even sometimes *celebrated* violence, for far too long. We need to rediscover the Gospel of peace. Think, for example, of the American fetishization of its soldiers. These men and women are indeed brave and deserve support, but the way Christians often praise and honor their inherently *violent* activities should give us pause. In the Church of my youth, I remember vividly when, especially on national holidays, we would go from singing worship hymns to patriotic hymns as if they were just as important. To celebrate the violence of American troops and then turn to praise the God who was executed by nationalistic violence is hypocrisy. The cross of the crucified Christ is incongruent with the blind support of state-sanctioned military violence. It was this same kind of violence that killed our Lord. Our doctrine of sin must be expanded to include the total renunciation of violence, for Christ's sake.

THE LOVE THAT OVERCOMES

Christ's commandment of nonviolence is *essential* to the Gospel. It is not merely a *suggestion* for how to be good, moral people. However, nonviolence is also so much more than just the passive renunciation of violence. In truth, nonviolence is the powerful resistance *against* violence. Nonviolence is *the love that overcomes violence.*

Moltmann writes on the effect of nonviolence:

The vicious circle of violence and counter-violence is broken. Non-resistance to evil shows up the absurdity of evil. Evil's strength is violence. Evil's weakness is its wrongness. Counter-violence supplies evil with its supposed justification, and often enough stabilizes it. It is only the non-violent reaction which robs evil of every legitimation and puts the perpetrator of violence in the wrong, 'heaping burning coals on his head' (Rom. 12:20).

— THE WAY OF JESUS CHRIST, 129

Nonviolence is not passivity, but courageous freedom. Only those who are set free from the fear of death by Christ's resurrection can embrace nonviolence, even in the face of death. Violence repays evil for evil, but nonviolence is *freedom* from violence and overcomes evil with good (Rom. 12:21, 27). Nonviolence reflects our faithfulness to the crucified and risen Christ who suffered and died without retaliation.

Nonviolence frees us to love our neighbor by overcoming the cycle of violence and counter-violence. Nonviolence is not merely the refusal to retaliate evil with evil, but the affirmative act of correcting evil with good. Nonviolence *is* how we love our enemies. As such, it means taking up "*responsibility for one's enemies*" (ibid.). Moltmann writes, "In loving one's enemies one no longer asks: how can I protect myself[...]? The question is then: how can I deprive my enemy of his hostility?" (ibid., 131). That is why the early Church Fathers took such a strong stance against Christians arming themselves with swords. Similarly, we might say today that gun ownership is excluded from the way of Jesus Christ because to own a gun is to premeditate retaliation (see chapter 8, sidebar). We cannot embrace our enemies with weapons of death in our hands.

Radical commitment to nonviolence is the way of Jesus Christ. It is not merely the renunciation of violence but the embrace of creative love. We have the assurance that even if we lose our lives in our commitment to nonviolence, we are in the company of Christ and share in His future. Nonviolence is a uniquely Christian obligation because it expresses our hope so profoundly well. The blood of the martyrs is the purest form of the Church's witness to Christ. In the face of a world of violence, we anticipate the coming of God's Kingdom through acts of nonviolent resistance against the powers that be. Even under the threat of death, we resist retaliation in the name of Christ. We stand together on the side of the oppressed and refuse to become oppressors. Even if we die for Christ's sake, we will not retaliate violence with violence. That is how we are Christ to this world.

8

ETHICS OF HOPE

SUMMARY: Ethics of hope are ethics *of life,* which prioritize the furtherance of life in a world of complicated possibilities. Like Moltmann's dialectic of cross and resurrection, his ethic recognizes both the realism of the unredeemed present and the hope of a better world. Therefore, we act ethically with an eye on both the sufferings of the present and the joys of the future.

IN MOLTMANN'S OWN WORDS:

A Christian ethic is an ethic of lived hope and is hence related to the horizon of historical change which is open to the future. It is not an 'ordering' ethic, nor is it a situation ethic. It is an ethic of change [...]. To do what is good means asking about what is better. For this ethic of change we need guidelines instead of laws and regulations. These act as signposts, steadily orientated towards the future, and offer changing responses to the challenges of history. Every *theologia viatorum* [theology on the way] demands an *ethica viatorum* [ethics on the way].

— GOD WILL BE ALL IN ALL, 285

Christian ethics are eschatological ethics. What we do now for people in

need we do filled with the power of hope, and lit by the expectation of
God's coming day.

— God Will be All in All, 289

Introduction

Moltmann initially planned his volume on ethics to follow *The Church in
the Power of the Spirit,* but it was delayed until the end of his systematic
contributions. At that time, Moltmann felt the limits of his knowledge
left him unequipped. The need to grasp more fully the medical and
ecological side of ethics was a particular concern for him. Now, at the end
of his series, Moltmann returns to articulate the ethics of hope. Although
this volume concludes Moltmann's systematic contributions to theology,
we are discussing it here, immediately after his Christology. We emphasized already that Christology and ethics are inseparable, for Moltmann.
To retain a natural order for that argument, I decided to place these two
chapters together.

Moltmann's ethic serves a particular purpose, being "related to the
ethos which has to do with endangered life, the threatened earth and the
lack of justice and righteousness. It is not a discussion of timeless general
principles; but in the face of these dangers, it focuses on what has to be
done today and tomorrow with the courage of hope" (*Ethics of Hope,* xii).
As such, it is a *"deliberately Christian ethics"* (ibid.). It is not a metaphysical attempt at universal ethics; instead, it is ethics by "the divine hope
and the claim of Christ" (ibid.). In line with the theology of life which
became increasingly important for Moltmann's later work, his ethics of
hope are at once *ethics of life.*

Ethics of Hope contains little new information. In fact, the book
mostly articulates a more precise ethic already present in the whole of
Moltmann's thought. These themes are merely drawn to the surface more
explicitly in this work. Therefore, this chapter will primarily focus on an
example of Moltmann's ethics, namely, the issue of abortion.

Ethics of Life

The strength of Moltmann's ethic is his emphasis on affirming and protecting life, which is particularly relevant for a post-war society marked by indifference and apathy. Albert Camus articulates the problem: "The secret of Europe is that it no longer loves life" (cited in *Ethics of Hope*, 45). Moltmann writes:

> Human life lives from being affirmed, since it can also be denied. For human life to be destined for eternal life means its unequivocal and unconditional affirmation by the living God. If God himself becomes a human being, and if in Christ eternal life appears among mortal men and women on this earth, then the human race is wanted by God, and every individual person can have confidence in his own existence. Every woman, every man, and every child is desired and wanted and expected. The creation of human beings in the earth's community of creation, the taking flesh of the eternal Word among us, and the outpouring on 'all flesh' of the life-creating Spirit are an affirmation of humanity within the community of all the living in the living space of the earth. Humanity is affirmed by God in this way not just for itself, and not for heaven, but in the community of life and for this earth.
>
> — ETHICS OF HOPE, 59

When in doubt, we choose life and resist apathy. Ethics of hope have this determination in mind: *to affirm life*. Politically, socially, and personally that is what an ethic of hope looks like in practice.

As disciples of Christ, we are called peacemakers—not peace-*keepers* but peace-*makers*—which implies acting courageously for the sake of life. As Moltmann writes, "Peace in history is not a condition in which one could sit back and rest on one's oars; it is always a way forward which has to be pursued, so as to create time for humanity, and so as to make life for coming generations possible" (ibid., 65). That is to say, peace is never a given, nor should it be presupposed in any situation. Just because an individual's life is relatively calm does not mean the world is at peace.

It is *necessary*, for the sake of life and in the name of Christ, that we resist oppression and injustice in all its forms. Civil disobedience is a Christian obligation in the midst of a world that does not value life. It is *justice*, Moltmann argues, that will create lasting peace, not security and comfort. Only a just society is at peace.

We refuse to plug our ears to the cries of suffering and death in this unredeemed world. In short, *we remember the cross*. That is how we live an ethic of hope. We remain sensitive to the suffering of God in and with the suffering of all creation, and in resurrection hope we act for the sake of God's coming Kingdom. Moltmann writes:

> 'God is dead—we have killed him,' Nietzsche maintained. Unfortunately he did not see *when* we kill God. We kill God when we make God's image the victim of our violence, for God is in God's image. We kill God when we shut out and drive away strangers, for God is in the stranger. We kill God when we choose death instead of life and secure our own lives at the price of the death of many other living things, for God is the living God. Anyone who infringes life infringes God. Anyone who does not love life does not love God. God is a God of the whole of life, of every life and of the life shared of us all.
>
> — A Passion for God's Reign, 18

Moltmann challenges us with this chilling image: "God in the victims of our violence [...] God, the victim in the victims, is 'the crucified God,' who looks at us with the silent eyes of abandoned street children" (ibid.). Indifference to the poor and the weak is indifference to God. The needs of the oppressed are the burden of the free and the privileged. It is in the name of the crucified Christ that we serve the needs of the oppressed, that we feed the hungry, that we take in the stranger. It is in the hope of a new creation that we resist death by standing against unjust systems which keep the poor penniless, the hungry hopeless, and the strangers homeless. It is *for Christ's sake* that we must listen to the cries of death and fully commit to an ethic of life. Because of the resurrection, a Christian in the world stands unequivocally on the side of life, and actively resists apathy.

AN EXAMPLE: ABORTION

Here we will examine the issue of abortion to show how Moltmann implements the ethics of hope. I want to preface these remarks by asking for your patience. I know this is a controversial issue. Moltmann's approach is nuanced and carefully balanced, and therefore well worth listening to. This debate, especially in America, is often reduced to strict black-and-white thinking so that good discussions rarely take place and nuanced conclusions are almost unreachable. Moltmann's guiding thought for the ethics of hope is this: when in doubt, *decide for life*. Moltmann moves beyond the polarization of "pro-life" and "pro-choice" camps with this principle in mind. Even if you disagree with his proposed solution, this example offers helpful insight into how Moltmann applies the ethics of hope.

We have to be clear what we are and are not discussing here. Moltmann writes, "Ethics is not a criminal code, and criminal law is not a substitute for ethics" (*Ethics of Hope*, 84). The issue is not the *criminality* of abortion, and neither is the issue its *permissibility*. Moltmann correctly notes that both sides of the debate fail by thinking of criminal law instead of ethical conduct. Criminal law is important, of course, but it should only come *after* ethical discussion. Legal considerations follow ethics. We far too often debate this issue with only the law in mind, but the main issue is not legal but ethical. The "pro-life" and "pro-choice" movements are often so passionate and angry towards each other because of this polarization. The debate has become a *legal* debate, rather than an ethical *discussion*. Only when we return to the core issue and examine the ethical complications of abortion will we listen to each other rather than talking past each other.

Within the context of an ethical discussion, there is room for a more productive dialogue because a multitude of answers become possible. In an ethical discussion, we are not forced to respond with a reductionistic "yes" or "no" answer but have the freedom to consider the complexity of the issue in all its facets. But that means giving up the black-and-white absolutism of "pro-life" vs. "pro-choice." Instead, we listen to the ethical concerns of the issue openly and form a legal decision only in the light of the ethical discussion. There is no one size fits all solution to such a complex problem, and admitting this will be a helpful step towards productive dialogue.

With this in mind, Moltmann begins by stating his essential agreement with Karl Barth on the issue:

Together with Karl Barth, I am starting from the assumption that 'every deliberate interruption of pregnancy ... is a taking of a human life, [not just] a ready expedient and remedy in a moment of embarrassment'. And yet 'there are situations in which the killing of germinating life does not constitute murder but is in fact commanded'. By this Barth means situations in which a choice must be made in order to protect life, because it is a matter of a life against a life. These are the situations we shall now look at in the context of various indications.

— ETHICS OF HOPE, 81

From this, Moltmann identifies three situations when abortion *may* be an acceptable ethical option. Since many of these situations fall into grey areas with no simple solutions, it would be unethical for the law to forbid abortion. Thus, these are three ethically permissible scenarios.

The first situation is in the event of a medical complication threatening the mother's life. Here a mother has an impossible choice: either giving birth and dying or surviving but terminating the life of the embryo. It would be unethical for the law to force the mother to give up her own life for the life of her child. In this context, a strict "pro-life" stance is, in fact, *against* the life of the mother. Although, this does not mean the mother may still decide to freely give up her own life for the life of the child, as some mothers have selflessly chosen. However, in this scenario, there can be no legal obligation to force a mother to give up her life to avoid abortion, since this would be unethical. Thus, this is the first scenario in which abortion is ethically permissible.

The second situation is in the event of ethical or criminal complications, such as the unfortunate, but sadly far too familiar, cases of pregnancy by rape. To force a mother to live the rest of her life with the haunting memory of her violent attacker would be unethical, and therefore, no law should forbid abortion for rape victims. That does not rule out the ethical possibility that the mother may still choose to keep the child, and that the mother may forgive her attacker and accept the good from the bad; but this can only be their freedom, not a forced conclusion. Ultimately, Moltmann thinks that in this scenario the best option would be to put up the child for adoption. The mother may not find the courage to love and affirm the child, but this does not mean someone else will not be willing and able to accept them. Although adoption should not be a force requirement, it the best alternative, and reforming the strict laws surrounding adoption is necessary to prepare for an influx of children. Social welfare systems and foster care homes would also need to more financial support for this to become a possibility.

The third situation is in the event of extreme social complications, such as severe poverty, limited means, or social detriment. Moltmann is clear, however, "As a method of birth control, abortion is irresponsible" (*Ethics of Hope*, 83). This possibility does not include the freedom to abort a child in merely *inconvenient* pregnancies. Abortion as *birth control* is wholly unethical. However, it is also unethical for the law to force a family into ruin from a forced birth—either socially, financially, or emotionally. Again, adoption would be the best alternative in these cases, but that is not always possible. Especially in America, where hospital bills are already far beyond the means of the millions of people who live in extreme poverty, giving the child up for adoption is sometimes just as financially demanding as raising the child. It would be unethical for the law to force families into ruin. Therefore, abortion may be an ethical choice in the protection of life, though second only to adoption. None of this, of course, would exclude the possibility that a family may *choose* to embrace their poverty and love their child despite their limited means, but it cannot force this. In the long run, the health care system needs to be restructured, so that giving birth would no longer be such an unbearable expense. That would make adoption a viable option for the severely impoverished.

After considering these situations in which it would be unethical to *forbid* abortion, Moltmann discusses the ethical reasons *against* abortion. Frankly, it is unethical to kill an embryo outside of these three conditions.

A divisive question in the abortion debate is whether or not an embryo is a human life. Moltmann argues that "inhumanity begins" when we remove the embryo from its concrete situation, that of human birth. In other words, inhumanity finds ground when we fail to identify an embryo as a human life. It is severely problematic to de-humanize an embryo in the name of a political debate. We must resist this reclassification of human life. Moltmann writes:

> We cannot take so easy a way out. It can very well be that a life has to be

killed in order that a life can be saved. But then one should justify the act of killing, not disparage the object to such an extent that it is no longer a question of killing at all. We are not living in an unscathed world but in a world with defects. In this world one must try to do what is better under conditions which are unavoidably anything but good. Life often costs other life, not just in the case we are discussing. That is a tragic situation in which is surmounted neither by the cry of murder raised by the moral rigorists, nor by the demands for liberty made by the liberals, nor by the striving for profit of the capitalists.

— ETHICS OF HOPE, 85

There is no easy answer to the question of abortion. The black-and-white dichotomy between "pro-life" and "pro-choice" camps only adds to the problem. The issue of abortion is far too complicated for a minimalistic political slogan. However, when in doubt, we choose in favor of life.

Ethically, life is primary. Legally, however, freedom is primary. It is legally unethical to force the death of mothers by refusing them the option of an abortion, to force the birth of rape-children, or to force financial or social ruin upon families. Therefore, legal permissions must exist for abortion in these situations. However, it is wholly unethical to de-humanize embryos as mere organic matter, and therefore to justify killing human life in the name of *comfort* or as a sort of birth control. The law should distinguish between *necessary* abortions and *comfortable* ones. The former should be permitted (but not required), and we reject the latter unequivocally. Corporate profiting from embryos is also wholly condemned. Human life is not for sale. Therefore, both the pro-choice and pro-life movements have a hint of truth in their rallying cries, but both fail to capture the nuance required for such a problematic issue.

Moltmann's position is a challenge to both "left" and "right" politics. Many Christians have sworn absolute allegiance to "pro-life" candidates, yet they have often failed to recognize situations in which abortion itself *is* the pro-life choice. We need brutal realism in our ethical decisions. We have no use for unrealistic, idealized ethics because they ultimately ignore the concrete situations of this fallen, unredeemed world. Moltmann pointedly writes:

Hope founded on the raising of the crucified Christ begins with the realities, not the illusions. It is only if we accept the tragic situation of having to act in the situations described that we shall work to change them, so that abortions and the killing of embryos are no longer necessary and no longer happen.

— ETHICS OF HOPE, 85

Abortions are undesirable, but they are sadly necessary in a corrupt world in which disease, rape, and poverty are present realities. Pro-life becomes anti-life when it fails to recognize the world as it is. We must keep our eyes open to the harsh realities of our world, but also work to change them and minimize abortion. Ethics of hope live in the dialectic of cross and resurrection—between the realism of an unredeemed world and an active hope in the new creation. The cross keeps our eyes fixed on the way the world *is*, while the resurrection draws us forward to anticipate the world as it *will be*. The brutal realism of the cross is often absent from pro-life reflections.

However, on the other side of the spectrum, pro-choice ideologies are morally corrupt in their de-humanization of embryos. A free capitalist system that permits the sale of human materials for profit is inhumane. Regulations should be in place against such inhumanities, for the sake of life. There is no ethical justification for profiting from the death of human life, even in its embryonic form.

In a strictly legal sense, we prefer to be pro-choice and to permit abortion, but in a highly regulated manner. Ethics take priority, which means the humanization of embryos is a necessary step to create an ethical system. It is unethical to bend a system to fit the wishes of those seeking release from the brute facts of reality or their guilt. Abortion, when necessary, should be considered soberly. It ends human life. Only when we recognize the reality against the idealization of reality can we make sound ethical decisions. Ethical decisions are complicated, but in uncertainty, we must decide for life with all the facts of reality in full view. Moltmann's preference for adoption is admirable, and there should be systems in place to make this more accessible as well.

Ethics "on the way"

Ethics of hope anticipate the future of God's Kingdom, while at once remaining true to the brutal realism of the crucified Christ. It is this dialectic of cross and resurrection, between brutal realism and expectant hope, that characterizes Moltmann's ethical reflections as well as much of his theology. Moltmann refuses to give up hope and live in apathy towards suffering. Therefore, he prioritizes the cause of life in the midst of an indifferent world. He remains realistic about the sad realities of the unredeemed present, however, and offers realistic solutions that favor life. Just as Moltmann's Christology emphasized the image of Christ's "way," so an ethic that is both Christological and eschatological is an ethic "on the way," from the realism of our present miseries to the hope of God's Kingdom. It means we have no perfect ethical system to cling to, no set of pre-established answers to life's difficult questions, and no roadmap. These are not the ethics of the homeland, but of the way. An ethic of hope lives in expectation of God's Kingdom but resists the illusionary claim of a perfect ethical system.

Moltmann ends his ethics with a reflection on their ultimate goal: doxology. Moltmann's unique kind of mysticism is implied here, which is mysticism *with open eyes* (more on this in the next chapter). Moltmann writes:

> The new Christian mysticism is turned towards the future, and with its hope for God awakens all the senses for the future of God's world. Those who have found God in their innermost being can forget themselves, go out of themselves, and do their utmost without losing themselves. The person who senses in himself the nearness of the risen Christ will be filled with a joy that embraces the world. He sees this disputed and suffering world as already in the daybreak glory of its eternal beauty.
>
> — Ethics of Hope, 239

Here in the embrace of God we are freed from fear and anxiety and give of ourselves freely with a joyful heart. From the stillness of quiet contemplation springs forth hope in God's coming Kingdom. This hope draws us *into* the world *as it is* so that we might change it in anticipation of how it *will be*. In contrast with a mysticism of escape, the mysticism of hope refuses to close its eyes to the sufferings of this unredeemed world and confronts the world in the security of God's presence. In the midst of a restless world, we root ourselves in the contemplation of God's presence, but we refuse to remain in the inwardness of our souls. We live with our eyes open to the suffering of this world, and with an expectation of its redemption.

A connection is found here between joy in God and revolutionary action, between doxology and justice. It is for the sake of *enjoying God* that we work to change the world. That is why Moltmann ends his *Ethics of Hope* in the spirit of doxology:

> Christian ethics is the human reaction to the coming of Christ into this world and is an anticipation of his future in the new world. That is why every good Christian ethics ends in doxology, so as with the praise of God to intensify the cry of hope, 'Amen, come Lord Jesus!' (Rev. 22:20). For in Christian ethics it must be clear that, we do not make use of God in order to change the world, but we change the world in order to enjoy God, as Augustine said.
>
> — Ibid., 229

God is not a tool for political or social activism. That is a criticism often made against liberation theologies, and it is perhaps not unfair to raise this concern. The cause of liberation can sometimes consume our attention so forcefully that we neglect the joy of God, which is the source and the goal of all our actions. Liberation alone brings us only halfway. The ultimate goal is the joy of God. Liberation culminates in doxology. However, this joy is also our strength to act. It is only in the joy of God that we find the courage to revolt against the injustices of our world. It is our source and our goal. Moltmann makes this connection when he writes:

> Joy in life's happiness motivates us to revolt against the life that is destroyed and against those who destroy life. And grief over life that is destroyed is nothing other than an ardent longing for life's liberation to happiness and joy. Otherwise we would accept innocent suffering and

destroyed life as our fate and destiny. Compassion is the other side of the living joy. We don't accuse God because there is suffering in the world. Rather, we protest in the name of God against suffering and those who cause it.

— "Christianity: A Religion of Joy," 13-4

May we be filled with a joy "that embraces the world," because in this world we see already "the daybreak glory of its eternal beauty" (*Ethics of Hope*, 239). In joyous anticipation, we thank God for what is to come and act in the expectation of God's faithfulness to the promise. We praise God for what God has done and is going to do, and in this hope, we act for liberation in the name of God. Here ethics and contemplation, action and praise, go hand in hand.

SIDEBAR: GUN VIOLENCE

As I write this, the heart-breaking news of yet another American mass shooting has just reached me. It occurred in a Florida high school and resulted in the deaths of seventeen people. It is now the 30th American mass shooting in 2018. (As of February 14, according to the Gun Violence Archive. I am referring to the shooting in Parkland, Florida.)

WHAT DOES AN ETHIC OF HOPE MEAN IN THE MIDST OF GUN VIOLENCE?

First, some statistics to consider:

The United States leads the world in mass shootings. While America claims only 5% of the world population, it contributes to 31% of its mass shootings (according to findings of the American Sociological Association, 2015). The country with the second highest mass shooting rate is the Philippines, but they lag behind by a sizable five-to-one ratio. The United States disproportionately leads the world in the number of guns owned by its citizens. There are an estimated 270-310 million guns in the USA. Moreover, with a population of roughly 320 million, that works out to nearly one gun for every citizen. Which also means that Americans own nearly *half* of all the civilian-owned guns in the world. India comes second in gun ownership with a meager 46 million, but India also has a much higher population (1.25 billion). India does not even make it onto the list of the top five countries for mass shootings.

Statistics have shown that those individual States in America with a higher average of guns per person also have more mass shootings and deaths by gun violence (CDC). The correlation between gun ownership and gun violence is a statistical fact. (This was proven decidedly by researchers Michael Sigel, Craig S. Ross, and Charles King III in "The Relationship Between Gun Ownership and Firearm Homicide Rates in the United States, 1981-2010", *American Journal of Public Health* 103, no. 11 [November 1, 2013]: pp. 2098-2105.)

The United States is *not* more violent than other countries. In fact, the world average is around a 6.3% rate of violent crimes, and the US is typically under that average at 5.5% (International Crime Victims Survey; Gallup Europe). The evidence is overwhelmingly clear that mass gun ownership and a lack of gun-purchasing restrictions is the primary cause of mass shootings in America. From an academic and statistical standpoint, this is an undisputed fact: more guns mean more gun-related deaths. It becomes even clearer when examining the States with stricter gun control laws, such as California and New York. More than any other factor, there is a verifiable correlation between gun control laws and fewer gun-related deaths (Richard Florida, "The Geography of Gun Deaths," 2011). That is not only true for the United States but also worldwide, since there is a verifiable correlation shown between countries with gun control and decreased gun violence (Epidemiological Reviews, 2016). Some argue that more guns in the hands of "good people" will cause fewer gun deaths and shootings, but this is statistically inaccurate. More guns and less restrictive gun laws unequivocally lead to more gun-related deaths and mass shootings. Mass shootings are *preventable.*

(Unsourced statistics can be verified by "Gun Violence by the Numbers"; see "Works Cited.")

If the Church in America remains indifferent in the face of these statistics, we will become complicit in a growing culture of death. The way of Jesus Christ is the way which leads to life. We must take a stand and work to enact policies and laws to prevent the rise of mass shootings. We must say

Yes to life in the face of violence and death. Machines purposefully designed for war and mass killing have no place in the life of a Christian, even in the name of self-defense. I would not go so far as to call it a sin for a Christian to own a gun, because I understand and respect the sport of hunting. (It is possible to allow guns with limited capabilities for the sake of hunting or sport, but the widespread production of automatic and semi-automatic weapons serves no viable purpose but mass death.) Gun ownership is often justified by fear, as a defense against others. Those who are led by the spirit of fear instead of the Spirit of Life will prepare for violent retaliation because of their fears, but this is not the way of the crucified Christ. To own a gun for self-defense is to premeditate retaliation, but this is against the way of Jesus Christ who called us to love our enemies and do them no harm. As we argued in the sidebar to chapter seven, nonviolence is not optional in the Christian faith, it is essential.

The personal desire to own a gun in the midst of a violent and unredeemed world is understandable, but we have to, as Christians, reconcile this desire for self-preservation with the ethics of Jesus' call to love our enemies. Does gun-ownership truly align with Jesus' command to love our enemies as ourselves? Is the premeditation to do violence by gun-ownership an act of love? The call to love our enemies is not mere sentiment but involves the conscious decision to reject violent retaliation. How can we love our enemies if we plan to do them violence, even in the name of self-preservation? We plainly cannot do both. There are other practical means of self-defense which will not make us murderers. I do not mean to imply we should become passive victims. Concern for personal safety is valid, but there are alternative outlets besides the ownership of deadly weapons. Taking self-defense classes or better securing our homes, for example, would be solutions that do not involve premeditated counter-violence against our enemies.

Finally, it is important to remember that there will be no easy solution to issues such as gun-violence in America (or anywhere). However, it will take all of us, our creativity and our strength, to help live out the ethical requirements of God's Kingdom in the world today. As Moltmann writes, "Christian responsibility for the world requires an ethics for changing the world, based on the righteousness and peace which we believe in and try to live, in the discipleship of Christ" (*Ethics of Hope*, 206). The Church cannot remain on the sidelines, as a culture of death multiplies around us.

When in doubt, we must stand on the side of life. With the statistics mentioned above, it is impossible to stand for life and support the "rights" of unlimited gun-ownership at the same time. Guns are tools of death. To call them anything else would be an unethical de-radicalization of their clear purpose. They are killing tools. Supporting unrestricted access to tools of death is unethical. Even if you disagree, the smallest possibility that gun-ownership will hinder life should cause us a moment's pause. An ethic of hope always strives to further the cause of *life*. We cannot faithfully walk the narrow way which leads to life if we hold in our hand's weapons of death (Mt. 7:13-4).

> Christians, instead of arming themselves with swords [or guns!], extend their hands in prayer.

> — ATHANASIUS

9

THE SPIRIT OF LIFE

SUMMARY: A holistic doctrine of the Spirit embraces the experience of God in daily life. It is a mysticism of the mundane, in which God is found not in the reclusiveness of the soul but the fullness of life and the body.

IN MOLTMANN'S OWN WORDS:

The more I love God, the more gladly I exist. The more immediately and wholly I exist, the more I sense the living God, the inexhaustible source of life and eternal livingness.

— THE SOURCE OF LIFE, 88

SECONDARY QUOTES:

[In the traditional mysticism,] God is experienced in turning inward and upward, while for Moltmann God is experienced in turning outward and forward.

— RICHARD BAUCKHAM: THE THEOLOGY OF JÜRGEN MOLTMANN, 220

INTRODUCTION

The Spirit of Life was not in Moltmann's original plan for the systematic contributions, but it fits well within the trajectory set out by previous volumes. It is interesting to note one of the reasons he offers for the change. He notes that it was, in part, because of the interests of his doctoral students, many of whom wrote their dissertations on the Holy Spirit. It reveals a sense of humility at the heart of Moltmann's project. As we have noted before, for Moltmann, dialogue is essential to theology. That is not an empty claim. He took the insights of his students seriously enough to change the planned structure of his systematic work. In the academic world, I find this remarkable. A hierarchy of professors over their students often plagues academia; lacking the right qualifications is sometimes cause for exclusion from the conversation. Personally, this is encouraging for my own work. I have no qualifications, in the academic sense, and have often felt excluded from "serious" academia as a result. Moltmann's willingness to listen and learn from his students is a beautiful testimony to God's solidarity with outsiders.

HOLISTIC EXPERIENCE OF THE SPIRIT

This book initiates a new emphasis in Moltmann's theology, which he calls a "new theology of life" (*A Broad Place,* 345). Albert Camus once said that after the mass deaths of World War II, "It is Europe's mystery that life is no longer loved" (cited ibid., 347). What is needed most in a violent, post-war society is a new love for life, a love which embraces life in its entirety. Moltmann writes:

> I wrote [*The Spirit of Life*] with great enthusiasm and new love for life, because the subject led me to sectors of theology and spirituality which until then had been unknown to me. I gave it the subtitle A Holistic Pneumatology, because I did not want to separate the spiritual from the physical life, or spirituality from vitality, in the traditional manner.
>
> — IBID., 346

A holistic pneumatology involves acquiring "once more a concept of theological experience" (ibid., 347). We seldom give the experience of God the systematic attention it deserves in theology, but it is vital we regain a theological appreciation of the experience of the Spirit.

Moltmann highlights a simple question that "embarrasses us," namely, "When did you last feel the workings of the Holy Spirit?" (*The Spirit of Life,* x). We are often overwhelmed by our distance from God or our lack of religious experiences in secular life. It is perhaps better, then, to ask this question: "[W]hen were you last conscious of '*the spirit of life?*'" (ibid.). Because "[t]hen we can answer out of our own everyday experiences and can talk about our consolations and encouragements. Then 'spirit' is the love of life which delights us, and the energies of the spirit are the living energies which this love of life awakens in us" (ibid.). The difference is profound. When we think of the experience of God, we tend to imagine a sort of out-of-body phenomenon. The experience of God is, we *assume,* foreign to our daily lives. It is "holy" and therefore remote and unnatural. We need a better definition.

When we define the experience of God as something outside our humanity, then we struggle to recognize the workings of the Holy Spirit in our daily lives. But instead, what if we presupposed the experience of the Spirit to be *already* at work in us, and in turn, discovered the presence of God in the fullness of life? From this perspective, Moltmann writes:

> The Spirit of God is called the *Holy Spirit* because it makes our life here something living, not because it is alien and estranged from life. The Spirit sets this life in the presence of the living God and in the great river of eternal love. In order to bring out the unity between the experience of God and the experience of life, I shall be talking in this book about '*the Spirit of life*', and I should like to invite readers to open themselves for their own experiences, and to look at them for what they are.
>
> — THE SPIRIT OF LIFE, X

That is a radical break away from what we usually imagine as the experience of God. Mysticism, for example, has a long history in the Church, but it has often sought escape from daily life by its pursuit of an "interior castle" (Avila) or a "seven storey mountain" (Merton). Moltmann presents a mysticism of *everyday life.* "Probably this mysticism of everyday life is the deepest mysticism of all. The acceptance of the lowliness of one's own life is the true humility. Simple existence is life in God" (*Experiences of God*, 76).

Moltmann refuses to limit the Spirit of Life to a foreign spiritual land called "the soul," as Augustine did. The Spirit is not somewhere else; the Spirit is here in the fullness of everyday life. Existence itself means life in and with God. The idea that experiences of the Spirit involve a mystical escape into the recesses of the soul is not in line with the Christian doctrine of the Holy Spirit, according to Moltmann. Instead, an appreciation of the bodily and earthly experience of the Spirit is as essential as the spiritual. Therefore, Moltmann writes:

> Where the Holy Spirit is present, God is present in a special way, and we experience God through our lives, which become wholly living from within. We experience whole, full, healed and redeemed life, experience it with all our senses. We feel and taste, we touch and see our life in God and God in our life. There are many names for God the Holy Spirit, but of them all the Comforter (Paraclete) and the well of life (*fons vitae*) are the names I like best.
>
> — THE SOURCE OF LIFE, 10

The experience of the Spirit permeates all of life and not just the small portion of life we often deem more "spiritual" than the rest. "By experience of the Spirit I mean an awareness of God in, with and beneath the experience of life, which gives us assurance of God's fellowship, friendship and love" (*The Spirit of Life*, 17). We have reversed the Lord's Prayer from "your kingdom come *on earth* as it is in heaven" into "let us escape up into your kingdom from the earth." Escapism is again one of Moltmann's chief opponents. There can be no experience of the Spirit which excludes any aspect of our lives, from the mundane and rudimentary acts we do mindlessly, to the mountaintop experiences, all the way down to the greatest sorrows and fears—the Spirit is present in all things. "The eternal life of God's Spirit is not a different life from this life here; it is the power that makes this life here different" (*The Source of Life*, 22).

This is perhaps best understood in contrast with Augustine. In the

Confessions, Augustine describes the love of God in the interior reclusion of the soul:

> But what do I love when I love you? Not the beauty of any body or the rhythm of time in its movement; not the radiance of light, so dear to our eyes; not the sweet melodies in the world of manifold sounds; not the perfume of flowers, ointments and spices; not manna and not honey; not the limbs so delightful to the body's embrace: it is none of these things that I love when I love my God. And yet when I love my God I do indeed love a light and a sound and a perfume and a food and an embrace—a light and sound and perfume and food and embrace in my inward self. There my soul is flooded with a radiance which no space can contain; there a music sounds which time never bears away; there I smell a perfume which no wind disperses; there I taste a food that no surfeit embitters; there is an embrace which no satiety severs. It is this that I love when I love my God.
>
> — CONFESSIONS, X, 6, 8

The Spirit of Life is not confined to the narrow spaces of the soul, however. Moltmann, on the night he first read Augustine's description of the experience of God, wrote this response:

> When I love God I love the beauty of bodies, the rhythm of movements, the shining of eyes, the embraces, the feelings, the scents, the sounds of all this protean creation. When I love you, my God, I want to embrace it all, for I love you with all my senses in the creations of your love. In all the things that encounter me, you are waiting for me.
>
> For a long time I looked for you within myself and crept into the shell of my soul, shielding myself with an armour of inapproachability. But you were outside—outside myself—and enticed me out of the narrowness of my heart into the broad place of love for life. So I came out of myself and found my soul in my senses, and my own self in others.
>
> The experience of God deepens the experiences of life. It does not reduce them. For it awakens the unconditional Yes to life. The more I love God, the more gladly I exist. The more immediately and wholly I

exist, the more I sense the living God, the inexhaustible source of life and eternal livingness.

— A BROAD PLACE, 350

The experience of the Holy Spirit in the fullness of life does not negate our humanity or circumvent our senses. We meet the Spirit of Life whenever we say Yes to life and reject apathy. The Spirit of God is not distant from the experiences of life, but God meets us in every moment. Our life springs from this Source, and our home is the vast spaces of the Triune life of love.

Contemplate the question Moltmann asks: "When were you last conscious of the *Spirit of Life?*" If we *begin* with the conviction that God is *already* active in every moment of our lives, then the Spirit will awaken our senses to the experience of God in everyday life.

THE SPIRIT OF HOPE

But lest we imagine that a kind of new-age spirituality is present here, Moltmann is clear that this is no other Spirit than the Spirit of Jesus Christ: "I am also choosing the phrase 'experience of the Spirit' as a way of understanding appropriately the intermediate state of every historical experience between remembered past and expected future. [...] The experience of the Spirit is never without the remembrance of Christ, and never without the expectation of his future" (*The Spirit of Life*, 17). It is a Christological pneumatology. The experience of the Spirit includes the remembrance of Christ and the expectation of His coming Kingdom.

Moltmann offers a brief "Meditation on Hope" in the short companion book to his pneumatology, *The Source of Life*. Here Moltmann writes that "the ultimate reason for our hope is not to be found at all in what we want, wish for and wait for; the ultimate reason is that we are wanted and wished for and waited for" (*The Source of Life*, 40).

Hope is a core element of Moltmann's theology, an insight upon which his reputation often rests. However, Christian hope is not primarily *our* hope in God. That is what we come to discover in the experience of the Spirit. In the Spirit, we experience hope because we experience *God's hope* for us, and thus we are awakened to a corresponding hope. We are not merely propelled ahead by the remembrance of Christ; we are *pulled forward* by the expectation of God's future. That is the experience of the Spirit; we live between the unredeemed present and the God who waits for us and hopes for us.

Moltmann writes:

> Whenever we base our hope on trust in the divine mystery, we feel deep down in our hearts: there is someone who is waiting for you, who is hoping for you, who believes in you. We are waited for as the prodigal son in the parable is waited for by his father. We are accepted and received, as a mother takes her children into her arms and comforts them. God is our last hope because we are God's first love. We are God's dream for his world and his image on the earth he loves. God is waiting for his human beings to become truly human. That is why in us, too, there is a longing to be true human beings. God is waiting for human human beings; that is why he suffers from all the inhumanities which we commit personally and politically. God is waiting for his image, his echo, his response in us. That is why he is still patient with us and endures the expanse of ruins in our history of violence and suffering. God isn't silent. God isn't dead. God is waiting. To be able to wait is the strongest strength. God is patient with us and puts up with us. God gives us time and gives us future.
>
> — IBID., 40-1

God awaits the homecoming of creation. God endures suffering because God is patient. That does not explain away suffering or ignore it. Instead, it is a powerful reminder of God's *co*-suffering love, the love which suffers with us and waits for us. In a reversal of Augustine's famous phrase, "Our heart is restless until it finds its rest in thee," Moltmann writes: "God is restless in his Spirit until he finds rest in us and in his world" (Ibid., 41). We are restless because of God's restlessness, and together we journey to the new creation of all things in which God will be "all in all."

Apathy, Hope, and the Deadliness of Death

In hope, we reject the apathy of modernity and once again say Yes to life. In the experience of the Spirit, we suffer the pain of an unredeemed present precisely because we anticipate the coming newness of all things. Thus the Spirit draws us towards the future without negating hope for the present. Hope is a *command*, then, to resist death and the powers of death. It is "a command to love life and cherish it" (*The Source of Life*, 39). Hope is resistance against apathy. "We experience the power of hope when we have to fight against our apathy of soul" (ibid.).

Saying Yes to life means we open ourselves up to the experience of suffering. That is, we do not shut ourselves off in a mode of impenetrability, but remain vulnerable and sensitive to life. "The way we live and the profundity with which we affirm life," Moltmann writes, "decides how we experience the deadliness of death" (*The Coming of God*, 77). The deadliness of death grows the more we embrace life and reject apathy. A truly apathetic person has no fear of death because they have no lust for life, but the person who embraces life will suffer more. Moltmann writes, "The more passionately we love life, the more we also experience the pain of life and the deadliness of death" (*The Passion for Life*, 25).

By rejecting the image of an apathetic (impassible) God, we recognize the need to fight apathy in ourselves. As those who embrace life, we suffer with God in tender love for the world. It is better to embrace life and suffer than to reject life and remain indifferent and cold to its effects. That is what it means for us to be the people of the passionate God, as Moltmann writes:

> If we were to live in a covenant with this passionate God, we would not become apathetic. Our whole life would be shaped by sympathy, by compassion. We would suffer with God's suffering in the world, and rejoice with God's rejoicing over the world. We would do both at the same time and with the highest intensity because we would love, and with the love of God we would go outside ourselves.
>
> — Ibid., 23

The people of God, those who are filled with the Holy Spirit and follow the way of Jesus Christ, share in God's *pathos*; they go outside of themselves and give themselves over in solidarity with the suffering and joy of others. That is the paradox of life in God: "Those who find their life will lose it, and those who lose their life for my sake will find it" (Mt. 10:39, NRSV). Apathy offers the illusion that we might escape the deadliness of death by diminishing love for life, but an unloved life is a life unlived. We must follow the passionate God into the love for life which includes the vulnerability to suffer personally and with others, to be moved by passion.

A NEW SPIRITUALITY OF THE SENSES

"The 'salvation of the soul' that belongs to the Augustinian tradition must be thrown open for God and the body, for social salvation and the salvation of groaning nature" (*The Living God and the Fullness of Life*, 159). This holistic and expansive vision of salvation is a sharp challenge to Western expressions of Christianity, especially the evangelical Church in America. The reclusive place called "the soul" cannot be the only focus of the Gospel, for Moltmann, and this leads him to develops a spirituality of the body and the senses. Our souls are not saved *from* the body but together *with* it; therefore, spirituality means the awakening of *all* our senses to life in the Spirit.

Spirituality has often been abusive to the body, and this is plainly recognized in mystical traditions of monastic reclusion from social and bodily needs. In extreme examples, it is also apparent in the physical acts of self-abasement such as the old Catholic practice of flagellation, in which a devout believer would beat their back with a whip. The Spirit is thought to be at war with the flesh, and thus we must subdue the flesh by its starvation or its abuse (both through mental or physical disdain). But that is a mistaken reading of Paul's famous dualism between the flesh and the spirit (Gal. 5:17). Paul does not use these terms in the same way we would use them today. "Flesh" has little to do with the muscles and organs of our body, and "Spirit" is not a reference to some higher nature or our brains. Instead, Moltmann notes, "Essentially the apostle was an apocalyptist, and he thinks about world history in terms of the two great world aeons. Here we have the transitory world-time of sin and death; there we shall see the new world-time of righteousness, justice and eternal life" (*The Source of Life*, 72). That follows the insights of Ernst Käsemann, the respected New Testament scholar who was also one of Moltmann's professors at Göttingen and later colleagues at Tübingen. The "flesh," then, is the unredeemed present that longs for the future, while the "spirit" is the new creation that is to come.

The new creation includes the new heaven and the new *earth*. It is not a gnostic or platonic vision of a purely spiritualized existence. As we noted in chapter two, Moltmann's hope is not in "going to heaven" when we die, but in the resurrection to new life. Resurrection means the redemption of the body and not its demise. Therefore, Moltmann writes:

> We shall not be redeemed *from* this earth, so that we could give it up. We shall be redeemed *with* it. We shall not be redeemed *from* the body. We shall be made eternally alive with the body. That is why the original hope of Christians was not turned towards another world in heaven, but looked for the coming of God and his kingdom on this earth. We human beings are earthly creatures, not candidates for angelic status.
>
> — IBID., 74

The Spirit is the "dawn of God's coming new world" (*The Living God and the Fullness of Life*, 158). The Spirit *sanctifies* our senses, making us alive to the presence of God. Paul implied this when he called our bodies the "temple of the Holy Spirit" (1 Cor. 6:19). If the "flesh" is the same as our bodily life, and if the flesh is at odds with the Spirit, then how could the flesh become the *home* of the Spirit of God? It is clear that the flesh is not our bodies or our human senses, but the age that is passing away.

What does this new spirituality look like? Moltmann writes, "We shall not withdraw into ourselves in order to seek God, but shall go out of ourselves in order to experience God's presence with all our senses in the world outside. [...] [T]he person who finds God awakens to life in its fullness" (ibid., 161). We smell, hear, feel, taste, and see the world in all its beauty—we meet God in the fullness of life's abundance.

However, we have become apathetic to our senses in the modern world. We flood our lives with distraction, hurrying from one experience to the next, but we experience nothing. We seek after "fast food" and fast living, but our haste leaves us malnourished. We place ourselves in a world of plastics and disposables, distancing ourselves ever further from the earth. That is not to say that this new spirituality is *materialistic,* but it is more aptly deemed the cure for our empty materialism. Materialism derives from the anxiety of missing out on life; we hoard things in a desperate attempt to give our lives meaning and purpose. We fill our lives with the "stuff" that promised to make us happy, but it does not and cannot. We fail to *enjoy* the simple, human experiences of life that are all around us and trade them in for cheap substitutes. The spirituality of the senses is a cure for materialism because we are no longer anxious about missing anything, and instead, we expect God in all things. We become content and celebrate life for its own sake. "The whole creation is a great and wonderful sacraments of God's indwelling presence" (ibid., 171).

There is something wonderfully spiritual about sitting in the park with our loved ones, with nothing else to do but laugh, look at trees, and listen to birds singing. There is mysticism in a moment of calm reflection, in the slow cadence of breathing. In this new spirituality of the senses, all of life anticipates God. In all things, God is expecting us, and the spirituality of the senses means cultivating an expectation of God in all things. Moltmann writes:

> When we wake up in the morning we expect the new day; and in the same way, the waking which springs from prayer to God also leads to the expectation of God in the life we experience. I wake up, and open all my senses for life—for the fulfilments and for the disappointments, for what is painful as well as for what gives joy. I expect the presence of God in everything I meet and everything I do. His history with me, and with us, is an on-going history. There is nothing more exhilarating than to experience this life-history with God in full awareness. [...] People who know that there is someone who is waiting for them and expecting them never give themselves up. And we are expected.
>
> — In the End—The Beginning, 84-5

The experience of the Spirit is possible because the Spirit of Life envelops our lives. We do not have to look into ourselves to find God. God is waiting for us in the fullness of life, expecting us and creating in us the expectation of the Spirit in all things. We embrace and are embraced by God through our senses.

An example of how this new spirituality applies to our lives is in the way Moltmann understands prayer. The call to "pray and watch" goes hand in hand. We pray *wakefully*, in anticipation of God's future. We pray in the posture of expectation, ready to act for God's Kingdom. The early Church prayed with their hands outstretched to God, their faces turned upwards, and their eyes wide open, leaning forward in a profound posture of expectation. This position resembles that of a child stretching out to be picked up and embraced by a loving parent.

To pray wakefully means opening our eyes to the world around us. To pray with indifference to the sufferings of this world is not a Christian way of praying. We do not shut our eyes to pray. Prayer does not mean arriving at a higher plane where we can ignore the cries of the hopeless and the oppressed. On the contrary, prayer awakens us to a sober recognition of the unredeemed state of the world, and prayer gives us the courage to act for the sake of God's coming Kingdom. It is a luxury of the first world and of the privileged middle class to pray blindly. We must pray and watch with open eyes turned to the sufferings of this world, so that prayer seamlessly flows into passionate action.

Joy, too, is awakened by this kind of prayer. While opening our eyes to suffering, we become sensitive to joy, too. Apathy robs us of both pain *and* comfort. To pray is to embrace the world and reject apathy for the sake of the the Spirit of Life and the fullness of existence.

WHAT IS LIFE FOR?

What is the meaning of life? For what "purpose" are we here? These questions often cause us anxiety and fear, but the new spirituality of life provides a freeing response: *life is its own end.*

Moltmann writes:

> Joy is the meaning of human life. Human beings were created in order to have joy in God. They are born in order to have joy in life. [...] There is

no purpose or utilitarian goal for which human life is required. There are no ethical goals or ideal aims with which human life has to justify itself. Life itself is good. Existence is beautiful and to be here is glorious. We live in order to live.

— THE LIVING OF GOD AND THE FULLNESS OF LIFE, 195

The modern world is full of people searching for their purpose in a job or some other utilitarian goal, but all these things are merely a way to use our lives, not their purpose. The Spirit of Life causes us to recognize the beauty of existence itself. Modern industrial society has painted life as a dreadful, horrible thing. Nihilism and existentialism have caused us to be miserable people. Working for a paycheck or for obtaining a high social status has caused us to miss the life in life. The Spirit of Life opens us up to embrace the joy of life for its own sake. It is redemption *into* life not redemption *from* life. We are awakened by God to love and celebrate life in all its glory.

Moltmann writes:

The working world of the modern industrial society already trains kindergarten children with threatening existential questions of this kind, according to which the meaning of life is to be found in purpose and usefulness. But those who find the meaning of their lives in purpose and utility inevitably end up in life crises once they become disabled or old. The 'meaning' of life cannot be found outside life but in life itself. Life must not be misused as if it were a means to an end.

— IBID., 195-6

May we learn to celebrate life, to see that life itself is its own end and purpose because God has blessed us with existence. May we go outside of our reclusive interior in the expectation of meeting the Spirit of Life in our everyday experiences. God is with us and in us. We cannot escape the presence of God. Cultivating an expectation of life in the Spirit presupposes God's goodness and faithfulness.

SIDEBAR: LIVE SLOWLY

I realized a growing dependence in my life on my smart-phone, and on various other tech devices including the internet. I found myself spending hours a day mindlessly scrolling Facebook, Twitter, or reading news stories. So I decided to do something about it, to consciously take a step away from the digital world and *enter life.* I decided to live slowly, even if just for one day a week, and to remember what life was like before instant distractions. Inspired by Moltmann's theology of life, I decided that every Sunday from now on I would live technology free: no internet, phone, or computer.

This experience has taught me that one of the greatest signs of our apathy to life is in how often we are willing to give in to distractions. On the first morning of my technology-fast, I was overwhelmed by how often I felt the urge to grab my phone or check my notifications. I began to realize that these distractions were nothing less than an escape from facing life head-on. Every time I choose distraction I reject life.

It was not long until my Sunday technology-fast became the highlight of my week. I re-entered life. I learned to live slowly. I embraced boredom and resisted every urge to ease boredom with distraction. I paid attention to the simple things. Uncomfortable thoughts or fears would sometimes confront me. Any other day and I would have reached for my phone and avoided these feelings. I resisted the temptation and met the Comforter waiting for me on the other side of my sadness. If we resist suffering we close ourselves off to joy as well; we reject the Comforter.

The modern world is blazing fast. It has no time for boredom, for melancholy, for imagination. *There is no time for life.*

> The modern world offers us countless opportunities for life and experience, but our lives are short. The unconscious fear of missing out on something, or of being done out of something, is a tremendous accelerator in the way we live—and it is not for nothing that the résumé we present on applying for a job is called a *curriculum vitae*—the 'race' of our lives. Everything about us is modernized faster and faster, and we hurry and rush from one place to another in order to experience something. We collect more and more experiences, and consume more and more rapidly without any apparent limitation of the speed. Fast food—fast life! But it is only the person who lives slowly who really experiences something of life. It is only if we digest what we experience that we have experienced something. It is only if we eat slowly that we enjoy what we eat. It is only if we can pause over an impression that we can absorb it. The unconscious fear of death hounds us through life, and life passes us by as we hurry past it. And yet we do not have to run after every possibility. One reality is of more value than a thousand possibilities.

> — In the End—The Beginning, 122

Technology can be a tremendous blessing, but more often than not it becomes an escape from fully embracing life. We have become slaves to the devices we use. We resist the sadnesses we feel and reach for distraction. We resist the melancholy feeling of growing old. We resist our deep fears of never being good enough, of failure or disappointment. We resist the fear of insignificance. However, when we distract ourselves from all these things, we distract ourselves from life. A culture of fast-living has led to a profound apathy for life. Indeed, "It is only the person who lives slowly who really enters into life" (*The Coming of God*, 57).

My technology-fast led me to realize how much I had become a slave to distraction and apathy. I cannot say I have become entirely free, but I have become aware of my apathy, and that is half the battle. The Holy Spirit, the Spirit of Life, is waiting in those moments of boredom and in the silent sadnesses and joys we distract ourselves from. If we do not let ourselves experience sorrow, how could we also expect to meet the Comforter? This apathy is nothing less than our resistance against the Spirit of Life, but God is gracious and faithful to us. God's Spirit will awaken in us a renewed love for life, in all its boredom and sadness, but also joy. That is what it means to experience the presence of God in our modern world of distractions and apathy, as Moltmann writes:

> To experience the presence of the eternal God brings our temporal life as if into an ocean which surrounds us and buoys us up when we swim in it. In this way the divine presence surrounds us from every side, as Psalm 139 says, like a wide space for living which even finite death cannot restrict. In this divine presence we can affirm our limited life and accept its limits. We will then become serene and relaxed, and will begin to live slowly and with delight.

— GOD FOR A SECULAR SOCIETY, 90

THE COMING OF GOD

SUMMARY: Eschatology is concerned first and foremost with the future of God, with *divine* eschatology. Every personal, historical, and cosmic eschatology depends on and is included in the hope of God's future joy. Here we pay particular attention to Moltmann's "universalism of the cross," but it is only within the context of divine eschatology that personal eschatology can be adequately understood.

IN MOLTMANN'S OWN WORDS:

The key promise for the development of my eschatology is to be found in Isaiah's vision: 'The whole earth is full of his glory' (6:3).

— GOD WILL BE ALL IN ALL, 39

I don't want to go to heaven. Heaven is there for the angels, and I am a child of the earth. But I expect passionately the world to come: The new heaven and the new earth where justice dwells, where God will wipe away every tear and make all things new. And this expectation makes life in this world for me, here and now, most lovable.

— "CLAREMONT LECTURE," 2014

The Christian doctrine of hell is to be found in the gospel of Christ's descent into hell [...]. He suffered the torments of hell so that for us they are not hopeless and without escape. Christ brought hope to the place where according to Dante all who enter must 'abandon hope'. 'If I make my bed in hell thou art there' (Ps 139:8). Through his sufferings Christ has destroyed hell. Hell is open: 'Hell where is thy victory?' (1 Cor 15:55).

— God Will be All in All, 46

Secondary quotes:

The greatest strength of Moltmann's universalism is that it is a universalism of the cross rooted in (an understanding of) what God has done in Christ. Questions of [...] whether God could have done otherwise than love us and save us become secondary to our responsibility as theologians to reflect on what God has actually done [...]. For Moltmann, therefore, God's freedom is certainly not eclipsed but is, together with God's nature, God's love, and God's will, revealed in (the redemption of) history.

In this sense, Moltmann's 'universalism of the cross', whether we agree with it or not, is first and foremost not a 'theological' proposal; it is a claim about what is revealed to us by God in Jesus Christ.

— Nicholas Ansell: The Annihilation of Hell, 371

INTRODUCTION

"In my end is my beginning." With this T. S. Eliot ends "East Coker" from his celebrated poem, *Four Quartets*. Moltmann borrows this phrase, calling it, "The dialectical mystery of Christian eschatology," and states, "Christ's end on the cross was not the last thing, but became his true beginning in the resurrection and in the Spirit who is the giver of life" (*Science and Wisdom*, 75). In the end is the beginning: this is the mystery of Christian eschatology.

Eschatology is hope, as we saw in chapter two. It is not the doctrine of "last things," as the term implies, but of the new beginning promised and founded upon Christ's resurrection. In *The Coming of God,* Moltmann presents an eschatological vision of the dawn of God's coming Kingdom. As the title suggests, the emphasis is not merely on the future of humanity or the earth, but Moltmann's emphasis is on *God's* coming, on *God's* new beginning together with all things. With a focus on divine eschatology, Moltmann discusses the personal, historical, and cosmic dimensions of hope.

We will first step back to see the big picture. Bauckham identifies seven characteristics of Moltmann's eschatology, which provide us with a helpful overview. From there we will explore two of the central issues in Moltmann's eschatology. First, we will complement our discussion on creation (chapter six) with an explanation of Moltmann's grand vision of God's de-restriction, in which God will be "all in all." Second, we will discuss a personal eschatology of hope for universal salvation, and thus explore Moltmann's universalism of the cross.

SEVEN CHARACTERISTICS

Richard Bauckham offers a helpful outline of the seven unique characteristics of Moltmann's eschatology (*God Will Be All in All,* 1-34). Moltmann's work is 1) Christological, 2) integrative, 3) redemptive, 4) processive, 5) theocentric, 6) contextual, and 7) politically/pastorally responsible. We will explain each of these in turn.

1. CHRISTOLOGICAL

Eschatology is best understood in the light of the history of Jesus Christ, just as the history of Jesus Christ is understood best in the light of eschatology. This interrelationship has always been a unique aspect of Moltmann's theology, seen as early as *Theology of Hope.* A central thesis of that early book was, "There can be no christology without eschatology and no eschatology without christology" (*History and the Triune God,* 193 n. 28).

It is helpful to see here that Moltmann's eschatology presupposes much of his early work, especially *Theology of Hope, The Way of Jesus Christ,* and *God in Creation.* As we saw in these books, there is an eschatological dimension to everything in the Christian faith, including creation and the person and life of Christ. It is "Jesus Christ and *his* future" that is the subject of Christian eschatology (*Theology of Hope,* 17). Moreover, as we saw, creation itself is eschatologically oriented, since God's self-limitation implies a coming "de-restriction" of God's presence.

Moltmann's eschatological reflections, therefore, are not speculative guesses about the future. Instead, it is crucial to see that the whole of Moltmann's eschatology is an extension of Christology.

2. *INTEGRATIVE*

By integrative, Bauckham means Moltmann's "fundamental principle" to be eschatologically "all-embracing" (*God Will Be All in All,* 10). As Moltmann writes:

> [T]rue hope must be universal, because its healing future embraces every individual and the whole universe. If we were to surrender hope for as much as one single creature, for us God would not be God.

> — THE COMING OF GOD, 132

Christian eschatology has far too often been individualistic or human-centric, focused on questions of personal salvation. However, Moltmann's vision of the future is all-embracing because our hope is not "heaven" but the new creation of all things. As Paul writes in Romans 8, creation "groans" for redemption. To exclude the future of the earth—or indeed anything or anyone—from our eschatological hope would be a mistake. Therefore, Bauckham writes:

> Integrative eschatology recognizes that the new creation must be all-encompassing. As Moltmann says of all the experiences of a human life, of all human beings and of the whole cosmos: nothing will be lost, all will be restored [...]. If God's soteriological (and so eschatological) work were a matter of redeeming some parts or aspects of his creation, while leaving the rest to perish, God would cease to be the Creator (cf. [*The Coming of God*] 269-270). Thus the unity and consistency of God's relationship to his creation requires that new creation be all-

encompassing. Indeed, if God were to allow any of his creatures to be lost, he would not be true to himself ([*Ibid.*] 255).

— GOD WILL BE ALL IN ALL, 11-2

Since God did not create human beings *alone* but brought an entire universe into being, then eschatology must include the whole of creation, or else God would not be faithful to Godself as the creator of all things. Moltmann presupposes his doctrine of creation which emphasized its *unfinished* nature. Creation, from the beginning, is oriented eschatologically towards the new creation. So here Moltmann insists that eschatology must have something to say about the redemption of creation, which includes the final Sabbath rest and unhindered Shekinah in which God will be at home in the world.

3. REDEMPTIVE

The coming of God means the ultimate end of sin, evil, death, and transience. For Moltmann, however, there is a unique distinction. While sin and evil disrupted God's creation, transience and death belonged to the original order of creation itself. Moltmann does not think that death is the consequence of sin, but that it reveals the imperfection of the original creation. Therefore, the coming of God means the *completion* of an incomplete creation. Death and transience will be no more, not because of sin, but because the original creation was incomplete. The new creation is not the return to a primordial state of perfection, but the redemption of creation into a new state of being, which includes overcoming death and transience.

4. PROCESSIVE

With this category, Bauckham articulates the fact that, "Moltmann speaks of an eschatological process which begins with the resurrection of Jesus and will reach its goal in the new creation of all things" (*God Will Be All in All*, 20). He notes that 1 Corinthians 15:20-28 is essential to Moltmann's vision, in which we read:

But in fact Christ has been raised from the dead, the first fruits of those who have died. For since death came through a human being, the resurrection of the dead has also come through a human being; for as all die in Adam, so all will be made alive in Christ. But each in his own order: Christ the first fruits, then at his coming those who belong to Christ. Then comes the end, when he hands over the kingdom to God the Father, after he has destroyed every ruler and every authority and power. For he must reign until he has put all his enemies under his feet. The last enemy to be destroyed is death. For 'God has put all things in subjection under his feet.' But when it says, 'All things are put in subjection,' it is plain that this does not include the one who put all things in subjection under him. When all things are subjected to him, then the Son himself will also be subjected to the one who put all things in subjection under him, so that God may be all in all.

— NRSV

This passage explores an eschatological *process*, which began with the bodily resurrection of Jesus Christ. Next is the resurrection of those that belong to Christ at His *parousia*, and finally the resurrection of all the dead and the end of death itself. This process is a part of the Trinitarian history of God, as Bauckham writes, "[T]he risen Christ is given the rule by his Father, and rules until he has subjected all things to his rule, when he finally hands back the kingdom to the Father" (*God Will Be All in All*, 21).

The importance of seeing eschatology as a process results in Moltmann's somewhat surprising argument for millenarianism. He argues it is necessary for Christian eschatology to retain hope in the millennium reign of Christ because this provides space for healing and growth before the reign of the Father. The millennium functions as a kind of transition.

However, he has been criticized for this decision. (In the companion volume to Moltmann's eschatology, *God Will be All in All*, many of the commentators criticized millenarianism as a weakness of his eschatology.) However, it is essential for Moltmann to include hope for *Israel* in his eschatological vision. There is no genuinely Christian eschatology which gives up hope for the Jewish people. Thus, the millennium reign of Christ is an essential aspect of the process of God's future. Furthermore, it is vital to affirm Christ's millennium reign because eschatological hope is chiefly for "combatants, not onlookers" (*The Coming of God,* 146). This move is also, then, to offers hope for *martyrs* to one day share in Christ's thousand year reign. We will not explore any further the details of Moltmann's millenarianism, but it was worth briefly noting why he considers it essential to retain.

5. THEOCENTRIC

The expectation of God's unrestricted presence in all creation is central to Christian hope. It is the "goal of creation as a whole and of all individual created beings" (*The Coming of God,* 318). All creation looks forward to God's indwelling presence, to the unmediated and direct manifestation of God's glory. The new creation of all things is the *result* of the arrival of God; God's coming is not merely a secondary aspect of Christian hope, it is the *essential* element. Creation is incomplete until God finds rest in it.

6. CONTEXTUAL

Eschatology is not an isolated consideration, but bound to the influence of history. With this Bauckham means Moltmann's awareness of the historical context shaping his eschatological reflection, as Bauckham writes:

> Contemporary eschatology needs to be self-aware and self-critical with respect to its relationship to its own tradition and its own context, and must engage in assessment and critique of the eschatologies, religious and secular, which are influential in its context.
>
> It is a merit of Moltmann's eschatology in *The Coming of God* that it incorporates a strong interpretation of its historical and global context. [...] In doing so it offers an eschatological critique of the distorted and destructive eschatologies of the modern period and brings the redemptive vision of an eschatology based on the cross and resurrection of Jesus Christ to bear on the damage that modern eschatologies have done and are doing.
>
> — GOD WILL BE ALL IN ALL, 25-6

Nineteenth-century eschatology is an example of what happens when eschatology fails to criticize the status quo. In this period, there arose a strong faith in the progress of history, both in its secular and religious form. Christian eschatology often gave into this faith in progress, but for Moltmann, this is the opposite of the contextual role of eschatology. Christian hope in the coming of God places us in conflict with the status quo, including the progress of history. Modern society, whenever it asserts power over history and faith in progress, must be confronted with the Christian hope of God's future reign. Secular hope often comes at the expense of the poor and weak in society, but Christian hope is precisely the hope *of* the poor and oppressed. That means, in other words, that Christian hope is a critic of all forms of worldly hope *in* history (we called this "utopian" hope in chapter 2). Where modernity promises a bright future at the cost of oppressing the weak, Christian hope is in the justice of God that causes the first to be last and the last to be first. Christian hope is incongruent with faith in "progress" for progress' sake.

7. *POLITICALLY AND PASTORALLY RESPONSIBLE*

This aspect is close to what we just considered, as Bauckham writes, "[C]ontextual eschatology and politically responsible eschatology are really two sides of a coin." (*God Will Be All in All,* 33). Eschatology not only has implications in its historical context, but Christian hope has profoundly helpful things to say to us personally and pastorally. It is never merely theoretical, and there is always a sharply pastoral edge to what Moltmann writes. The big questions and fears we face tend to be eschatological, such as the fear of death and questions about the fate of loved ones. Any eschatology worth the paper its printed on will have something to say to these questions and fears.

DIVINE ESCHATOLOGY

What does eschatology mean *for God?* That is the question Moltmann considers in the final chapter of *The Coming of God.* Here Moltmann presents divine eschatology in the context of God's glorification. What does God's glory consist of? Moltmann considers four proposals: 1) the self-glorification of God, 2) the self-realization of God, 3) the interactions between divine and human activity, and 4) the fullness of God and the feast of eternal joy. Only this final answer, for Moltmann, fully expresses the true glory of God's future.

With a bit of poetic flourish, Moltmann describes what he means by describing God's future glory as the fullness of God and the feast of eternal joy:

> The feast of eternal joy is prepared by the fulness of God and the rejoicing of all created being. [...] Inappropriate though human analogy is bound to be, in thinking of the fulness of God we can best talk about the inexhaustibly rich *fantasy of God*, meaning by that his creative imagination. From that imagination life upon life proceeds in protean abundance. If creation is transfigured and glorified, as we have shown, then creation is not just the free decision of God's will; nor is it an outcome of his self-realization. It is like a great song or a splendid poem or a wonderful dance of his fantasy, for the communication of his divine plenitude. The laughter of the universe is God's delight. It is the universal Easter laughter.
>
> — THE COMING OF GOD, 338-9

Moltmann would sometimes quote Athanasius, who said, "The risen Christ makes life a continual festival, a festival without end" (cited in *Experiences of God,* 31). This is the Christian hope: to join in God's glorious festival of life without end. The "universal Easter laughter" of God's delight is not only the goal of creation and existence but God's goal and therefore God's glorification. This vision has been implicit in all of Moltmann's work but receives individual attention here. Moltmann hinted towards this vision of glorification in the very first of his systematic contributions:

> To throw open the circulatory movement of the divine light and the divine relationships, and to take men and women, with the whole of creation, into the life-stream of the triune God: that is the meaning of creation, reconciliation, and glorification.
>
> — THE TRINITY AND THE KINGDOM, 178

Moltmann's eschatology centers around the Sabbath rest of God in and with creation, God's Shekinah. In the end, God will be "all in all." All existence will be permeated with God's delight, bask in God's love, and swim in the ocean of the Triune *perichoresis.*

PERSONAL ESCHATOLOGY

Moltmann writes, as we noted above, "If we were to surrender hope for as much as one single creature, for us God would not be God" (*The Coming of God,* 132). Naturally, we might ask: What about hell? Does this mean the redemption of all things (universalism)? The short answer is yes, though it should be qualified. Moltmann's universalism is uniquely a *universalism of the cross.*

It will be helpful if we begin with the "confession of hope" Moltmann learned from Christoph Blumhardt:

> The confession of hope has completely slipped through the church's fingers ... There can be no question of God's giving up anything or anyone in the whole world, either today or in eternity ... The end has to be: Behold, everything is God's! Jesus comes as the one who has borne the sins of the world. Jesus can judge but not condemn. My desire is to have preached this as far as the lowest circles of hell, and I will never be confounded.
>
> — CITED IBID., 254-5

"Behold, everything is God's!" is a startlingly triumphant declaration, but empty speculation is not its root. Trust in God's sovereignty is a strong driving force behind much of Moltmann's theology. If God is sovereign and wills for none to be lost, then our hope is all-embracing. Moltmann once confessed, "If I examine myself seriously, I find that I have to say: I myself am not a universalist, *but God may be one*" (*Jesus Christ for Today's World,* 143; emphasis mine). It is important to notice that the question is ultimately *God's* question. Even in the example above, the problem of giving up hope for anything or anyone is ultimately a breach on the Godness of God. In the end, it is the faithfulness of God which is at stake. The question is not, "Are we universalists?" The proper question is, "Will God give up on anyone? Will God remain faithful to creation?"

Moltmann's understanding of what it means for human beings to be created in the image of God is helpful in this regard. The image of God in humanity is not limited to the soul, as Augustine thought. Instead, to be in the image of God is to be relational. We saw this in Moltmann's social doctrine of the Trinity. We are not correctly God's likeness when we are in isolation from others, but only in fellowship with others. And the most essential relationship of our personhood is the one we have with God. However, it is not merely *our* relationship with God that is essential; it is God's relationship to us. In other words, while the relationship we have with God may become strained or full of doubt, *God's relationship to us remains unchanged.* Our very identity is found here in God's faithfulness. We are those whom God loves, and to whom God will be faithful. Even in death, even in sin, even in the darkness of our suffering—God is faithful.

So the question is not, "Who is in a relationship with God?"—as if to imply that our ability to maintain this relationship is what saves us. The question is, "Will God give up even a single atom of creation? Will God's faithfulness fail anyone?" What it means to be a human being, in other words, is not defined by the relationship *we* have with God. It is unequivocally God's relationship with us that matters most. Universalism is simply a consistent trust in God's faithfulness to creation. It is the hope that the end will be: "Behold, everything is God's!" (Blumhardt). If God were to give up on anything or anyone that God has made, it would be against the very Godness of God. *That* is why the question is not "Are we universalists?" or "Is Moltmann a universalist?" The only question that matters is, *"Is God?"*

The strength of Moltmann's universalism of the cross is that it is not a speculative conclusion to his theology but rather a presupposition based on the revelation of God in Christ. It is a certain hope which plainly confesses: *this is what the crucified God is like.* The God who was in Christ "reconciling the world to Himself" is the God who will remain faithful even in the sharpest contradiction of our sin and darkness. It is thus a universalism of the cross that Moltmann argues.

It is important to recognize that this is not a "hoping for the best" kind of universalism, as if this is just a nice idea we hope to be true.

No, it is a *confident* hope fixated on the faithfulness of God. The same God that raised Christ from the dead, from the pit of hell and suffering, is the same God who promised to do the same on a cosmic scale, who promised the new creation. It is the theology of the cross that offers the strongest defense of universal hope, and more specifically, Christ's descent into hell is central for Moltmann. Ansell calls this is a "pre-theological" position, meaning it is not a conclusion of Moltmann's theology but a presupposition derived from the cross. Ansell writes:

> [Moltmann] insists that because the revelation of God's purposes in the Christ event has already taken place, a hope that is rooted in the cross is not simply an expression of what we would like to happen. Given God's decisive action in Christ, we can be confident of the outcome: 'What Christ accomplished in his dying and rising is proclaimed to all human beings through his gospel and will be revealed to everyone and everything at his appearance.' [...] This has nothing to do with merely 'hoping for the best'. For hope, in Moltmann's theology, provides the way to certainty. And the cross provides the way to hope. In 'submerg[ing] ourselves in the depths of Christ's death on the cross,' Moltmann writes, '...we find the certainty of reconciliation without limits.'
>
> — THE ANNIHILATION OF HELL, 39-40

Universalism is a "certain hope," for Moltmann, because of the cross of Christ. Because Christ suffered the torments of hell, of God-forsakenness, and was raised to new life, we proclaim with certainty Christ's triumph over hell.

Therefore, Moltmann *does* believe in "hell," but only as that which Christ has overcome. In an interview, Moltmann was asked about the role of hell in his theology of hope. He replied:

> I believe in Christ's Descent to hell. He came back and declared: 'I have the keys to death and hell!' What does He does with these keys? He opens them up of course! When you think of hell, you should never think about it in the context of the question whether you yourself or

someone else is going there, but always look to Christ. In His wounds, death and hell have been overcome.

— BERNDT: "AN INTERVIEW WITH MOLTMANN"

If we ask ourselves, "Do we know anyone who is in hell?", the only Christian response is one name and one name alone: Jesus Christ. Moreover, since it is only possible to say with certainty that *Christ* entered hell, then hell is not without hope. A theology of the cross, of Christ's descent into hell, is the most potent defense of our universal hope. Moltmann writes:

> The *Christian* doctrine about the restoration of all things denies neither damnation nor hell. On the contrary: it assumes that in his suffering and dying Christ suffered the true and total hell of God-forsakenness for the reconciliation of the world, and experienced for us the true and total damnation of sin. It is precisely here that the divine reason for the reconciliation of the universe is to be found. It is not the optimistic dream of a purified humanity; it is Christ's descent into hell that is the ground for the confidence that nothing will be lost but that everything will be brought back again and gathered into the eternal kingdom of God. *The true Christian foundation for the hope of universal salvation is the theology of the cross, and the realistic consequence of the theology of the cross can only be the restoration of all things.* [...] Christ gave himself up for lost in order to seek all who are lost, and to bring them home. He suffered the torments of hell, in order to throw hell open. [...] Through his sufferings Christ has destroyed hell.

> — THE COMING OF GOD, 251, 253-4; ITALICS ORIGINAL

This link between Christ's descent into hell and universal hope is not an insight original to Moltmann. It has roots in the Apostles' Creed, which confesses Christ's descent into hell, but it may also be discovered all throughout the Christian tradition. In the ancient city of Aquileia, Italy, for example, the universalism of the cross was professed through a unique Easter Eve tradition (also known as Holy Saturday). Moltmann highlights this fascinating example of early Christian universalism because their confession centered around Christ's descent into hell. The *Credo Aquileiensis*, pronounced on Holy Saturday, declares:

> When Christ, the king of glory, entered the underworld to destroy it, and the angelic choir called upon the princes to lift up their gates before his face, the people of the saints, held captive by death, cried out with tears: Thou hast come, O desired One, for whom we have waited in darkness so that this night thou might lead us captives out of the dungeon. To thee our sighs have risen, thee we sought with abundant lamentations. Thou hast been the hope of the despairing, the mighty consolation in our torments. Alleluia.
>
> — CITED IN SUN OF RIGHTEOUSNESS, ARISE!, 147

Above the entrance of hell, Dante supposed we would find the inscription, "Abandon hope all ye who enter here." However, if Christ has descended to the land of the dead, then hell itself is not without hope. "Theologically," Moltmann writes, the question of universal salvation "can be decided only in the framework of christology" (*The Coming of God*, 237). It is not empty speculation that leads Moltmann to arrive at his universal hope, but devotion to Christ and His cross. Christ holds the keys to death and hades (Rev. 1:18). Hell is not without hope.

It is interesting to consider here how the *pathos* love of God takes on new light (chapter 3). What is the great equalizer? Undoubtedly, death and suffering. There is nothing more universal. Moreover, if Christ has entered into our suffering and death so that no one suffers or dies apart from Christ, then to maintain a doctrine of hell would be to deny Christ the due "reward of His sufferings" (to borrow a phrase from the Moravians). That is to say, suffering and death are indeed the only universal guarantees in life, and Christ has embraced us in precisely those moments. Precisely in the darkness of the "hell" of our suffering and death, Christ has joined us there because His unquenchable love for us; we are not alone. Universalism begins here with the recognition of God's solidarity with every victim of suffering and death. Their future is also *God's*.

We recognized this insight when we related God's suffering to the victims of Auschwitz (chapter 3). The stories of those who suffer are not their's alone, but also God's. To give up hope for anyone would be to give up the very Godness of God, to give up the cross of Christ and God's solidarity with the victims of suffering. Moltmann's doctrine of God has at its center the cross of Christ (recall the icon we considered in chapter 5). Which means, in this context, that God has identified Godself unequivocally with the victims of suffering and death. The essence of who God is in Godself is revealed in God's solidarity with humanity. That is why if we surrender hope for anyone it would be at once to give up the Godness of God. It is for *God's sake* that we must not resign our hope to anything less than hope for all creation.

Moltmann's universalism of the cross regains the glorious triumph of Christ's sufferings. In the end, if anything or anyone is lost, then Christ's sufferings were insufficient and the cross failed. Indeed, "There can be no question of God giving up anything or anyone in the whole world, either today or in all eternity. The end must be: 'Behold, everything is God's!'" (Blumhardt). God is faithful to His promises. Nothing will be lost; God will abandon no one.

There are two possible objections, however, to this universal hope. First, that it denies free will. Second, that God does not desire the salvation of all, but instead, ordains some to reprobation and thus to hell. We will now turn to these objections.

FREE WILL?

What does this universal hope mean for free will? Are we *forced* to accept grace? Some have the idea that free will means we can choose to damn ourselves or save ourselves by accepting or rejecting grace. However, this relies on a wrongful idea of mutuality between God and human faith/unbelief, as if God's grace and human faith are on the same level. For Moltmann, "The doctrine of universal salvation is the expression of a boundless confidence in God," but the idea that free will results in a double-outcome (heaven and hell) is simply "the expression of a tremendous self-confidence on the part of human beings" (*The Coming of God*, 244).

It is a high form of pride and human-centric egotism whenever we imagine that *we* can make such a decision. It essentially makes God *dispensable* for salvation. According to free will, God is ultimately just a *tool* we use in deciding *for ourselves* whether to be saved or damned; God is not the determining factor, *we are*. We are the venders of our own bliss or torment. That is why Moltmann concluded, "The logic of hell is, in my opinion, in the last resort atheistic" ("The End of Everything is God," 264). When it comes down to it, it is a question of where our confidence lies. In the end, is personal faith/unbelief more powerful than God's will to save?

In the same way that no shadow can resist the light, so no sin can be too severe that it keeps us from God's grace. Moltmann writes, "It is not [God's] anger which is everlasting; it is his grace" (*The Coming of God*, 243; see Psalm 30:5). Our response to God's grace matters, but the relationship is wholly unbalanced. God's grace and the human response to it are simply not on the same level. The former gives space for the latter, but it is not subject to it. God's grace far outweighs the human will in either faith or unbelief. In a letter, Moltmann writes, "Grace is universal, faith is particular, [but] we are saved by God's grace" (Merritt: "A Letter from Moltmann," 2014).

Finally, Moltmann offers a biblical example for why the notion of free will is no excuse to assume a double outcome. Frankly, our will is not truly *free* until it is redeemed. If according to Romans 8, God is for us and no one can stand against us, then not even *ourselves* can stand against us. If God is for *me* then even *I* cannot truly stand against *myself*. An unredeemed will is never truly "free" enough to undo God's will to be so for us that nothing, not even ourselves, can stand against us. The critical question is this: *Can we be so against ourselves that God gives us up for loss?* Do we have the power to *overcome God* by turning God's "for us" into an "against us?" Are we then somehow *stronger than God* in our delusional self-opposition? The answer must be *no*, or else God is not a free God but a God subject to the corruption of our unredeemed will.

A double outcome eschatology is an *atheistical* doctrine. If "everyone were to forge their own happiness and dig their own graves, human beings would be their own God" (*The Coming of God*, 243). If we could decide for or against God, then God is merely an idea we project from ourselves, and when we say "God" we mean the power of our own self-determination. We cannot have more confidence in our ability to reject or accept God than we do in God's ability to save. We sometimes say that universalism takes away free will. However, is a "free will" truly free if it remains unredeemed and sinful? Can our sinful will separate us from grace? The ultimate question is not, "Did so-and-so accept Jesus as their savior before they died?" The ultimate question is this: "If God is for us, who can be against us?"

> Who makes the decision about the salvation of lost men and women, and where is the decision made? Every Christian theologian is bound to answer: *God* decides for a person and for his or her salvation, for otherwise there is no assurance of salvation at all. 'If God is for us, who can be against us …' (Rom. 8:31f.)—we may add: not even we ourselves! God is 'for us': that has been decided once and for all in the self-surrender and raising of Christ.
>
> — THE COMING OF GOD, 245

Ansell summarizes this well: "Universal salvation is rooted in the sure promise that in the kingdom of glory, we shall all be(come) truly and finally free" (*The Annihilation of Hell,* 206). It is in the expectation of a will finally set free from our sinful self-hatred and self-condemnation that we discover, in the end, that not even ourselves can separate us from God. In a sense, this is the eschatological appropriation of Augustine's *interior intimo meo*—God is closer to us than we are to ourselves. Moltmann writes, "[E]ven if I am lost to myself, I am never lost to the faithful God. Even if I give myself up, God never gives me up" (*The Source of Life,* 33).

DOUBLE-PREDESTINATION

The second objection to Moltmann's universal hope comes from within his own tradition. It is the proposal of double-predestination, in which God decides to elect some while rejecting others. To this Moltmann asks an important question: "Does theology not involve the Christian faith in inward contradictions if what is expected of the great Judgment is something different from what God has revealed in Israel's history and the history of Jesus Christ?" (*The Coming of God,* 236). That is to say, will God's judgment be at odds with God's self-revelation? Moltmann summarizes the problem:

If *the double outcome of judgment* is proclaimed, the question is then: why did God create human beings if he is going to damn most of them in the end, and will only redeem the least part of them? Can God hate what he himself has created without hating himself?

— IBID., 239

Double predestination is inconsistent with the God revealed in Christ. Ansell offers a summary of this argument: "In taking the cross and descent into Hell as so central to God's revelation to us, Moltmann's challenge to other positions is clear: 'Do not tell me that some people may or must go to Hell on the basis of some theological system (indeed some theological 'necessity'); say that (if you can) in the light of the cross, in the face of the crucified God'" (*The Annihilation of Hell*, 206). Moltmann thus rejects any system that contradicts the cross of Christ.

The heart of this issue is in how we define God's judgment. What does coming judgment entail? If the same Christ who suffered and died for our salvation is also the Judge, then who will be condemned? To condemn any person to damnation would be the ultimate act of self-contradiction. The judgment which is to come must correspond to the One who suffered for all and with all in His Godforsaken death. We can only proclaim a double-outcome if we cut this vital link.

Moltmann writes at length:

[I]n trying to measure the breadth of the Christian hope we must not wander off into far-off realms, but must submerge ourselves in the depths of Christ's death on the cross at Golgotha. It is only there that we find the certainty of reconciliation without limits, and the true ground for the hope for 'the restoration of all things', for universal salvation, and for the world newly created to become the eternal kingdom. It is only the person who understands what Christ suffered in his God-forsaken death who understands what, by virtue of his resurrection, is manifested in his present rule and in his future 'to judge both the quick and the dead'. In the crucified Christ we recognize the Judge of the final Judgment, who himself has become the one condemned, for the accused, in their stead and for their benefit. So at the Last Judgment we expect on the Judgment seat the One who was crucified for the reconciliation of the world, and no other judge. The person who in the history of Christ has experienced the righteousness of God which creates justice for those who suffer injustice, and which justifies the godless, knows what the justice is which at the Last Judgment will restore this ruined world and put everything to rights again: it is not retaliatory justice, Ulpian's *suam cuique*, to each his due—the justice that gives everyone their 'just deserts', which requites the wickedness of the wicked and repays the goodness of the good; it is the righteousness and justice of the God of Abraham, the Father of Jesus Christ, who creates justice, puts things to rights, and justifies.

— The Coming of God, 250

The Judge whose judgment is ahead of us is none other than Jesus Christ who suffered and died for the world. To divorce Christ's self-giving love from His judgment is a profound inconsistency that we must not allow. The same motivation behind Christ's death is behind His judgment; the "last judgment" is not for ruin and destruction but salvation and restoration. If this judgment is according to the terror of law which punishes sin, then we have no hope. But if it is indeed *Christ's* judgment, then we have a certain hope in the universal restoration of all things. The judgment that is before us is not according to the *retaliation* of the law but the *restoration* of Christ. How can the same Christ who proclaims non-retaliation (Mt. 538-42) at once be the eschatological perpetrator of the greatest act of eternal retaliation imaginable?

Judgment is not the ultimate but the penultimate act. As such, the last judgment ultimately serves the new creation. It makes right the wrongs of history and heals our wounds. It is for the sake of the new creation that Christ judges, not for the sake of condemnation.

Universalism for God's sake

Moltmann makes an insightful plea regarding the universal glorification of God, and this serves as an appropriate conclusion to this chapter. He writes:

Every theology of grace tends towards universalism because it issues for

God's sake in the triumph of grace. Every theology of faith tends towards particularism because it starts from the decision of the believer, and hence issues in the separation of believers from the unbelieving. The theology of grace makes us humble and unites us with all human beings, for 'God has consigned all men to disobedience, that he may have mercy upon all' (Rom. 11:32). The theology of faith, in contrast, is in danger of self-righteousness on the part of believers towards nonbelievers, because the difference between them depends on the human beings themselves. These traditional differences can be surmounted if the salvation of the world is seen in *the universal glorification of God*, and if it is theocentrically orientated, not anthropocentrically.

— Sun of Righteousness, Arise!, 148

We overcome the conflict between universalism and particularism when we take our eyes off of ourselves and return our gaze to God. The beginning of this chapter showed the theocentric emphasis of Moltmann's eschatology. Likewise, I have tried to show that Moltmann's universalism of the cross does not center around the question of individuals, but it is fundamentally a question about God. When eschatology becomes less concerned with the fate of individuals and is more concerned with *God's* future, then universalism is not only an acceptable hope but an *essential* hope. It is for *God's sake* that we refuse to give up hope for anyone or anything. It is for the sake of the universal glorification of God that we repeat Blumhardt's confession of hope: "'Behold, everything is God's!'" Thus, a universalism of the cross is universalism *for God's sake*.

A BRIEF READING GUIDE

There are a few different ways you could tackle the ten major works we focused on in this book. As you will recall, these ten are either from the "early trilogy" and the "systematic contributions to theology." I recommend beginning with the systematic contributions. Even though the early trilogy tends to be the most well-known, I have found that the later contributions are easier to read. *Theology of Hope* is typically the first book people pick up (it was my first), but it is also one of Moltmann's most difficult books. I would not recommend it right away for newcomers of his thought. You are certainly free to read in chronological order, but this is what I would recommend instead, particularly if you are entirely new to Moltmann:

Begin with *The Way of Jesus Christ*. It is one of Moltmann's best works, and reading it first will introduce you to many of the essential themes in his theology. Together with this book, you should read the short volume *Jesus Christ for Today's World*. These two compliment each other quite well, and reading both will give you a good overview of Moltmann's significant insights.

From here I would recommend reading either *The Trinity and the*

Kingdom or *The Crucified God* (or both, ideally). With these, you will be introduced to the core of Moltmann's doctrine of God, especially his unique emphasis on God's *pathos* or co-suffering love. The volume entitled *History and the Triune God* compliments these well.

Next, I would dive into Moltmann's later works, particularly his mature "theology of life." One of the best books to begin with is the recently published *The Living God and the Fullness of Life* (2015). This book is a continuation of Moltmann's *Spirit of Life*, and it is a clear and helpful introduction to the later insights he emphasized. From this, I would read both *The Spirit of Life* and *The Source of Life*. The former is a more detailed look at pneumatology, while the latter is a short, more accessible work on the Spirit. *Experiences of God* is also an insightful volume on a similar theme that could be read in conjunction with these.

After you have gone this far into Moltmann's theology, I would recommend reading his autobiography, *A Broad Place*. Moltmann's theology is inseparable from his own life and experiences, making this volume indispensable. I would compliment this text with *Experiences in Theology*, Moltmann's methodological book. Together these two volumes will give you an excellent overview of what the task of theology means for Moltmann. *A Passion for God's Reign* and *Theology and Joy*—which is a slightly revised reprint of *Theology of Play*—would compliment a study of Moltmann's methodology.

From here you could fill in the gaps however you like, based on your interests.

Tackling Moltmann's eschatology is a daunting task, but this would be a crucial next step. *In the End—The Beginning* is a good volume to begin with. It is a short work that covers many of Moltmann's major insights in an accessible way. *The Coming of God* and *Theology of Hope* may be read in conjunction with each other. The complimentary volume edited by Richard Bauckham, *God Will be All in All*, is very helpful in clarifying many of the themes from Moltmann's eschatology. An early text, *The Experiment Hope*, works as a kind of transition book between *Theology of Hope* and *The Crucified God*. As such, it is perhaps more accessible than *Theology of Hope* and could be read in conjunction with that text.

God in Creation could also be read alongside Moltmann's eschatology since the two doctrines are connected. However, it is also an insightful study on its own. *Sun of Righteousness, Arise!* and *The Future of Creation* would complement it well.

Moltmann's doctrine of the Church is often overlooked, but I hope I peaked your interest enough in chapter 4 so that you do not skip over it. *The Church in The Power of the Spirit* is accessible enough to read, but you might compliment it with *The Open Church* and *The Passion for Life*.

Moltmann's *Ethics of Hope* makes explicit many of the themes that are implied throughout his work and is well worth exploring for these insights. For shorter volumes on the more ethical/political aspect of Moltmann's theology, I would recommend: 1) *God for a Secular Society,* 2) *Religion, Revolution, and the Future,* 3) *On Human Dignity,* 4) *Creating a Just Future,* and 5) *Science and Wisdom.*

Elisabeth Moltmann-Wendel is well worth reading for her own sake. *God His & Hers* is a good introduction that was co-authored by both of the Moltmanns. Her most famous work, however, seems to be either *The Women Around Jesus* or *I Am My Body.* Her book *Rediscovering Friendship* is also quite enjoyable, as was *Humanity in God* (co-authored with Jürgen Moltmann). She should not be overlooked, nor should her influence on Moltmann be undervalued.

Moltmann has published two books of early sermons, *The Power of the Powerless* and *The Gospel of Liberation.* Both texts offer insight into Moltmann's early thought. Another example of an early text is his contribution to the volume *Two Studies in the Theology of Bonhoeffer* (with Jürgen Weissbach).

That does not cover all of Moltmann's work, but it covers his major texts. There is really no "wrong" way to read Moltmann. I would say just dive in with what interests you most and go from there.

There are two books Moltmann has published recently which remain untranslated. These are the 2017 *Hoffnung für eine unfertige Welt* (*Hope for an Unfinished World*) and the 2018 *Über Geduld, Barmherzigkeit und Solidarität* (*On Patience, Compassion and Solidarity*). (Title translations are my own and thus subject to change.) Keep an eye out for their eventual appearance in English.

There are a number of great secondary studies now available on Moltmann, most of which were written as subject-specific dissertations. Two
texts, however, offer an overview of his work. A helpful book is *The
Kingdom and the Power* by Geiko Müller-Fahrenholz. Müller-Fahrenholz
was one of Moltmann's first doctoral students in Bonn. Richard
Bauckham is arguably the leading interpreter of Moltmann, and since
Moltmann himself highly praised his work, he is the perhaps the best
secondary source to read. The most complete of his two books is *The
Theology of Jürgen Moltmann,* which collects many helpful essays on his
theology. His other book focuses on the "early trilogy," especially on
Theology of Hope and *The Crucified God.* This book is *Moltmann: Messianic
Theology in the Making.*

Beyond these texts, secondary literature tends to focus on specific
themes in Moltmann's theology. Depending on your interests, any
number of these books would be a helpful study (listed in no particular
order):

The Annihilation of Hell by Nicholas Ansell studies universal redemption in Moltmann's theology. I would highly recommend it to anyone
skeptical of Moltmann's "universalism of the cross," or who might be
interested in studying it in depth.

The Transformative Church by Patrick Oden studies Moltmann's ecclesiology in conversation with the Emerging Church movement in America.
This book is helpful because it highlights an overlooked aspect of Moltmann's theology, and provides reflections on how we might implement
the proposals found in his doctrine of the Church.

Origins of The Theology of Hope by M. Douglas Meeks studies the
development of Moltmann's *Theology of Hope.* A helpful study on the
influences of Moltmann's first great book.

Theology as Hope by Ryan A. Neal is a more critical examination, but
it still does a relatively good job of assessing his major contributions.

Embraced: Many Stories, One Destiny: You, Me, and Moltmann by
Mark French Buchanan is a compelling collection of stories which articulate Moltmann's theology in everyday life. A short but pastorally significant example of Moltmann's theology in action.

Indwelling the Forsaken Other by J. Matthew Bonzo and *Jürgen Molt-*

mann's Ethics of Hope by Timothy Harvie study ethics in Moltmann's theology.

The Future of Theology ed. by Miroslav Volf is a collection of essays written in Moltmann's honor for his 70th birthday. Like most books of this kind, there is a mixture of greats essays with decent ones.

Pilgrimage of Love by Joy Ann McDougall studies the Trinity and the Christian life in Moltmann's theology. It has been highly praised for its constructive reading of Moltmann's mature thought.

God, Hope, and History by A. J. Conyers studies the important theme of history in Moltmann's theology.

The Logic of Promise in Moltmann's Theology by Christopher Morse is an early study of Moltmann's thought.

Jürgen Moltmann and Evangelical Theology ed. by Sung Wook Chung contains essays from several Evangelical theologians. While a few essays were disappointing, I was pleasantly surprised with most of the contributions.

BOOKS TO COMPLEMENT A STUDY OF MOLTMANN

There are several titles that would complement a study of Moltmann's thought quite well. These are either books that directly influenced Moltmann or that take his insights into new territory. I have highlighted four in particular that I recommend, and list some others that may be of interest to you. (These are in no particular order.)

Night by Elie Wiesel is one of the most moving books I have ever read. It is one of those books you cannot read without being affected by its content. Wiesel was a holocaust survivor and writes about his experiences.

The Cross and the Lynching Tree by James H. Cone is a classic text of Black Liberation Theology, which is one of the most important movements in American theology. This text is also one of the best examples of liberation theology for the unacquainted.

"On Preparing to Die" is a 1519 sermon by Martin Luther which Moltmann often cited. Collected in *Martin Luther's Basic Theological Writings* ed. by W. R. Russell and T. F. Lull.

The Hardest Part by G. A. Studdert Kennedy. Moltmann highly praises this as a book of "prophetic and radical force rather like that of

Barth's *Epistle to the Romans*." It is a pastor's reflections on his wartime experience and offers a moving account of God's co-suffering love.

Commentary on Romans by Ernst Käsemann.

The Theology of the Old Testament by Gerhard von Rad.

Foundations of Dogmatics by Otto Weber.

Theology of the Pain of God by Kazoh Kitamori.

The Prophets by Abraham Herschel.

The Principle of Hope by Ernst Bloch.

Church Dogmatics by Karl Barth.

Letters and Papers from Prison by Dietrich Bonhoeffer.

Action in Waiting by Christoph Friedrich Blumhardt.

Poverty of Spirit by Johann Baptist Metz.

A Theology of Liberation by Gustavo Gutiérrez.

God as the Mystery of the World by Eberhard Jüngel.

Orthodox Dogmatic Theology by Dumitru Staniloae.

The Silent Cry by Dorothee Soelle.

The Creative Suffering of God by Paul S. Fiddes.

Being as Communion by John Zizioulas.

Tragic Sense of Life by Miguel de Unamuno.

Exclusion & Embrace by Miroslav Volf.

WORKS CITED

Works cited are listed in order of appearance, by chapter, and have not been repeated by sequential use.

Introduction:
Wyatt Houtz: "Jürgen Moltmann at 90: A Recap of the Unfinished Worlds Conference at Emory" - October 23, 2016. https://postbarthian.com/2016/10/23/jurgen-moltmann-at-90-a-recap-of-the-unfinished-worlds-conference-at-emory/

Biography:
J. Moltmann: *A Broad Place: An Autobiography* (2009). Minneapolis, MN: Fortress Press. Translated by Margaret Kohl.
Dion Forster: "An interview with Jürgen Moltmann by Selina Palm VLOG 63" (Youtube) - April 5, 2017. https://youtu.be/5BA_IPIOG34 - Forster transcript: https://ofthemakingofmanybooksblog.wordpress.com/2018/01/21/transcript-an-interview-with-jurgen-moltmann-by-selina-palm-vlog-63/

Overview of Works:
Richard Bauckham: *Moltmann: Messianic Theology in the Making* (1987). UK: Marshall Morgan and Scott Publications.

Chapter 1:

J. Moltmann: *Religion, Revolution, and the Future* (1969). New York: Charles Scribner's Sons. Translated by M. Douglas Meeks.

J. Moltmann: *Experiences in Theology: Ways and Forms of Christian Theology* (2000). Minneapolis, MN: Fortress Press. Translated by Margaret Kohl.

Miroslav Volf, Carmen Krieg, Thomas Kucharz (edited by): *The Future of Theology: Essays in Honor of Jürgen Moltmann* (1996). Grand Rapids, MI: Wm. B. Eerdmans Publishing.

Karl Barth: *Evangelical Theology: An Introduction* (1992). Grand Rapids, MI: Wm. B. Eerdmans Publishing. Translated by Grover Foley.

B.A. Gerrish: *Thinking with the Church: Essays in Historical Theology* (2010). Grand Rapids, MI: Wm. B. Eerdmans Publishing.

J. Moltmann: *A Passion for God's Reign* (1998). Grand Rapids, MI: Wm. B. Eerdmans Publishing. Edited by Miroslav Volf.

Richard Bauckham (editor): *God Will be All in All: The Eschatology of Jürgen Moltmann* (2001). Minneapolis, MN: Fortress Press.

J. Moltmann: *The Church in the Power of the Spirit: A Contribution to Messianic Ecclesiology* (1993). Minneapolis, MN: Fortress Press. Translated by Margaret Kohl.

J. Moltmann: *The Trinity and the Kingdom: The Doctrine of God* (1993). Minneapolis, MN: Fortress Press. Translated by Margaret Kohl.

J. Moltmann: *God for a Secular Society: The Public Relevance of Theology* (1999). Minneapolis, MN: Fortress Press. Translated by Margaret Kohl.

Chapter 2:

J. Moltmann: *Theology of Hope: On the Ground and the Implications of a Christian Eschatology* (1993). Minneapolis, MN: Fortress Press. Translated by James W. Leitch.

Walter Rauschenbusch: *Christianity and the Social Crisis* (1907). Public domain.

Richard Bauckham: *The Theology of Jürgen Moltmann* (1995). Edinburgh, UK: T&T Clark.

J. Moltmann: *The Source of Life: The Holy Spirit and the Theology of*

Life (1997). Minneapolis, MN: Fortress Press. Translated by Margaret Kohl.

J. Moltmann: *The Living God and the Fullness of Life* (2015). Louisville, KY: Westminster John Knox Press. Translated by Margaret Kohl.

J. Moltmann: *Jesus Christ for Today's World* (1994). Minneapolis, MN: Fortress Press. Translated by Margaret Kohl.

J. Moltmann: *The Gospel of Liberation* (1973). Waco, TX: Word Incorporated.

Anup Shah: "Poverty Facts and Statistics" - January 7, 2013. http://www.globalissues.org/article/26/poverty-facts-and-stats

Chapter 3:

J. Moltmann: *The Crucified God: The Cross of Christ as the Foundation and Criticism of Christian Theology* (1993). Minneapolis, MN: Fortress Press. Translated by R. A. Wilson and John Bowden.

J. Moltmann: *The Experiment Hope* (1975). Philadelphia, PA: Fortress Press. Edited, translated, with a foreword by M. Douglas Meeks.

Ryan A. Neal: *Theology as Hope: On the Ground and Implications of Jürgen Moltmann's Doctrine of Hope* (2015). Eugene, OR: Pickwick Publications.

Kurt Vonnegut, Jr.: *Slaughterhouse-Five* (1969). New York: Dell Publishing.

Elie Wiesel: *Night* (2006). New York: Hill and Wang.

"God weeps with us so that we may one day laugh with him." The source of this quote is unknown, though it is a popular remark often attributed to Moltmann. I have used it here, even though it may be a misquote, because it fits well within Moltmann's argument.

Augustine: *The City of God*. Public domain.

Tobias Winright: "Jürgen Moltmann on Capital Punishment" - October 24, 2011. http://catholicmoraltheology.com/jurgen-moltmann-on-capital-punishment/

J. Moltmann: *The Power of the Powerless: The Word of Liberation for Today* (1983). New York: Harper & Row.

Benjamin Merritt: "Protest Hope" - February 26, 2014. Transcript: http://moltmanniac.com/protest-hope/

Mark Oppenheimer, The New York Times: "A Death Row Inmate Finds Common Ground with Theologians" - February 27, 2015.

https://www.nytimes.com/2015/02/28/us/a-death-row-inmate-finds-common-ground-with-theologians.html

Peter Foster, The Telegraph: "US Torture Report: CIA used discredited Cold War techniques" - December 9, 2014. https://www.telegraph.co.uk/news/worldnews/northamerica/usa/1128387 7/US-Torture-report-CIA-use-discredited-Cold-War-techniques.html

Chapter 4:
Patrick Oden: *The Transformative Church* (2015). Minneapolis, MN: Fortress Press.

Chapter 5:
Karl Barth: *Church Dogmatics* (2004). New York: T&T Clark. Edited by G. W. Bromiley and T. F. Torrance.

J. Moltmann: *Sun of Righteousness, Arise!: God's Future for Humanity and the Earth* (2010). Minneapolis, MN: Fortress Press. Translated by Margaret Kohl.

J. Moltmann: *History and the Triune God: Contributions to Trinitarian Theology* (1992). New York: The Crossroad Publishing Company. Translated by John Bowden.

C. S. Lewis: *Mere Christianity* (2001). New York: HarperCollins.

J. Moltmann: *The Future of Creation: Collected Essays* (2007). Minneapolis, MN: Fortress Press. Translated by Margaret Kohl.

J. Moltmann: *The Passion for Life: A Messianic Lifestyle* (2007). Minneapolis, MN: Fortress Press. Translated by Margaret Kohl.

Elisabeth Moltmann-Wendel and J. Moltmann: *God, His & Hers* (1991). London, UK: SCM Press. Translated by John Bowden.

George Hunsinger: "*The Trinity and the Kingdom* by Jürgen Moltmann (review)." *The Thomist: A Speculative Quarterly Review*, Volume 47, Number 1, January 1983, pp. 129-139. Published by The Catholic University of America Press.

Chapter 6:
Ton van Prooijen: *Limping but Blessed: Jürgen Moltmann's Search for a Liberating Anthropology* (2004). Amsterdam: Rodopi B.V.

J. Moltmann: *God in Creation: A New Theology of Creation and the*

Spirit of God (The Gifford Lectures 1984-1985) (1993). Minneapolis, MN: Fortress Press. Translated by Margaret Kohl.

J. Moltmann: *The Way of Jesus Christ: Christology in Messianic Dimensions* (reprint, 1993). Minneapolis, MN: Fortress Press. Translated by Margaret Kohl.

J. Moltmann: *In the End—The Beginning: The Life of Hope* (2004). Minneapolis, MN: Fortress Press. Translated by Margaret Kohl.

J. Moltmann: *Ethics of Hope* (2012). Minneapolis, MN: Fortress Press. Translated by Margaret Kohl.

Chapter 7:
Geiko Muller-Fahrenholz: *The Kingdom and the Power: The Theology of Jürgen Moltmann* (2001). Minneapolis, MN: Fortress Press.

Brian Zahnd: *A Farewell to Mars: An Evangelical Pastor's Journey Toward the Biblical Gospel of Peace* (2014). Colorado Springs, CO: David C. Cook.

Jason Poterfield: "40 Early Church Quotes on Violence" - http://enemylove.com/40-early-church-quotes-on-violence-enemy-love-patriotism/

J. Moltmann: *The Spirit of Life: A Universal Affirmation* (2001). Minneapolis, MN: Fortress Press. Translated by Margaret Kohl.

Chapter 8:
J. Moltmann: "Christianity: A Religion of Joy" - September 7-8, 2012. https://faith.yale.edu/sites/default/files/moltmann_christianity_a_religion_of_joy.pdf

"Gun Violence by the Numbers" - https://everytownresearch.org/gun-violence-by-the-numbers/

Chapter 9:
J. Moltmann: *Experiences of God* (2007). Minneapolis, MN: Fortress Press. Translated by Margaret Kohl.

Augustine: *Confessions.* Public domain.

J. Moltmann: *The Coming of God: Christian Eschatology* (2004). Minneapolis, MN: Fortress Press. Translated by Margaret Kohl.

Chapter 10:

Benjamin Merritt: Claremont Lecture - "I Don't Want to Go to Heaven" - May 1, 2014. Video: http://moltmanniac.com/new-jurgen-moltmann-video-at-claremont/ Transcription: http://moltmanniac.com/i-dont-want-to-go-to-heaven/

Nicholas Ansell: *The Annihilation of Hell: Universal Salvation and the Redemption of Time in the Eschatology of Jürgen Moltmann* (2013). Eugene, OR: Cascade Books.

J. Moltmann: *Science and Wisdom* (2003). Minneapolis, MN: Fortress Press. Translated by Margaret Kohl.

Florian Berndt: "An Interview with Moltmann." http://www.tentmaker.org/biographies/moltmann.htm

J. Moltmann: "The End of Everything is God: Has Belief in Hell Had its Day?" (1997). The Expository Times, pp. 263-264.

Benjamin Merritt: "A Letter from Jürgen Moltmann," March 5, 2014. http://moltmanniac.com/a-letter-from-jurgen-moltmann/

ABOUT THE AUTHOR

STEPHEN D. MORRISON is a prolific American writer, ecumenical theologian, novelist, artist, and literary critic. A strong sense of creativity and curiosity drives his productive output of books on a wide range of subjects.

This book is the third in his "Plain English Series." Previous volumes include *Karl Barth in Plain English* and *T. F. Torrance in Plain English*.

For more on Stephen, please visit his website. There you can stay up to date with his latest projects and ongoing thoughts.

WWW.SDMORRISON.ORG

ALSO BY STEPHEN D. MORRISON

Plain English Series:

Karl Barth in Plain English (2017)

T. F. Torrance in Plain English (2017)

Jürgen Moltmann in Plain English (2018)

Schleiermacher in Plain English (forthcoming)

For a complete list of the projected volumes in this series, please visit:
www.SDMorrison.org/plain-english-series/

―――――――――

Other titles:

Welcome Home: The Good News of Jesus (2016)

10 Reasons Why the Rapture Must be Left Behind (2015)

We Belong: Trinitarian Good News (2015)

Where Was God?: Understanding the Holocaust in the Light of God's Suffering
(2014)

Made in the USA
Columbia, SC
30 May 2018